Evie Branthes

ISBN: 0-9649290-0-7

Illustrations: Joyce Herringshaw

Cover illustration: Adam Turner

Dedicated To

*A special sister, Irene,
my bridesmaid, and my friend.*

Life's Road

I did not know how steep the trail, I was about to start.
I just knew that I could not climb, if only I took heart.
I waddled through my childhood days and loitered by each
    flower,
I picked a rose, some cowslips, and the wild daffodil.
And then I paused to smell the great wild perfumed air,
I did not need to hurry for I had time to spare.

My tiny feet made footprints, after cool refreshing rain.
Oft times I stepped on thorns, that caused a pang of pain.
With parental guidance along the crooked way,
My legs grew ever stronger when I faced a stormy day.
One day I had to start on that shaded path alone,
I was so determined, there would be no unturned stone.

I paused to watch a butterfly and listen to meadowlark,
I'm grown now and must hurry on, I have no time to park.
Those giant rocks that were much too large for me
Became the bridge I needed, to cross life's troubled sea.
I stooped to clear the path, and found gold nuggets there.
If I would have turned back, where would I be? Oh where?

A Letter to Mom

As I paused to dust your picture on my dresser top today

My memory reversed back to days, you brushed dust and tears away.

And then I gazed a moment, at the pillow that you made,

And each little stitch spoke of patience, that you so often displayed.

I can just see you resting, as you read for your black worn Book.

While I stand here by dresser and look and look and look.

—Your Loving Daughter,

Evie

Acknowledgements

With deepest gratitude to our daughter Jill and husband Mark Herringshaw for editing this book.

To the talented Joyce Herringshaw, for the illustrations.

To my husband for his encouragement and patience during the long evenings I spent at the computer.

To all the readers of *Strawtick Memories*, who kept plodding me to "hurry up and finish that book." Without your encouragement. It may not have become a reality

To all my family that inspired and performed in the stories.

Table of Contents

About The Author

The author was born in a rural area home, near Hewitt Minnesota. The couple now live in a suburb of St Paul, Minnesota. She is married and has fourteen granchildren.

Her husband once asked, "What will you do when our family is grown?"

Evie now asks herself "Will the Lord grant me healthful days to complete all I desire to do?"

The finishing touches and last minute decisions on a project, such as *Life's Rugged Beauty,* cause anxious moments. The day she sees the finished project will be the day she will be found seated at her computer.

In her previous book, **Strawtick Memories,** Evie shares her childhood with you.

Foreword

The nostalgic story of Evie's childhood begins in her first book, *Strawtick Memories*. The multiple human interest stories that transpired in the lives of Evie and her fourteen siblings will touch your heart.

The fascinating story of personal griefs and triumphs are contained in *Life's Rugged Beauty*, the sequel to *Strawtick Memories*. This book is written in honesty and sincerity and in a warm, down home style. It allowed us to experience the happy times and the difficult three years of separation during World War Two.

We enjoyed a glimpse of their courtship, attended their wedding, and visited their home on the farm, as we walked through rugged, yet beautiful paths with Evie and Ray.

We laughed aloud and then shed a tear while immensely enjoying this delightful collection of inspired stories. Enjoy!

Dr. Marshall and Betty Daniels
Shoreview, Minnesota

Evie Branstner is a writer that captures the people and times. She has lived her life to the fullest with purpose and meaning as a woman devoted to God and her family. Her book gives us an insight to a special time in history that few remember. She combines hard life reality with a sense of humor in her writing.

She is a dynamic speaker, encourager and motivator for other people. Evie has made a difference in the lives of many people. She has been a mentor, advisor, and a very dear friend to me over the years.

Pamela Stewart
Elementary Teacher, Pastor's Wife

Introduction

It was with mixed emotions the author sat before blank pages and lay her entire life for others to witness. Recalling many of the chapters brought laughter, and tears. Had it been penned on parchment, some of the pages would have stained with both tears of joy, and pain. Reflecting on the entire picture she visualized more sunshine than shadow. *Life's Rugged Beauty* paints the verbal picture of her life. It was not written as a biography of a famous person, but to portray a lifestyle that is foreign to following generations, a lifestyle that will perhaps never be repeated.

The desire of the author is to preserve life in the Forties through the late Nineteen Hundreds. She is often reminded that many of her contemporary's can no longer relate their life stories. At the age of seventy-one, Evie shares *Life's Rugged Beauty* based on reality.

The fictitious names of many of the characters used in the story are based on real life. The dialogue employed in the book is as true to life as the author's memory can recall. Evie is very much alive, and the story is based on fact.

The changes in Evie's life span were even beyond her scope of imagination. Living during World War II was perhaps the most difficult period of her life.

In 1996, Evie and Ray will celebrate fifty years of married life. To the youth they would highly recommend saving all your old love letters. While looking for information to include in *Life's Rugged Beauty,* the box of letters was dusted off. They sat by Ma's old range and laughed and cried together. It reminded them of the long years of separation, and how precious each day that they remain together. Evie had forgotten that Ray would rather die than live without her. Of course she often reminds him of that fact.

They trust that in sharing their lives in these pages will be an encouragement to someone.

A more detailed account of her heritage is contained in the introduction to her first book *Strawtick Memories*.

1
Autumn Reflections

The seasons continued to bring winter with its white holidays and everydays as well—spring, with its cowslips, wild plum and choke cherry blossoms, baby rabbits, the return of the robin and numerous signs of its "great to be alive feelings." Fall crept in so quietly in all its splendor.

Evie's first long trip to Whitefish, Montana was a happy memory. She was on hand to welcome Joy's baby into this world. Letters from Joy found their way to the house at the end of the lane and oft reminded Evie of the beauty of the west. One Christmas Baby Robert splashed the cards with a million dollar smile as he played with his toes. He was the special attraction on every card, his proud Daddy's hobby being photography.

Elizabeth gave birth to her last child ten days before Joy's baby Robert was born. Little Jane weighed about five pounds and entered the world with the symptoms of a down syndrome child. She needed so much care, so Elizabeth continued to depend on Evie to manage the busy household. Jane made slow progress, making a weak cry when hungry. Her skin was as tender as the

Mother's heart that cared for her. Elizabeth's long siege of changing diapers for fourteen babies ended by the time Jane reached her third birthday.

The multiple shades of the woods behind the tar papered barn and unpainted corn crib were breath taking. The leaves were at their peak of color. Fall was Gus and Elizabeth's favorite season. "Maybe the reason is just the pure beauty of autumn," thought Elizabeth. "Then again, could it just be that the end of canning and gardening is such a relief that I can take time to drink in the scenery?" Elizabeth almost asked herself audibly. With no one around to answer her questions she continued to take a mental inventory of the two filled bins of potatoes and the piles of squash and pumpkin that were covered with straw. "We won't put it in the cellar until we have warning of a hard frost," she thought to herself. "I'm so proud of the rows and rows of canned goods, and that fifteen gallon crock of sauerkraut will taste wonderful with spare ribs, which reminds me," she continued her silent dialogue, "it is time to quit day dreaming and check to see if Evie has supper in the makings."

Elizabeth livened up her step and hurried on. She had one arm out of her overall jacket as she opened the homemade kitchen door. She took a deep breath as she questioned, "What smells so good Evie?" "It's a new recipe Joy sent me for apple crisp," was her quick response, and added, "I baked the potatoes, and we have enough ham left for one more meal." She continued to chop the huge head of cabbage for cole slaw. A pan of golden brown biscuits and ten loaves of bread were cooling on the kitchen work table. The entire batch was sending a heavenly aroma and signals to get washed up for supper. Elizabeth made the supper call as her flock left their work or play. As Evie was dishing up the cole slaw Elizabeth had to step out the kitchen door for one more look at the magical beauty of an early fall sunset. "Where did the summer go? It seems like I just planted the garden." Enchanted, she paused longer than she realized, "It grew as fast as my children. I can't believe that Mae and Joy have left us for homes of their own, and I am Grandma." She almost choked on these thoughts. She longed to see her first little grandchild, Russell more often. Michigan seemed almost as far away as China, and grandson Robert was in the heart of the Rockies.

Elizabeth's last long trip was her return trip from the University Hospital to have one kidney removed. That trip was lost in a sea of memories, though the dreadful experience was often recaptured in her dreams. She would never forget the long ride by wagon to Henning to catch a train to Minneapolis. Nor could she forget the painful thirty days in the hospital. Since that chapter of her life, neither time nor funds would allow for travel with raising her large family.

Irene and Chuckie were Gus's right hand. They were next younger than Evie and were up early to help with the morning chores. Then breakfast feeding the calves, pumping water by hand, and then rushing in to brush off the hay seed and leave for the walk to school. Their school lunches were neatly packed in a 1/2 gallon syrup pail. Home made bread sliced evenly cradled the peanut butter and jelly. There were usually oatmeal cookies or doughnuts hidden beneath the sandwiches. It was carefully wrapped in the wax paper rescued from the corn flake boxes, and if it was apple season there may be fruit in the pail. Every evening the dinner buckets were carefully washed and placed upturned on the warming oven to avoid rust under the rim of the precious pails and prevent the growth of any foreign substance. The Branstners may have been poor, but they took pride in taking care of even the string that was ripped from the flour and feed sacks. It came in handy whenever a package was wrapped. It was also employed to make an entertaining game. You placed the string around the palms of both hands placed your middle finger through the cord and soon had a puzzle to make different design by having a partner pull the strings a certain way to make still another puzzle. The string was passed back and forth until the artists had explored every pattern, or they were called to do something more constructive. You had to be there to understand the proper procedure.

Home spun games replaced the need for a video. There were no electronic or video games, and no money to waste. Steal sticks, dodge ball, or catching fire flies to light up their world, were seasonal after supper games. Jumping rope was still another after-dishes-and-chores pastime. In a few weeks the barefoot soles of the children's feet were thick and tough. Gus would often remind them to save their shoes for school. He was not the least worried that they may outgrow them, for perchance the shoes did get tight they would always fit *someone.*

A stair steps of little girls filled the house with activity and joy. Ruthie was as petite as her younger sister June. Donna, Orpha Ann and the two gems, Pearl and Ruby were next in line. Then to break the spell Willy and Benjamin surprised the family before Baby Jane joined the large family.

And so we pick up the story from *Strawtick Memories.* The romance and struggles of the real world in the life of Evie are perhaps in living color in God's great recording studio.

2
Strawtick Memories

Change was part of life. Evie thought of all that had happened since Joy and Mae left home. She sat by the dining room table lighted by an aladdin lamp. It was her hall of silence after everyone had drifted off to bed. She had the best excuse to be the last one to bed, as her bed was the sitting room couch. It was a bed at night and a couch by day. It was letter writing time. With at least eight friends and cousins out preparing to, or defending our country, letter writing was the least Evie could do.

Words were not flowing tonight. Evie bit the end of her pen and stared at the darkness through the paned window. Scenes from the past two years flooded her memories while the clock ticked in the quietness. She thought of her school mates and cousins, and memories of their time together, and then of the uncertain future. The fire in the airtight stove cracked as if to interrupt the silence.

Dad had just gone over to check on Uncle Chris. "We haven't heard from Howard for about eight weeks," Chris tried to state in a matter of fact way, though his countenance betrayed him. His face looked gaunt and tired. It was difficult to sleep with your only son out facing the bullets, somewhere in Africa. Uncle Chris was as kind a man as you could find this side of the Rockies. He was of medium build. His clean bib overalls fit perfectly. He seemed to breathe the very law of kindness.

Auntie Nell was short and enjoyed her tasty food. She walked with a limp. Her hair was thinning, and she usually found something to laugh about. "She is not herself today," Gus thought to himself. Aunt Nell was busy washing up her milking dishes. She pulled her apron to wipe a bead of sweat from her brow, as she casually tipped her round rim glasses up to catch the tears that were sneaking down her cheeks. Yes, World War II was for real. It was touching the heart and homes in this valley.

Gus returned home and told Elizabeth, "I am so glad we had girls first and Chuckie is not yet old enough to go to war. I hope it is over soon," he sighed.

"I must write," Evie convinced herself as she paused to pray for her big cousin. "I will have faith that he will be alive," she whispered to herself as a big yawn escaped and the lamp flickered.

My Dear cousin Howard;

It is does not seem possible that you are so far away. I just thought of you so much today after I closed the wooden gate that you carved on every time you loaded another spreader of manure. I could almost hear you telling us the joke about the old Model T that had the sign on the bumper that said, "Constipated Can't Pass Anything." I wish I could bring you an egg sandwiched between home made bread."

And on and on the letter went about the past. Just then Evie noticed how low the oil was getting in the aladdin lamp. One glance at the clock she decided, "I must say something about the future to give hope of a brighter tomorrow and homecoming." She added, "Just thought I would let you know the hens are still laying and I will be waiting to make you that egg sandwich. I am having lots of practice baking bread, I can assure you of that.

She lit another lamp, turned the wick down low, and made sure the aladdin lamp was out. "It'll be time to get breakfast before I get settled in my bed," she thought. The bed had to be made up nightly. There could not be a wrinkle in it. No one, but no one, could perform this task for Evie.

Morning came, it seemed, as soon as her head hit the pillow. Evie tried to orient herself before she crawled out of her warm nest. "I better add wood to that kitchen range, the troops will soon be ready for breakfast."

As Chuckie finished his breakfast he reminded Evie that it was corn picking time. "Dad is going to be gone today, Evie. Will you help me pick corn?"

Evie twirled a negative thought or two around in her mind and then consented to grant his request. It would be a change to get out of the house beyond the clothes line. Chuck harnessed the faithful team while Evie hunted up her bib overalls and one of her Dad's old flannel shirts. Grabbing a hat from a nail behind the kitchen door, she hopped on the back of the wagon box as it headed for the field. In no time her gloves were wet.

"I think we should wait for the sun to dry the dew before we pick this corn," was the suggestion from someone that was in the habit of giving free advice on how to run a more efficient household.

"This corn will dry off as we pick it, and the days are getting shorter. I would rather pick before the snow flies." The serious answer came from Chuckie.

The sun did come out. "I miss Old Fan," Chuck commented in dead seriousness. "She was the best old horse to have on the wagon when we were picking corn or potatoes. She always knew when to stop." The complete episode was a flashback of memories, as though it was a live theater on the edge of the wooded area with the floating clouds as a back drop.

The scene had been a perfect summer day, until

Chuck came rushing in the house short of breath. Everyone knew he had witnessed something terrible. "F-F-F-Fan is so sick, Dad," his voice broke. "She is down in the barn yard and can't get up!" He gasped again. Fan was considered a member of the family after all her faithful years of horse power.

Gus realized she was getting up in years and was careful not to over work her the past spring. Fan was the mother of Babe, who was now sharing the work load. Babe was young and frisky, but being on the same set of eveners, Fan held her in stride.

The older children of the family followed Dad and Chuckie to see for themselves.They found her lying on her side with her head thrown back. She opened her eyes to the call of her master. Irene squatted to study the situation, as though she could personally communicate. "She is so thirsty Dad," and took action immediately by pumping a pail of ice cold water and placing it beside Fan. With a surge of strength she lifted her head and drank one third of the water. Irene just knew when she batted her eyes, she was saying thank you.

Fan was tenderly cared for the next few days. The children took turns keeping vigil by her side. They curried, petted and pampered the worn horse. She never lacked love or sympathy.

Irene ate her dinner as fast as she could, and ran to check on her patient, but was unprepared for the next scene. Fan was lifeless. "Fan, Fan!" pleaded Irene. "You can't be! You can't be . . . " She could not complete the sentence. She ran crying as though her heart would break. She crawled through the fence, not thinking to dodge the top barbed wire.

The relaxed dinner conversation was silenced, as Irene slammed the screen door. There had to be a reason for all those tears and blood. "F-F-Fan is . . . ," the word could not be verbalized. Irene stood unaware that blood was mixed with her tears. "What in the world did you do to your forehead?" Elizabeth questioned, noticing the half

moon shaped cut. Elizabeth quickly shifted Irenes attention to herself. She reached to her head, looked at the
blood on her hand and turned white. It occupied her mind
for a while. The wound was washed and dressed. When
Irene was assured she would live, they all gathered on a
grassed area 'neathe the shade of the old oak tree.

Opportunities of showing kindness to Fan had
ceased. Gus put a rope around Fan's body and somehow
the muscles of the family rolled the lifeless thin horse on
a stone boat. Fan's own daughter was privileged to be pall
bearer. Her daughter, Babe pulled as though she counted
it an honor. A deep hole was dug between two evergreens,
in the heart of the forty acres that Grandpa Chase had
homesteaded. A grave side funeral was conducted, with
all the family in attendance. It was a solemn occasion
that would long be remembered.

Chuck and Evie had just relived the entire day, and
hardly realized that they had picked four long rows of
corn and it was now high noon. They conveniently ended
up on the end of the field where they could almost smell
dinner.

"How did we get started on that subject?" Chuck
asked as they unhitched the team and led them to water.

3
The Wood Chopper

"Irene and Evie, would you girls go down to the early potato patch?" Elizabeth questioned, rather than commanded. It being such a perfect afternoon, the girls did not mind that assignment. They grabbed their straw hats off a nail and took a cold drink of the most wonderful pure water in the world, then headed out the screen door. Sport, the spotted mongrel dog, joined them down the path to the barn. The rusty pail they used would no longer hold milk. They picked up a short handled fork for digging the potatoes. The girls were skipping along as they swung the empty pail while dragging the pitch fork behind them. The sisters continued to discuss the subject that Ma had interrupted. Dad had come home from the school board meeting the previous evening and announced the need for a custodian for school district #150. "Annie doesn't want the job anymore," he said. "And it's a good job for Irene and Evie, and heaven knows they need every penny they can earn. They could clean the school once a month for three dollars," Dad stated in a matter-of-fact way. Evie and Irene were delighted with the prospect. They continued to work for Uncle Fred and Aunt Maggie whenever there was extra cooking to do. Cousin Jane was now old enough to baby-sit her little siblings. Earlier, Mae and Evie had taken turns staying by the week to help Aunt Maggie when Jane was too small and insecure to stay in the house alone during milking time.

"It will be so great to have some money to spend of our very own," Irene said in her most excitable tone. Evie agreed and proceeded to spend the first months pay check. "We both need anklets and underpanties," costing about ten cents per pair and the latter at thirty nine cents each. "We will need to save back 15 cents each for the offering on Sunday," the girls agreed, having heard a few sermons on tithing ten percent of your income. "And then we'll have some *pants and anklets!*"

Evie sighed. Not that they had been without such necessities in the past, but the prospect of having store bought clothing to replace the bloomers made from flour sacks was inviting. First the printing had to be soaked from the sacks with kerosene and Grandma's home made lye soap, and rubbed on the wash board. The girls were definately not willing to advertise for the Dakota Maid Flour Company. At any rate when you swung by your knees on the bars at school you wanted your bloomers (Ma's definition) to be snowy white. The potato pail was filled, and the girls headed down the lane toward home. They had been so busy spending the future paychecks that they hardly realized the pail was overflowing. The wire handle was cutting into the palm of Evie's hand. She switched the pail to her left hand. Irene knelt to pick up the potatoes that fell in the transaction and grabbed a hold of the heavy load. By the time they reached the kitchen they had also spent their October paycheck.

Cleaning Island School was a big job. It never entered the mind of the farm girls that it would be such a major undertaking. Visions of new clothes blurred these facts. The school desks were attached by two long boards connecting about five of the desks together. The long rows of desks were all moved to one side of the

school building. Sweeping compound was tossed around
to absorb the dust as though you were spreading grain
to the chickens. The room was first swept, and then it
was scrubbed with a long handle mop, and rinsed with
clear water. Next, after drying, a coat or two of Johnson
wax was applied to the gray painted floor. While the
wax was drying the two cleaning maids washed the
blackboards on the other side. They cleaned the
teacher's desk and the platform boards. The dusty
erasers were pounded on the rail of the steps. "I will put
more wood in the stove," Evie informed Irene. "A warm
temperature will hasten the drying process." "As if I
didn't know that," Irene murmured under her breath.
The fire also had to heat the water for scrubbing.
Building the fire, and carrying the water from the out
door pump had been a prerequisite of the entire project.

While the second half of the floor was drying the
girls each cleaned the boys' and girls' halls. The ledge
that supported the dinner buckets was scrubbed, as
well as the the dirty floor. There was always a crust or
two of bread or an apple core to toss out to the grateful
sparrows or chickadees. In the sub-zero weather the
lunch buckets were placed under the black stove. After
a long walk to school most of the students had frozen
sandwiches. The slippery waxed floor lightened the load
of sliding the rows of seats to the other side to repeat
the triple steps of the last half of the job. "Let's have our
snack," the suggestion came from Irene and landed on
Evie's very receptive ears. The hot chocolate was heated in an aluminum pan with a short handle. For lack of
a holder Evie grabbed her mitten. "These peanut butter
sandwiches never tasted better," the sisters agreed.
What better way to wait for the last layers of Glo Coat
to dry? The seats were then placed as straight as an
arrow. A few scratches on the waxed floor were touched
up after scooting the seats in rows,and the girls looked
over the room with a sense of satisfaction. Evie verbalized her thoughts. "I wish it would stay this clean," with
just a tinge of doubt about such a rare possibility. Irene,

as always with her business head piped up with, "Then we wouldn't have a job."

The girls were anxious to reach Williams to make out the check before he left his dinner table for field work. The drafts on the stove were closed to make sure the school would be standing on Monday morning and both doors were locked securely. The tired feeling seemed to disappear as they walked on home with the coveted paycheck in their water-soaked hands. They arrived home in time to help prepare the evening meal. Meatballs, baked beans, and potatoes really hit the spot. "Elizabeth you really got a good scald on those beans," Dad remarked. Ice cold raspberries topped off another country supper. Remembering the hot summer days the wild berries were picked warmed you to the core.

By the first of December Irene and Evie had earned nine whole dollars. It was mutually decided to spend three dollars on the other sisters and brothers for Christmas gifts. "I think we should buy under clothing and stockings," of course that thought was firmly stated by Irene, as only she could be so sensible. "I think we should put a few sticks of gum in each stocking," Evie piped back.

Williams was a large serious man with dark penetrating eyes. He made out the third check without a hint of emotion. As he handed Evie the check he asked, "Would you girls be interested in washing the ceiling and walls of the school during Christmas vacation? That is if you think you can handle a big ladder." The answer was in a strong affirmative, "Of course we can handle a big ladder!" Irene was quick to answer. "How much do you pay for that big job?" she asked, with ne'er a negative thought of having to spend Christmas vacation scrubbing ceilings and walls.

Gus always made sure his family was as snug and warm as possible in an old farm house. There was always a pile of wood cut, sawed, and dried in advance. The wood was just the right length for the parlor furnace, the airtight (that was in the dining or "other room" as it was often referred to) and the kitchen range. Elizabeth was fussy about the length of wood that was in the wood box for cooking, for that was an important part of life on the farm.

That Fall a large family moved into the Valley. Chucky often brought a new friend home after school. "Do you have any big brothers?" Dad asked the curly haired lad? "Yes! I have lots of big brothers, but three have left home," was the proud response. "I have a big brother, Ray, that is home part of the time". Gus did not let any grass grow under his feet. He was soon driving in the Miller farm, hiring a wood cutter.

It was Evie's eighteenth birthday, and the very day that she and Irene began their big cleaning project, Ray started off in the woods with a freshly sharpened ax. The girls left early that morning. Elizabeth suggested in a rather firm tone, "You girls better come home for a hot dinner, that job will take lots of energy." After three hours of scrubbing on metal decorated ceiling, the girls were ready to carry out Ma's suggestion. The wind was blowing the sub-zero temperature in their faces, as they waded three-fourths of a mile through the snow banks. They wrapped their scarfs around their face until you could barely recognize them. They arrived before the dinner's finishing touches were completed. Irene set the table while Evie picked up the ironing project where Elizabeth left off. It was an excellent time to warm by the kitchen fire and kill two birds with one stone. You also had the aroma of dinner that near the range. The dinner smelled heavenly. The pork gravy was bubbling through a brown smooth consistency. Ma was just mashing the potatoes as Dad opened the door, with the wood cutter behind him.

Ray was a shy thin young man of twenty years. With the removal of his overall jacket his blue plaid shirt was reflected in soft blue-gray eyes that was a close match to his faded bib overalls, a proper attire for every farm boy working in the woods. Evie sized him up as being about five foot ten inches and a waistline of thirty two. Of course she would never allow anyone to know her observations or that she even cared. She was surprised that he did not have brown eyes and dark hair like his fourteen year old brother Kenny.

"This is my wife Elizabeth, and our daughter Evie," Dad said. Evie paused long enough to return a greeting and hurried on lest the sleeve on the shirt she was ironing dry before the wrinkles were ironed out. Evie detected a smile spreading across Ray's face as he greeted her. She covered the remaining sprinkled clothes and assisted in dishing up the creamed carrots. It did not take long for everyone to be in their designated places.

The little ones were a wee bit bashful, having had to share the meal with a perfect stranger—well, a stranger anyway. The blessing on the food was requested by Elizabeth. "Help yourself to some more potatoes and meat," Gus said as he passed the food to the wood chopper. After working in the cold, Ray was easily persuaded to second helpings. Elizabeth was busy feeding the baby in the high chair. "Will you go get the doughnuts in the warming oven, Evie?" Elizabeth asked. Donna had coined the word "defruit" instead of dessert. The family quite often used Donna's version. On this day with a stranger in their midst it did not seem quite proper to use the term. Dessert was served as Ma suggested.

Irene and Evie were soon on their way back to the coal mine, or rather, the school, and Ray back to the steady chopping of trees. "I wish that someone would invent a good cleaner that was kind to your hands, yet powerful enough to cut this smoke and dirt," the wish was that of Evie's. Visions of a ten dollar bill in their rough red hands, and energy from Ma's good dinner gave the girls renewed strength and determination to work a few more hours and days. Everyday was quite repetitious; the girls went home for lunch and so did the wood chopper. Gradually the girls talked a little more to the hired man, and Evie caught him looking in her direction more each day. Meanwhile Evie tried to convince herself she was not one bit interested. Elizabeth sensed an unusual bit of interest on the part of Ray, and often reminded Evie, "Ray certainly spends a lot of time looking across the table at you". Evie tossed her head of dark curly hair and changed the subject.

The wood was cut by the time vacation was over, and life went on as usual for Evie and Irene. They had lots of time to decide the most practical way to spend ten dollars, as the snow storm plugged the long driveway. Irene went back to school, and Evie continued ironing with the old sad iron and a few other daily tasks that filled her day. Practicing on the organ was her one escape from the humdrum. After all, she did learn a few of the basics of reading music in eight lessons. Rena, a friend from church, had kindly offered free lessons a few years before. Evie rode the bike over five miles of sandy roads each way. It was such a delight to go home to practice on the old church organ that had been donated to the Branstner family. Then Evie became ill, which was nothing new, having had bouts of kidney infections as long as she could recall. Dr. Will ordered complete rest. No bike riding! Her dreams of being a noted pianist were shattered. It was much too far to walk, and Gus was too busy to leave his farm work to take her for lessons. By this time Evie found a second hand piano, and had time to spend practicing. She kept trying to figure out the sharps and the flats to her favorite hymns. She discovered she could change some sharp keys to flats, but not knowing what key she was playing a song in, she just knew it sounded great. One decision was final. "My kids *will* have music lessons!" she murmured under her breath. The winter months were long for Evie and nothing exciting happened in the valley.

Ray continued working for Pete Graff on the farm, and spent his spare time dreaming of the girl by the ironing board. His brother Kenny visited the home often. "Did you see Evie this week?" Ray asked when he went home. He spent what idle time he had trying to gain courage to ask Evie out.

4
A New Dawning

Easter came. Evie and Elizabeth made print dresses for the little ones that had outgrown their clothing and did not have a hand-me-down to wear for Easter Sunday. Elizabeth beamed with pride at the perfect french braids that Donna and Pearl paraded as they marched around the *other* room. June and Ruby preferred long curls. The stiffly starched frocks, brand new anklets and polished shoes would have made any mother proud. They crowded in the car and went to Union Corners Church. A timely sermon was delivered after the Sunday School chorus and study.

"Isn't it a beautiful Easter?" Elizabeth shook Mary Eckmans hand as a smile stretched across her face. Mary and Elizabeth were old school chums. After an exchange of greetings with others Elizabeth gathered her flock together "as a mother hen would gather her chicks" and they hurried on home.

"You children all change your clothes as soon as we get home," Elizabeth commanded. They must take the utmost caution with their Sunday "go to meetin" clothes.

Two big roosters were also neatly dressed and filling

the kitchen with a great aroma of sage dressing. Elizabeth first added kindling to the coals in the range. The potatoes were in a kettle, awaiting to be boiled and mashed. A large casserole of scalloped corn was placed in the oven to bake. A pan of homemade rolls sent out pleasing scents as they heated in the warming oven. Elizabeth's chow-chow (a mixture of fall pickled vegetables), orange marmalade, two pumpkins, and one chocolate pie decked the pantry shelf awaiting their destiny. A linen tablecloth covered the bountiful table. Elizabeth gave thanks as the family bowed in silence. Perhaps she was comparing this scrumptious spread with some of the holiday meals in bygone years of beans and biscuits.

Another day, another month past before Evie went to the big town of Bertha to work for the Hartungs, who owned the only hardware store in town. The house was like a mansion to the new maid with so many bedrooms and a huge summer bedroom built on the back of the house over the back porch. It had windows on three sides.

Mrs. Hartung was bedridden. Evie stood by her bedside as she gave her specific directions, in a firm but not unkind tone. "Your time to get up will be 6:00 a.m. I would like the furniture dusted every morning before you start breakfast." She continued to give her the daily routine each morning as Evie delivered her breakfast to her bedroom. Evie soon learned to make cookies with fat from the bacon. She had to admit it worked very well. The spicy oatmeal cookies tasted fine. The bacon fryings were always consumed in the fried potatoes back at the farm. She soon caught on why there were rumors of the family being the richest folk in town.

"You will have every other weekend off," was the promise when Mr. Hartung came to the farm to select his hired girl. Two long weeks had past, and Evie had already discovered a way to get home. Grace (Evies' old bosom friend) worked at the hospital just a few blocks away, as did her nurse sister. Evie ran over every evening she could to visit or go for a walk with her childhood schoolmate. "You can ride home with Hester and I every week that you get time off," Grace volunteered. Hester was her *big* sister with a car of her very own.

Evie could hardly wait to get home. It was so lonely without her younger brothers and sisters. The first two weeks seemed an eternity. It was wonderful to get back to the six-room house with all her family. Saturday was always busy, getting food ready for Sunday. A 1931 black Chevrolet drove into the yard. Elizabeth announced, "It is Ray! I am sure he is here to see you, Evie." "How do you know that? I am not going out there," Evie stated emphatically. "He hardly knows me!" Elizabeth and a few of the little ones went out to greet him, only to return and say, "I told you so!" Evie glanced in the mirror while brushing a lock of curls in place, and opened the screen door. She was not usually at a loss for words, but was not sure what to say. What did he want anyway?

"Hi! I just heard from my sisters that you were home for the weekend and I was wondering if you needed a ride back to Bertha on Sunday night," he asked. "Not really," was the curt reply. "Hester plans to pick me up. She makes the trip every Sunday." "I am taking my sisters and brothers to Sunday School tomorrow, and I will see you in church," Ray stated just before he started the motor on his car. Evie ran back to the kitchen and her scrubbing. "What did he want?" was the question that was fired from all directions. "I told him I already had a ride back to Bertha." "Why did you disappoint him? You could let Hester know you had a ride," Elizabeth insisted. "Ma why does it make any difference? I don't really know that guy. I am not ready to go with anybody." "I was sure he liked you, Evie." "It took him six months to show any signs of it," Evie retorted. She scrubbed the white birch floor with renewed vigor. She was on her knees using lye water and a scrub brush.

It was a gorgeous day on June 14, 1942. Ray brought his younger sisters to Sunday School and church. After the service he quickly followed Evie out the door and again insisted on taking her back to Bertha. What was a girl to do? Elizabeth looked Evie in the eye, and

Evie could read her mind. That afternoon Evie walked over to inform Hester she did not need a ride back to Bertha. Evie was tempted to stay home and help her mother, but knew in her heart a sick lady was depending on her. "I really need to earn some money," she rationalized. "And I *may* enjoy getting to know Ray." It had taken Ray from January 18 to June 14th to get up courage to ask Evie to do anything with him. There was really not much to ask her to do. The town of Bertha was like a ghost town on Sundays. No one had ever heard of a Burger King or a Dairy Queen. It even lacked a park to walk around in. At last he found an excuse. She needed a ride back to work. His brother Kenny kept him posted on everything that transpired at the Branstner ranch.

"It is my twenty-first birthday today," he proudly informed the girl by his side.

Evie had no intention of going beyond the friendly stage with this farmer. She had not sorted out in her mind exactly what was in store for this country girl. She carefully watched the fate of her own mother, and that of other women in the valley, including Ray's Mom. She did not know if she would ever marry. "I don't want to just get married and have babies every year until I reach my mid-forties," she told her mother on several occasions. She and Joy decided they may as well manage an orphanage, until Joy changed her mind and was swept off her feet by a young preacher. After all, if it was experience working with children and washing diapers, Evie felt skilled in this field. Perhaps it was all those ideas that made deep grooves in her brain, and caused the rather cold treatment on that so-called date. It was not a real date as far as Evie was concerned, or why did he bring his brother along? Kenny was sleeping in the back seat before they reached their destination. Evie made an effort to converse, but that was as far as she planned to go. Ray was already deeply in love, and Evie could not believe that you could love some one you barely knew. "No! I do not want a good night kiss," she promptly informed the pursuer. He walked her to the door in silence and bid her good night with a gentle touch on her hand. Evie unlocked the front door to the mansion.

Mr. Hartung had his ears tuned to the parlor radio, hardly noticing Evie as she entered the room. President Roosevelt's voice penetrated the air waves. He spoke of the need for reinforcements on all battle fronts. "We all must sacrifice, we must unite and forget our differences." His vibrato voice echoed through the rooms. Evie was now aware of how Ray must feel about Uncle Sam's call. She sat in the front hall for the special bulletin and then heard the song, "Don't Sit Under The Apple Tree With Anyone Else But Me," as she trudged up the open stairway with mixed emotions.

She was happy that Ray admired her, but to fall madly in love your first ride to town was more than she could comprehend. Ray fell for the farmer's daughter the first time he laid eyes on her at the ironing board. He spent the previous six months dreaming of her as his bride. He walked slowly back to his black Chevrolet and felt he was far from first base.

It was not characteristic of him to be overly persistent, but as the old Chev made its way back to the Valley he determined in his heart to be everything he thought Evie would want in a young man. It was always a pleasure to take his family to church. In fact he could hardly wait for the Sunday that Evie would be home. One weekend Evie did not come home on her scheduled trip. Ray was soon on his way to the Hartung residence. He cautiously rang the door bell. Evie answered the door and was so surprised to find the young farmer dressed in his Sunday best. He was in his only navy blue suit, white shirt and tie. "I thought you may like to go for a ride. It is such a beautiful July day," Ray tried to sound convincing. "No, I have other plans," Evie said, knowing very well a telephone call could change her plans with Grace. She was reluctant to further encourage Ray that she planned to be a steady friend of his, much less his special girl. There were things she admired about him. She had time to calculate a few good points. He did not have habits that

annoyed her, like his brothers and father. He was courte-
ous and thoughtful. "I don't think he should be so aggres-
sive about being my steady right off the bat," Evie mused
to herself while Ray waited nervously for her to change
her mind.

"I am sorry I can't go today," Evie repeated. She was
not going to give in and allow him to think he could drop
by on the spur of a moment and expect her to be exuber-
ant about it.

Ray made one more attempt to solidify some sort of
a date. "When is your next weekend off?" "I am going
home next Friday night," Evie replied. "May I come to get
you?" Ray asked. Evie sensed a sincere sad expression in
his faded blue eyes and could not utter a negative word.

"I do have a ride, but what time would you come?"
was Evie's way of reluctantly consenting.

"I can be here at seven then we will have time to go
to Wadena and have a root beer float or a banana split."

Evie had never more than heard of a banana split.
"That sounds good to me," Evie agreed.

Friday night finally arrived and Ray was not one
minute late. On the way to Wadena the conversation was
soon on the subject that was most prominent on Ray's
mind.

"My classification is now 1-A, and I will be joining
my three brothers in the service. I can work on the farm
for the summer months and then I will be leaving," Ray
said quietly with a note of sadness. "I meet the kind of a
girl I've dreamed about all my life and then I have to
leave her. I hope we can become better friends before
fall." Evie was speechless when he added, "I have wanted
to spend time with you ever since the first day I met you.
I have loved you from the day your father introduced us."
Evie could not say the feeling was mutual, but was learning to know and admire Ray more than she dare admit to
herself. The conversation drifted to family situations,
both the banana split and the evening were soon history.

"My folks will wonder what happened to me. I usually get home about seven thirty when I ride out with Hester." Ray knew it was time to go back to the valley but he somehow felt that he had made it over the first hurdle.

From that evening on, Evie discovered it was very difficult to refuse a date with Ray. Every other weekend the two found somewhere to go together, if nothing more exciting than meeting some of Rays favorite aunts and cousins. Hours of weekends were spent together. He was working as a farm hand for the largest farmer in the valley. Evie had also worked for that same farmer as second cook for a short time." I remember Pete would always come in the evening and put his easy chair near the kitchen range and rest his feet on the oven door," Evie told Ray. "He still does," was his response.

Evie and Ray had a few things in common besides both having worked for the richest man in Oak Valley and being from large, poor families. Their births each numbered the fourth, on the list of offspring; they both had learned the meaning of hard work, and were of mutual faith. Would this suffice to cement their friendship?

5
War in The
South Pacific

She continued to correspond with Ray. At times it seemed only a dream that the two would ever embrace again. Over thirty-three months had passed with no promise of a tomorrow. V Mail was the most information received. That was a one page letter, reduced in size and written on the inside of the tiny envelope. At times the V Mail was eight weeks apart. "You begin to feel you are writing to an imaginary friend," Evie said sadly. A blank letter was on the dining room table before her.

She stared into space and the darkness through the window. The children were all tucked in, and Evie had waited for it to quiet down. She opened the window to enjoy the fresh air, the songs of the birds and crickets, and the cool breeze whistling through the plum trees.

Ray had been living in a world he never thought would exist. The need was urgent for men on all fronts. Young men had to grow out of their boyhood almost over night. Thanks to an Auntie, Ray graduated from Marshall University High in Minneaoplis in nineteen forty.

It was before daylight, on Friday September 1, 1939, that the German Armies ate a midnight breakfast, prepared a sneak attack, and crossed the Polish frontier. Two days later Britian and France declared war. It was a war that interrupted families all over the world. Congress passed the Lend Lease Act on March 11, 1941. United States began as a Supply Sergeant, and by November of 1941 America was involved in a very tangible way. The surprise attack of Pearl Harbour on December 7, 1941 was the last straw as far as Ray making any great plans for the immediate, or any, future.

It was Friday, November 13, 1942 that he was to leave Fergus Falls. The train broke down in Staples, and Ray was separated from the Ottertail recruits. Only eternity will tell what this separation may have caused. He perhaps would have been shipped to the European conflict. Evie and her two best friends, Lois and Rena, also left to seek their fortunes in the Twin Cities. Ray was sure Evie could spend a few hours with him, while awaiting his orders at Fort Snelling. His brother Murley was on furlough at the time. Murley, his fiance', Mary, Evie, and Ray enjoyed their first and only double date. Evie was invited to spend the night at Aunt Anna's already full house. It was November 14, 1942. The following day Ray took her back to her rooming house on Beacon Avenue. They said their sad goodbyes. Evie and her roommates had found a job at Griggs Cooper. Evie was helping prepare the candy that went into the ration packages. Lois and Rena were working on a belt line, stuffing those boxes for hungry service men on both fronts.

It was Sunday, the 16th of November. The sun was just setting. The phone rang for Evie. Rays' voice sounded so urgent. "I am just leaving Fort Snelling for the St. Paul depot. Please come down! They will not tell us where or when we are going, but I am sure we will be at the depot in an hour or so. We'll soon be on our way somewhere." Only the officers in charge knew where their tracks lead. For the protection of all their military cargo, no one could know that they were on their way to Camp

Wolters in Texas.

Evie was not familiar with St Paul. She did not know where the depot was. Fear welled up. "I've got to go now," Ray hung the receiver before Evie could admit her fear of finding the depot by herself.

She confided to her roommates. Lois piped up, "If you don't go to the depot, I am going to go by *myself!*" It was a last attempt to make Evie go! Lois found a street-car schedule and they were off.

It was a sea of army uniforms throughout the large train station. Evie wondered how she would ever spot the soldier she loved. Every soldier was marching restlessly. Ray's eyes were searching for one girl that was five foot two with eyes of blue. Evie was soon in his arms. As private as Ray liked to be, he did not worry about an audience. "We will only be here five minutes, and then we have to load. Why couldn't you have been here earlier?"

Evie tried to explain. "The street cars and buses do not run as often on Sunday and we had to change from one to the other."

Ray softened and said, "Let's just enjoy the five minutes we have. It may be a long time before we see each other again." Little did he know how long that last embrace had to last. It was good he could not see beyond that day.

After thirteen weeks of intensive training and ready or not, a thousand troops were on a pullman train headed for Pennsylvania.

Two long weeks were spent in waiting to replace troops in Europe where most needed, perhaps to invade North Africa. The recruits were confined to the barracks, packed and ready to leave at a moment's notice. Early in the morning, orders came to board a train. Thinking they were heading for the east coast and on their way to cross the Atlantic, they discovered the train was heading west.

"Keep your shades lowered as we enter cities," the message was handed down throughout every pullman.

Ray had always dreamed of seeing his country, but never with the shades pulled down, and not knowing his destination. Five days later he was privileged to see the Pacific Ocean. The troops were transported by barge to a large Dutch Merchant ship, off to see the world. The crew was as Dutch as the merchant ship itself. The guns on the ship were manned by the Navy and the chefs were dressed in white. You can bet they had beans for breakfast, dinner, and supper. Ray had always wondered why his mother referred to them as navy beans. Ray was assigned to swab the deck. The bunks were stacked four high where formerly cargo was stacked. It was off on a twenty-seven day journey. The trip was zigzagged (a precautionary measure to escape Japanese submarines) heading toward the French island of New Calidonia. It took a little longer that route. Crossing the equator was the highlight of that expedition.

Landing in a semi-tropical island they slept in pup tents until pyramidal tents were in formation. This was set up for troops that would come to protect the island later.

When the camp was set up, it was on to more important tasks, and on to the Solomon Islands. It was on the Russell Islands that they were assigned to the 169th Battlion and Forty Third Division. With only thirteen weeks of basic training for the war in Europe, the ship itself was shaking with anxiety.

"I did not have this in mind. Think of all the hours I spent in school wishing I was grown up," Ray's mind wandered back. The tables had turned. Ray was wishing he was still a little boy and was already sick of the ocean. He had spent hours leaning over the rail. That was the only convenience of swabbing the deck. His combat clothes hung loosely at his waist. "I could get sick swinging! How, and why, am I out here in the middle of an ocean? I don't want to kill anybody."

The soldiers were not in the habit of displaying their fears. That would only show signs of weakness. Secretly, they would all rather have awakened to the smell of bacon and eggs, and their mother's tender voice calling up the stairway, "Breakfast!!" In contrast, the loud voice of the Sergeant reminded Ray he better stop wistful dreaming and be at attention.

They were now on a World War I destroyer, dressed for combat. Their bags were packed, their guns were cleaned and loaded. And it was not to play cops and robbers on the back forty.

They landed in pitch dark on a small island. In the twilight hours as they were unloading boats by hand, they spotted three Jap soldiers setting up machine guns. One Japanese soldier was killed, two escaped in the thick jungle. A patrol was sent out, but did not find the two enemies. With only two lucky Japanese on that small island, the 143rd was soon on its way to more opposition. Those two may still be in hiding, having never heard of the fate of Hiroshima, or Nagasaki.

The next island was New Georgia. Ray, like other soldiers, was on a landing craft when a squadron of Japanese bombers soared overhead. The ship they had just left opened fire. Not one bomber made it through the battle. One U.S. transport went down with all it's crew. Ray did not have time to give it a lot of thought at that moment. Would his craft land safely? What lies ahead? The center of the jungle had been cleared by the British and underneath that jungle was the most beautiful solid coral landing field. But the Japanese had control of that coral airport.

Ray was placed in the front lines. Struggling through the heavy jungle, the going was tough. He witnessed the fall of many of his comrades. A bugle boy, who was not trained for jungle fighting, was the first to fall. "Fall down! "Fall down!" his buddies commanded. Falling only on one knee made him a perfect target. He never blew his bugle again.

Each soldier carried a folding handle shovel that fit conveniently in his pack. During the day the temperature was one hundred degrees plus. They dug fox holes to sleep in when they could not be on the slow move. The enemy could not tell exactly where in the dense jungle they were, but made sure the night guards would make plenty of noise to keep the GI's awake; thus not alert for fighting the next day. The Japanese soldiers were taught it was better to die than be taken a prisoner of the U.S. army. These brave soldiers were not buried. The humid hot air left only the skeleton in two days.

For two or three days they met up with stiff resistance as they tried to take a hill that was close to the airport. The battalion commander gave the orders to take the hill at all costs. The captain was from Minnesota. He planned to lead, instead of follow, to the top of the hill. His brave act cost him his life, but perhaps saved the life of one of his men.

There was more than fresh air to breathe. The soldiers had not had a bath for over twenty days. Their water was from mud holes with drops of chlorine to make it safe enough to drink. The American bodies were taken care of with dignity, as soon as possible. After six weeks another unit joined them to replace the losses. They occupied a hill near the airport. When it was nearly dark they were attacked. Too many troops made the mistake of being in one spot when a mortar shell hit. They did not live to see the light of a new day. Compared to the loss of the enemy, Company B's loss was minor in number, leaving over one hundred and fifty dead Japanese. Every American soldier had real worth, and death caused a hush to come over the company. After the battle, strong men bowed with unkempt hair, and folded their rough hands, while tears rolled down their overgrown beards. It was with sorrow and mixed emotions Ray opened his C rations and bowed to give thanks as he remembered his fallen comrades.

Replacements were sent in and the company started back, thinking they had conquered the jungle. Suddenly they were ambushed and faced another battle. The first Sergeant was one of the first to fall. Ray and three other soldiers carried him back to a camp near their landing. Ray knew little about him. He was large and from Italian descent, about fifty years old, and from Connecticut. Without a shave or hair cut for twenty eight days, it was hard to guess his age. He perhaps had a family that he had not seen for three or four years. He was suffering and scared. The load was heavy, but so were the hearts of the four hungry soldiers. Why did he make it through the long battle and then land on a stretcher, by the bullets of a few stray Japanese?

They dug another fox hole, ate their rations and fell in their usual bed. The next morning they were given a razor blade and took the hint. The sun heated water for a bath. Is that what it feels like to be clean? It wasn't long and their clothes were wet from the heavy humid climate. Before they left the next day Ray saw them remove the body of the Italian soldier.

The objective of the Forty Third was to take over the Munda airport. The task was accomplished. "I can't believe I am still alive," Ray thought to himself. He reached for a pencil and paper and decided to let the world back home know he was still kicking. This letter was sent to Ray's brother, Dock.

August 31, 1943
Dear Dock;

I received your letter of August 11, yesterday. The censorship restrictions have been modified. I think you knew that I first landed in New Calidonia. What a place that was! At the time I was there I hated it. I would just as soon be back there now. You perhaps know that the Island is under French domination, and there are still a few French there and the greater part of the population is natives. There are more soldiers now than anyone else. Those natives really hold you up! Fifteen cents for a small glass of lemonade or a dip of ice cream. Everything you buy cost five times more than it does at home. We can buy candy at the PX cheaper.

But back to New Calidonia. In peace time this Island would be considered beautiful. We were not looking for beauty. There is a chain of mountains running through the center of the Island, practically all mountains and hills. There was a stream running through the camp. We were located in a valley. It was a good location. We built a camp there. You can imagine the type of work we did there, digging grubbing and chopping. About the same work of the CCC, only we worked about as hard as the WPA workers did. We had a few ball games there and our chief entertainment was movies, two or three times a week.

I took part in a parade. It was quite a parade, the occasion being French Independence Day. It was at Naumea, the capitol city. The French, the Navy, and New Zealand Troops also took part.

I took part in the New Georgia Campaign. I was lucky and came out without a scratch. You perhaps read the details in the newspapers. I can tell you some of my personal experiences.

I will never forget my first night on the front. We dug in on a hill taken from the Japs that day. The place stunk from dead Japs. When darkness came the Japs also came. Not to attack but to torment us. They really did a job of it, too. I did not sleep a wink, I was so scared. Their objective was to keep us awake at night, and fire at them so they would know our position. We did not shoot at night, at least for the first fifteen days. They threw hand grenades and shot twenty-five calibre rifles. They would also get in foxholes with some of the fellows and cut them up.

We dreaded the nights more than advancing during the day. We finally got used to the noise and slept. We were three or four men in fox holes . That made it easier for us also. They kept up those tactics for two and one half weeks. We were attacked two nights in a row by the best Jap troops called the Imperial Marines. They are dead ones now. Our battalion was credited with killing three hundred those two nights. I fired about eighty rounds. I saw two drop. What really saved us was our mortars. One mortar shell (About 60 MM) dropped in a hole full of Japs. There were twenty three Japs in that hole the next morning. Those MI rifles are really good. Mine was full of mud but worked like a charm. They really take a beating.

We were relieved for a few days, but came back for the final push. We dug in a hill overlooking the airport. The Japs still occupied the hill. Artillery was dropping on them and they ran like lunatics. Some of the fellows took pot shots at them but they were a thousand yards away. They can't fight in open country. They had lots of pill boxes dug, and would put coconut branches around them and would plaster it up with coral rock. That is why it was so hard to knock them out. They even had tunnels dug in the side of the hill, through solid coral. The little devils would not give up. They killed some of our wounded men on stretchers and even the bearers. At one time our supply line was cut off and we were without food for two days. We only had about half enough that week. There was also a scarcity of water throughout the campaign. We drank water from shell holes that horses would not even drink from.

That is all in the past now. We camped on Munda airport for a few days, I am not permitted to tell you where I am now. There aren't any Japs here, an occasional air raid. They don't drop bombs here though. We see plenty of dog fights. Our boys really knock them out. We saw one Jap Bomber attack our fleet. Forty Jap bombers came in. Thirty nine went up in flames,and the other was shot down. The total for that day was ninety eight fighters and bombers. Our losses were very small. We saw what our Air Force can do. Most were shot down by anti-aircraft. I have also seen our dive bombers in action. Pictures cannot do justice to scenes like that.

Brother, don't wish you were here. This jungle fighting is hell, with nothing but jungle flies and pests. You can't see what you are shooting at. It drives a guy nuts. It isn't a healthy country. I will be glad to get out of here. Stay in Camp Young.

You asked me how it felt to shoot some one. I didn't have any feelings. I was too scared. It was my spirit that did the shooting. Don't let anyone ever tell you they were not scared. They would be lying. When the mortars start flying and the enemy is sneaking up on you, you are *scared. So much for that campaign.*

I don't know when I will see you again. It has been three years now. We'll both be old men.

Love, Your Brother Ray

6
Evie Leaves The Valley

World War II, with it's ugly reality, weighed heavily on the hearts and lives of almost every family in the Valley. The entire family crowded around the radio at news time. President Roosevelt's voice penetrated the lowly homes in America. The war seemed endless, and Evie was getting restless. Was it going to take the life of every red-bloodied American to defeat both Hitler and Japan? There was no time schedule to look forward to homecoming for members of the armed forces.

The invitation from Mae in Michigan came as a breath of fresh air. Mae was expecting her second child. Her husband Gene worked in a defense plant. "How lucky can a sister be, married and having a husband home by her side," Evie said to Elizabeth. As she sat on the wood box and read the letter, Ma turned the sizzling pork steaks and lifted the cover from the big kettle of boiling potatoes, just in time to save the stove and the wonderful aroma in the kitchen from a burnt odor.

Mae's little boy had just turned two. The letter was an invitation to Michigan to care for little Russell while his Mamma took her maternity leave. Evie was soon packing her black suitcase with all her worldly possessions, including an old Bible. "I am going to buy myself a new Bible the first pay check, when I start a new job," Evie stated. Elizabeth and Gus saw her off at the Wadena train depot. Again it was sad to tell all the family good-bye. Michigan was on the other side of the world as far as the little sisters and brothers were concerned.

The train was filled with wives with squalling babes in arms, and toddlers hanging to their mother's skirts. The seats were loaded with diaper bags, bottles, teddy bears, and cracker crumbs. Evie later learned that many had bid their husbands farewell and were now going home to hope and pray that Father would return. Evie recalled Ray wanting to marry before Uncle Sam called him. Just observing the scene on the train reminded her how fortunate she was. "I have a difficult time trying to hang on to my purse and a magazine," she thought to herself. "What would I do with a baby?"

The Waves and Waac uniforms really looked classy. She sat and tossed the idea of joining with them just to wear the uniform. Service men occupied the greater share of the coach. Body language was a dead give away if they were heading home or had just said good-byes.

Evie dialogued with everyone who showed a wee bit of interest. She secretly worried about transferring to another station in Chicago. "How far is it?" she inquired of the conductor.

"You have two hours to get there," was his short and grumpy reply.

The train reached the Windy City on time. "I have never seen so many soldiers, sailors and Marines." Evie was in awe. Cabs lined the front of the station. Evie rushed to catch one.

"All armed forces and their families served first," a goliath in uniform shouted. Every cab was filled and when more cabs arrived they too were packed.

"Maybe I should join the Waacs," thought Evie. She spotted a clock on top of a tall building and ran to catch an approaching cab, just as military personnel crawled into the restless cab. One sympathetic sailor motioned for her to hop in. It was a first, both for a cab ride and the privilege of sitting on a sailor's lap. It was the last bold attempt to catch the train to Lansing. Alas, it was too late; the train had just departed. Evie was heartsick, hungry and alone.

Fearful of looking for a hotel in a strange city, and trying to save the few dollars in her purse, Evie spent the next ten hours watching a new world revolving around a nation at war. "How can there be any soldiers on the front or sailors at sea with this many in Chicago?" she seriously wondered. And where in the South Pacific was her dear soldier?

The clock ticked slowly. It was in the middle of the night. Her sleepy mind wandered back to the Valley as she fought falling off the chair. The hours passed as though an eternity, then *finally* it was time to board the train. A man in uniform again repeated the orders for civilians to please step back until all military were serviced. Evie's dog eared ticket was in her hand. Numerous times she checked it to be sure it was not lost. Finally, she was on the last lap of her journey. She had every intention of eating in the diner car but she could no longer fight sleep. The first audible sound was the voice of the conductor, "Next stop: LANSING." She ran to the ladies room, splashed cold water on her face, and quickly combed her tangled dark curly hair. She gave her teeth a swap and a promise. It was with a deep sigh she stepped from a nightmare, back to reality. Gene and Mae were at the station for the second time. Seeing family and her first little nephew compensated for the darkness of Chicago.

Mae and Evie had time to catch up on the news from the Valley before delivery pains separated them. Mae was quite the same sister except for the expanded waist line. The beautiful brown-eyed nephew bonded with his Auntie in time to feel comfortable with Evie as his Nannie.

The rented cottage bordered a five acre grape

orchard. "Be careful not to allow Russy to go in the orchard alone," Mae cautioned. The power of suggestion carried to little ears. A day or so later, Evie took her eyes off him and Russy was nowhere in sight. Evie's heart skipped a beat as she ran through the orchard.

"Russy, Russy! Russel Eugene Hauser, answer me!" Her mouth was dry and her mind raced over the forewarning. "What will Gene and Mae think of me?" How could short legs travel so fast? Russy had just recovered from polio. Evie raced up and down the rows and rows of grapes. No pot of gold could have been more rewarding than the sight of that little boy with a grin stretched across his face as though he was playing his first game of hide and seek.

Mae made it to the hospital, and the proud father came home to announced the birth. "What did you name her," Evie asked?

"Her mother wants to call her Grace Eloise." Evie decided she liked that name, she wondered if the war would end, and would she ever experience the mystery of creating a new life? She was content to enjoy and love the little bundle that invaded Mae's home.

Mae and Evie kept very busy taking care of a wee one and little Russy. Evie was experienced in washing diapers, after having ten sisters and brothers younger then herself. Trying to keep up with that big brother and having meals on the table when the day closed made the time pass quickly.

The sisters would be the first to confess there was time for reminiscing. "Remember the time you wanted me to chase you until I caught you?" Evie queried. She chased Mae until she could barely breathe. Mae was then to chase Evie, but she was tired of running and just flopped in the shade of a tree in Martin's pasture, refusing to budge.

"No, I will never forget that chase," Mae responded. "You had an old board in your hand." Mae's strength was renewed; she ran as though her life depended on it (which it may have). Just then a wonderful tune on the radio set Evie's feet in time, and she was dancing across Mae's living room. Mae's laughter encouraged Evie to continue till the last note faded into advertising .

"What are your plans?" Gene asked of Evie. "Why don't you find a job in Michigan? There is no job for you back in Minnesota!" Mae was now feeling capable of taking over the household without a maid. With Gene's sane advice, Evie went to Lansing to apply for work. A large bakery advertised for help. With the shortage of workers Evie was to start work immediately. Gene and Mae lived outside of the city, and Evie had no transportation to Lansing on Sundays. The bakery crew all worked on Sunday in order to supply sixteen trucks to leave early on Monday morning. The defense plants employed almost all able bodied workers. Evie had the special privilege of arriving an hour earlier in the morning and working ten hours daily and working on Saturday mornings instead of Sundays.

Along with other behind-the-scene jobs, Evie's duties included lining the cake pans and stacking them on heavy racks, ready to be filled with dough. Archie, the tall thin baker, came early to start the dough for stacks and stacks of rolls. The cake pans were framed together in groups of ten with five pans on each side. A dispenser was set to release two exact amounts of cake dough at a time. The conveyer belt was timed to move the pans along. It was Evie's job to see that the next set of pans were placed on the belt as Irene moved the full pan from the other side of the contraption. Time and noise did not allow idle chatter, nor did you dare miss a beat. Cake dough was a sorry mess to have on the conveyer belt.

A tall lanky seventeen year old boy ground nuts, dates, and raisins. He also took sweet dough and stretched it in a long slender shape with a large electric roller. The dough was then placed on a conveyer. Two other girls worked with Evie and spread cinnamon and sugar over the dough.

Childhood small pox left Irene with a pitted face.

She had large beautiful blue eyes and black curly hair that detracted from that problem. Cindy, her partner at the conveyer, was a tiny little red head, with a temper to complement the freckles. Evie and the two girls took over the project from there, while Rodney prepared the next twelve feet of dough. The dough was then rolled together and the conveyer transported the dough through a sharp roller that cut the rolls in uniform size. The girls kept perfect time arranging the rolls on large sheets for baking. Again, you must work fast or rolls fell on the floor. Skip, the head baker, was short, fat, and jolly; with thinning curly hair. The only time he was crabby was when too many rolls landed on the floor.

One morning Rodney came running and screaming, "Skip! Skip!" His left ring finger was grinding with the raisins. With young men as scarce as hen's teeth, and Rodney incapacitated, the girls had to take turns handling forty or fifty pounds of dough. That was fine until the novelty wore off.

"This is hard work, Skip," grumbled Irene. Cindy and Evie agreed. The following day Cindy and Irene went on strike. Evie had been drilled to do what she was told. Day after day she tugged at the long strips of dough but was reminded that Rodney had made a lot more money than she was being paid. Break time came and Evie headed for the rest room, but instead she went in the big office.

"I would like to speak to the boss," she said to a receptionist. She had not seen him since the day he hired her. Evie explained to him that the other girls refused to take turns on the roller. "It is a man's job, and Rodney was paid thirty cents more per hour then I am getting. I will continue working, if I receive the pay I deserve."

"The boss wrinkled his forehead and said, "I will increase your pay, but whatever you do, don't let Irene and Cindy know about it." Evie made a solemn promise. She could hardly contain herself until she could tell someone. Gene and Mae rejoiced with her at the supper table.

Irene and Cindy could not figure Evie out. "How can you work on that conveyer day after day, and why?" On pay day Evie forgot all about the hard work. She laughed all the way to the bank. "I will never tell." One day she took her check to the rest room, tore off the stub and forgot to put it in her purse or locker.

Irene and Cindy then took their break, but not for long. "We found this in our rest room? Whose pay stub is this? We've worked here a lot longer than Evie! Why should her pay check be more than ours?" Answering their own question by shouting, "It is Evie's, we know! We are going straight to the office and demand equal pay." The two employees came out of the office crying, and ran to their lockers. They left in the middle of the afternoon.

It was difficult to find someone to replace the "mad hatters" and Evie felt badly about being so careless with the stub of her pay check. The cakes, rolls and other baked goods continued to be ready for loading in the sixteen trucks each morning, as the remaining crew carried the load. Two weeks went by when who should appear but two disgruntled workers. They had been to the office begging for their jobs back. "Under one condition, you start at beginner's wages for the first two weeks," said the Boss. "Leave Evie at the dough roller and don't make any trouble." With no money to pay next month's rent, what more could they say?

Summer brought with it a longing to go back to Evie's roots. Letters from home were a reminder of all her family that she truly missed.

Little Grace Eloise was a bubbly little bundle of joy, and Russy shared in every project that Mae had going on in the old farm house that the family had just purchased.

"I don't think you should go home," her brother-in-law advised. "You'll never come back." His predictions proved to be almost true.

Evie boarded the bus with the same black suit case, and very little increase in baggage. Tucked safely in her purse were six hundred dollars in saving bonds and more cash than she ever dreamed of possessing. She was now the proud owner of a beautiful Bible, and had spent money on a huge package to send back home for Christmas. It contained sweaters and toys for all the children, and clothing for Elizabeth and Gus. It was the only spending splurge during those months. Evie's goal for spending was in the future. "This war *will* end, and I will need furniture and a home of my own." She dreamed of a brighter future as the old bus rattled on, and she wondered again which of the service men she knew would be coming home. Letters from home had brought news of one school mate killed his first day of action in the South Pacific. Another school mate lost one leg, and a brother of Ray's was wounded in action in France.

War was again touching lives close to home. "We cannot lose faith in a future," Evie breathed to herself. News of destruction in Europe reminded Evie how grateful she should be that no shots could be heard at any back door in America. She would soon be home once again! The bus sped on, and the passengers were unaware of all the dreams that crossed Evie's mind those many hours. She had less fears of traveling alone. She fell into a deep sleep during the night only to discover her precious purse had fallen under her feet. She woke up in dismay until she found it. Wadena never looked so inviting. She hurriedly picked up her shopping bag of leftover apple cores, old maids from some popcorn, her diary, and a letter she had written to Ray; a letter filled with sweet nothings and hopes for tomorrow .

No place seemed as safe as the end of the lane, known as home to Evie, in the heart of the valley—the center of the world, where Elizabeth gave life to Evie and her fourteen brothers and sisters.

7

What Next?

Evie returned from Michigan to discover changes in all the children. Each one had grown into the next step up in sister's clothes and shoes. Little sisters proudly displayed the new garments they had sewn for their new dollies. Big sister had sent them dolls for Christmas. Evie unpacked her old black suitcase and brought out a few surprises. Gum was impossible to find. Evie could only bring flavored wax.

Elizabeth noticed her unhealthy complexion. "Evie, you don't look like you are feeling very well," she commented. In all the excitement Evie did not give much thought to her physical condition. She decided it was just from the long trip home. In a few days Evie was very sick. One look at her and Dr. Will hospitalized her with yellow jaundice. Working ten hour days at the bakery, the temptation to eat fresh baked goods, and the anxious moments over the war had taken its toll on Evie's health. After seven days in the Bertha hospital, Evie was released though unable to eat a meal. She was served only liquids the seven days she was hospitalized. How proud she was not to burden her parents with the hospital bill. It did steal from the money she saved for furnishing her dream house.

Elizabeth brought her bedridden, bronze daughter a small dish of jello for supper. Broth was her main diet. Gradually the farm food sounded inviting. In a few weeks Evie gained strength and joined the family around the table. She spent hours in the country air, shelling peas, snapping beans, and walking to the mail box, each day hoping for another V-Mail. The oriental color gradually disappeared from her skin, but deep sadness plagued her. Though Evie was recuperating from yellow jaundice, every inch of the farm brought back memories. Some escapades took place while Evie was in Michigan. Evie was given a synoptic and detailed account of each human interest story as the children prepared for bed. Evie lent a listening ear, as though she had never witnessed, participated in, or heard the story before.

With fourteen children, how could there be a dull moment? "Do you remember the Sunday morning everyone piled in the Ford to attend the church?" Evie asked. All of the sisters contributed wee bits, as they plugged into their memory bank . "If you don't all talk at once, I will make notes to record this for our children," Evie promised.

Luckily Gus was an early bird, for on this particular day he needed extra time to perform an errand of mercy. While on their way to the country church they spotted two bucks, competing for leadership. Their horns were locked together, and they were completely exhausted. The dip in the fighting ring indicated it had been an all night battle. Gus quickly removed a long pole from the Ross farm gate, to pry the limp warriors apart. They appeared to be very submissive, and were as still as death. They remained on the ground a few minutes, as though they could not believe they were free. Slowly they raised on their wobbly legs, and walked to a wooded area. Neither buck was really a hero. It should have made headlines in the Wadena Pioneer Journal.

It was planting time, then harvest, before you could catch your breath. Gus planned to clear more land for

next year's crops. Willy followed barefoot at his father's
heels. He carried a hatchet along to help cut trees. The
partners worked silently together for a short time and
when Gus looked up Willy was missing. He had been cautioned to be very careful. The hatchet missed it's target
and wham! Willy's big toe was sliced nearly in two. He did
not want his father to know of the accident and left the
scene without explanation. His toe bled profusely, as he
ran through the corn stubble and dirt. His sister, Orpha
met Willy while swinging a karo syrup pail with goodies
and fresh water.

Willy was crying, "Orpha, bring some epsom salts in
warm water to the barn to soak my toe. Please don't tell
Ma! Just get some clean rags and some cord to wrap my
cut". (Cord was the string ravelled from flour sacks for
such purposes. You never threw the cord away. The sack
may be used for a dish towel, pillow case or a pair of
bloomers. On this occasion the cord came in handy for a
stubbed toe.)

You couldn't keep secrets from Ma; she had eyes in
the back of her head, and ears that no sound escaped. She
peeked out the kitchen door as Orpha and Willy were
running to the barn, and surveyed the damage. "Orpha
run to get your dad at once," commanded Elizabeth, in no
uncertain terms. Several stitches had to be taken by old
Doc Will. Luckily the Ford started right off and had plenty of gas. Willy was never anxious to play Paul Bunyan
again. He vowed he would choose a safer trade.

Eleven year old Willy did not search for trouble, but
some how it found him. On one occasion he hopped on the
running board of his cousin Arnold's car. Arnold speeded
up and Willy fell off the moving monster. It ran over his
leg. Arnold frantically reversed the car, picked his wounded cousin up and took him home. Orpha was out by the
wood pile and ran to the rescue.

"Get me something to soak my knee in and bring it
to the barn!" Willy begged.

"Willy, you have to see a doctor," Orpha screamed

when she saw the wound. Ma always seemed to be just around the corner for such moments. Again he was rushed to Bertha. This episode cost Willy thirty eight stitches and his Dad a doctor bill, and a pair of crutches. The knee did heal, and there was a short period of rather dull life for the family—until Willy had a sudden urge to see the world from the peak of the garage. One slip and he was seeing stars from the ground. The wind was knocked out of him and he was left with a fear of heights (at least for overnight).

However, he was not the only adventurous member in the family. Gus stacked hay by the barn for winter's feeding. He arranged two long stacks very close together. They were rounded to perfection so that rain or snow would not penetrate the stacks. Twine was weighted with sticks of wood and anchored over the hay stacks. It was *so* out of character, but one day Orpha could not resist temptation, as she spied a ladder on the end of the hay stack. She crept quietly to the top of the stack.

"Orpha you come down this minute! You know Dad told us never to play on the hay stack," Donna warned, cupping her message with her hand around her mouth toward the sky.

"I will just run across the stack one more time," Orpha promised and giggled. "This is so much fun!" She slipped between the large stacks of slippery hay. June and Ruthie heard Donna screaming. They ran from the house. Sport was barking and pawing at the hay. All they could hear was the muffled cry of Orpha between the two stacks. It was a hot summer day. The girls tried to dig between the stacks. They were soon exhausted, and could not see their sister. "Hold your hands up, Orpha and keep them up!" June hollered. They could then see the tip of her fingers and know how much more hay had to be moved to reach her. Playing on the hay was no longer a temptation. Sisters brushed the tell tale hay from her golden curls and raced to the house to quench their thirst.

"Please don't tell Dad," Orpha begged. A pledge was sealed. Blood ran thick among the children. They would risk their lives to protect one another. They were always ready to share the last piece of cake, the crust of the bread, or a tub of used bath water.

Excitement was not limited to the younger children. It was long before Mae left home, when gum was a rare commodity. In the evening Uncle Leon would stop by Lyman Store and cousins would come over with a juicy wad of gum in their mouths. It smelled so good. When the Branstner children would have a stick of gum, some would treasure it unopened for days and others rip the stick open and mix saliva with it pronto.

Mae would harvest spruce gum from the tree and cook it a while. It usually stuck to your teeth but with a wild imagination you could taste wrigley's spearmint. She boiled it in the cover from Ma's canning jar on top of the range. One day it crusted over on top and exploded to the ceiling. She had big plans to invent a new flavor for the Wrigley Company but could not get the formula off the kitchen ceiling.

Joy worked for a family in Minneapolis while attending Bible school.

During summer vacation Joy came home with three children that craved country air, Janie, Bud, and Phil Hauser. No matter how crowded around the table, or how cramped for bed space, Elizabeth permitted Joy to bring the children. Sixteen hungry mouths surrounded the table three times daily.

In the long summer evenings the children played outdoor games. They caught fireflies and put them in small glass jars or played steal sticks, dodge ball, or perhaps they invented a game. A very favorite pastime was playing church on top of the lumber pile behind the chicken coop. Gorgeous weddings ceremonies and baptismal services were also conducted in that sacred place. An old Ford car was their only means of transportation to and from these events, though it never moved an inch. One day June had the misfortune of getting her fingers caught in the door. Gus forbade them to play in the car from that day on, and so ended the rides in the cool of the day. They now had to walk all the way to the services and also to town. "It isn't fair," they all agreed when the car set idle.

Phil was always the dignified preacher. It is not possible to record how many times Bud married Ruthie, even though they did not believe in divorce. June was chosen as bridesmaid, and the Hauser children's cousin Robert Foreman (the local Pastor's son) was best man. All older members had a very prominent place for each function. Funerals were not as popular, but there were a few; perchance a cat, dog, chicken, bird or pet crow may die. They all deserved a proper burial. At each church service an offering was taken. A sardine can made an excellent offering plate, and the loud clunk from the stone contribution indicated the generosity of the donor. The service always boasted a large attendance. When the evening meeting was dismissed the entire congregation marched to the farm home to find lodging for another night. It was a most economical motel, with bed and breakfast all at one low price. Everything in the country was free. It was a garden of Eden for the city dwellers.

Bedtime stories from the past were now entertainment. They had read every book in the Island School library, but human interest stories were created every day at the end of the lane.

"It's time for you kids to settle down." The sobering voice came from Elizabeth, as she was trying to rock Jane to sleep. And so the story book was closed for another day.

Evie dismissed herself from the foot of the children's bed, and sneaked off to spend time alone with her parents; then to think of something to cheer her dear soldier on the far off Island of *somewhere*.

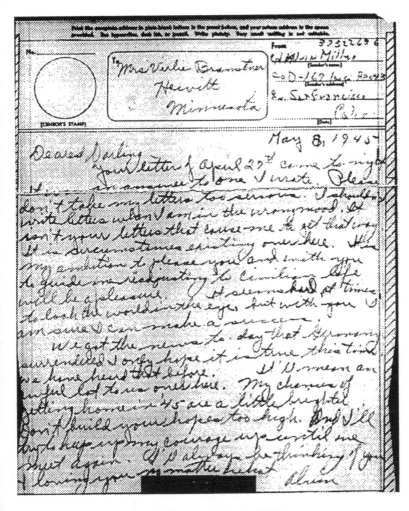

V Mail letter of May 8, 1948

8
Reflections

A cool summer breeze soothed the lonely spell that came over Evie. She tried to visualize where Ray was, and what he was doing at this very moment. She missed him desperately. She thought, "Perhaps it is a blessing his situation is unknown." The wind blew her curly brown hair over her freckled face, and billowy clouds were floating so gently in the spotted blue sky. It was early in August nineteen forty-five. She was lying on an army blanket under the shade of the old elm tree. It was a tree that shared many memories. A rope swing hung from one of its strong branches. She couldn't count the times she had swung a baby to sleep, or swung herself high in its branches, while reciting the old poem,

> *How do you like to go up in a swing,*
> *up in the sky so blue?*
>
> *I do think it the most wonderful thing*
> *that ever a child could do!*

She had memorized every word, and she agreed with the poet. Her many sisters and brothers also loved the swing. Sometimes they took turns and pushed each other for one hundred pushes. Evie reflected on her life and she thought of Aunt Maggie who was like a second mother to her.

Uncle Fred and Aunt Maggie's children were all younger than Evie. They lived just across Martin's pasture from Elizabeth and Gus. There was always a well worn path across that pasture. Both sisters Mae and Evie, loved to stay with Aunt Maggie. She hired them to help with the house work, and as Nannies to care for the little ones. The pay was one dollar per week during school months, and increased to two green-backs during the summer months. Aunt Maggie, being a fair minded person, settled the matter. Mae and Evie would work every other week, giving both an opportunity to make some spending money.

Evie descended the ladder to a pitch dark cellar as items were added to the list. "Bring up a quart of dill pickles, and toss in a few carrots with the potatoes." Aunt Maggie was making up the menu for the evening meal.

Evie continued her trip down memory lane as she remembered there always seemed to be a baby in diapers. Both Nannies were accustomed to the distasteful job of changing diapers. Winter or summer you could also bet on one assignment: "Would you get the clothes off the line before it turns dark?" Paring vegetables, carrying in wood for the range and heater, cleaning the lamp shades, refilling the lamps with oil, and setting the table were their main daily duties. It was more than the weekly pay that made the position so desirable. Aunt Maggie's cooking was also a draw, and how they loved her chocolate fudge.

Aunt Maggie was generous with last minute instructions as she left for the barn to help Uncle Fred milk the twenty four holsteins. "Now Evie don't allow the children to pull on the table oilcloth. If they pull the lamp off you would have a terrible fire!" She instilled a holy fear of the toddler's grabbing the oilcloth, and the lamp along with it. Evie and Mae took their responsibility very seriously. "Jane you wipe dishes for Evie, and Dickie you watch Harvey and Betty," Maggie continued instructions while she buttoned her milking jacket and buckled her overshoes, shut the door and went out to face the elements. Evie or Mae were ten to twelve years old then, and in full charge.

"Can I wash dishes tonight?" begged Dickie, as he began pushing a chair near the stove. The kitchen range was always in operation. A large dish pan was placed on the center front to wash the dishes in. This kept the water as hot as your hands could stand.

Evie thought to herself, "I will give Dickie about a five minute interest span." To her surprise he washed every dish, down to the old black skillet. She placed the wash pan over the reservoir, lest Dickie fall on the hotter part of the stove. Making sure the rinse water was scalding hot, she gave each dish a good extra rinse, in the event the little seven year old missed a particle of food.

Maggie used potato water in her bread. She often reminded Evie to save the water when she drained the potatoes for supper. "Is Mamma going to bake bread tomorrow?" he asked as he finished with the last pan. Dickie confused the source of the water she used. The incident was often repeated to guests. Aunt Maggie would begin telling the story and little Sir Echoes would pipe up with, "Dickie thought you made bread from dish water!" And all the children would join in laughter. Children were the prime source of entertainment, and there was *plenty* of that.

It was a hot summer day. Evie was in charge of keeping track of her cousins. Harvey came in sweaty and tired. He had to have a drink first and then said breathlessly, "I can't find Betty."

"Has anyone seen Betty lately?" the serious Auntie asked. Evie looked up from ironing the dish towels.

"No, I haven't."

"She may be lost in the corn field," Aunt Maggie exclaimed. The hay mow was another possibility except she had always been afraid to go up there alone. "Run over and get Annie and the boys to help!" Aunt Maggie was talking loudly. When the neighbors arrived they were staggered between the long row of corn. The search went on for two hours. Finally, Betty emerged laughing, from the under brush of an old shade tree near the outhouse. She and Harvey, her younger brother, had been playing hide and seek. It amused Betty to think the neighbors joined in the game. While the search went on Betty was so very still, she fell asleep. She would perhaps be hiding to this day, had she not become hungry and thirsty.

Uncle Fred was not at home for a few days. Everyone was snug in bed. Evie slept on the day bed in the living room. Aunt Maggie leaned over her bed, with her hand at her side, bending over with her face revealing severe pain. "Evie! Evie! Wake up." She shook Evie's shoulders and tried not to awaken the entire family. Evie tried to adjust to the lamp light.

"Go get Annie! My side is killing me." Evie dressed as fast as skat. She did not think to light the lantern, besides she would not have wasted the time. She ran barefoot through the kitchen and the dark shed and on to the end of the driveway. Every fence post and every bush left her breathless; she was sure it was a wild animal and she heard unusual noises. Her heart beat faster when she remembered Martin's dog. He began to bark as she reached the path to the house. She ran as fast as two short legs could carry her with Fido at her heels. She knocked frantically. Roy came to the door and shouted, "Who is there?"

"It's me, Evie!" Roy was a middle-aged neighbor. He was a short, thin, quiet man and was in his long underwear. He had known Evie from birth. Evie revealed her mission. "Aunt Maggie is so sick! Can Annie come at once?" Roy lit the oil lamp and alerted his wife. Annie quickly dressed in a faded house dress. She and Evie went racing to the rescue.

"You go back to bed, Evie," Annie suggested after conferring with Maggie. Evie obeyed, but could not get to sleep with a dear old Auntie groaning as though the death angel was at her door. By five o'clock in the morning it grew quiet in the bedroom. Evie could no longer contain herself in bed. She entered the kitchen in time to see Annie closing the lid to a two pound cheese box.

"Annie what did you put in that box?" Evie asked, knowing she had used the last of the cheese at supper time.

Annie whispered in Evie's ear. "Get me a shovel and come with me." A deep hole was dug back of the grove. Annie looked weary as she put the last mound of earth over the cheese box. "Get a big stone Evie," Annie requested with tears running down her cheek. The marker was placed, as Evie witnessed the private and secluded burial of one who should have been another cousin. They walked in silence back to the house. The night was far spent. The children were waking each other. It was time to face a new day.

Evie pondered over the events of the night and went to Aunt Maggie's bedside. She looked pale and gaunt. Not a word was said about the nightmare. "Will you go over to Martin's and ask Clayton and Ted to come over and do the morning chores?" Evie ran, but this time could plainly recognize a fence post for just that.

In the warm summer Evie begged, "Aunt Maggie please may I sleep upstairs?"

"Well, Evie you know there are no banisters around that stairway, and what's more you have been known to sleep walk. You could fall through and break your neck!" she added. There was something adventurous about sleeping in that spooky upstairs. Adjoining it was the walk-in attic, that stored Uncle Fred's World War One uniform, old photos of bearded men, furniture in need of repair, and maybe a bat or two. Evie's courage grew, as they pushed a trunk at the high end, and placed chairs along the edge of the stairway . She then tied one foot to the post of the bed, by folding a diaper on the bias. Fluffing her pillow she gave a deep sigh and settled in for the night. The musty odor and imaginary figures kept her awake for an eternity. Her thoughts finally carried her to dreams of the future. She dreamed of a most romantic husband, beautiful children, and a castle. To her amazement she fell sound asleep, and even *lived* to write about it.

The old army blanket had carried Evie down memory lane. Her strength was renewed as she rested under the elm tree. She could not believe the length of time her mind had wandered. Jumping up as though there was a fire, she shook the grass off the blanket, as she ran toward the house. It was time to live today, and help Ma with supper.

9
More of The South Pacific

Company B was now in control of the coral airport. It was wonderful to clear the mud from their combat boots and put their feet on the solid ground. How nice it would be to sleep without the threat of death, or screaming Japanese. There were no enemies in sight. The solid coral would make a perfect dance floor. With wives and sweethearts worlds away, that was just a happy thought. Their real dream was to have a home cooked meal, sleep between white sheets, and drink pure cold water. And oh! to get some mail from someone back home. The beaches and airport were guarded around the clock. Ray's company remained on New Georgia for one month. At last the good news from the Staff Sergeant, "Company B will go to Auckland, New Zealand for a 'rest'."

It was the winter season when they landed in New Zealand. Cleveland was one of Ray's close buddies. "Let's volunteer for KP," Cleveland suggested. Just getting to smell the food, have extra ice cream, fresh bread and real meat was unbelievable. Their main meat had been canned lamb's tongue, and the GI's wondered what happened to the rest of the sheep. They washed dishes, and peeled vegetables without a complaint. After three months in New Zealand, Cleveland and Ray carried twenty extra pounds under their belts, while trying not to think of what may lie on the rugged path ahead.

There were not many signs of Japanese on the islands of New Guinea. The company patrolled islands along the way for three or four months, and then on to Luzon. There they remained out at sea far enough to escape the Pazuooko (rocket type bombs) that were preparing the way for the land invasion of the infantry.

Here Ray was assigned to the Battalion Head Quarters (an Assault Platoon). With no training with this weapon Ray questioned, "Why are they issuing me a Brownie automatic gun?" These questions and many others flooded his mind. The twenty pounds of ammunition, automatic Brownie, and other gear weighing over fifty pounds were almost more than he could carry on a smooth trail.

It was January of 1945. The Seventh Fleet steamed north toward Lingayan Gulf, but not without opposition by the Kamikaze Planes. The fast Carrier Task Force rushed to their aid, but not before there were heavy losses. They prepared the way for the Infantry Division to wade ashore on January the ninth. The protective Air Forces overhead gave the soldiers renewed hope and courage.

Ray went in with the fifth wave of soldiers on Lingayan Gulf and went north. The Japanese were dug into the hills. Days ran into each other; it was almost impossible to keep track of them. Sundays you did not wear your best suit. It was another day that you hoped you would make it through. Ray was a guard by night and took ammunition and supplies to the front by day.

One day while trudging up hill with a load of ammunition, water, and rations Company B was preparing to attack the enemy. The supply sergeants could see the Japanese at a distance. Company B's second platoon was leading the attack (Rays old Company & Platoon). They had suffered over fifty percent casualties. The second squad was to lead the attack. The Squad leader had called Max to be the lead scout. Max joined the squad at eighteen. He was a handsome, tall, lanky Jewish boy and not a candidate for the infantry. Though uncoordinated, the squad leader sent him as lead scout. Max never complained but accepted orders without question. The first shot fired took his life. He was too tall to be lead scout. He was Ray's version of a hero. Nearly a half century later Ray's thoughts return to the day Max's life was taken. On Memorial Day, Ray pauses to remember the hero who never made it home to accept the medal he deserved.

A day after Ray was transferred to Company D, the company he left advanced to a point and dug in. One soldier that lived to tell Ray the story began by stating, "Boy am I lucky to be alive." He continued on as though he was telling a wild dream. "The weary gunners went to sleep on the job last night. The enemy made a sneak attack and over twenty of the Company were killed. Another guy and I played dead. An enemy actually sat on me, thinking I was dead." When the Japanese left and it was safe to move back, the two soldiers crawled back to safety.

Ray soon toughened up. The battles on New Georgia now seemed like a Sunday picnic. He later learned that the day after he was assigned to Company D, the company he left was nearly wiped out. "I don't mind this heavy load, and I would have had to say farewell to many of my comrades anyway," Ray pondered. "It is much easier this way." He paused with grateful heart to wonder why his life was spared.

Ray's twenty extra pounds of weight had disappeared by now. At times he could almost smell pork chops sizzling on the old kitchen range at home and see his mother in her apron peeling potatoes. It was only a dream. He reached for his C rations and was grateful that there were no Japanese staring into the two man foxhole with three weary men in it.

"Just think," he told his fox hole partners, "my baby

brother is almost four years old and I hardly know what he looks like." He was secretly happy that it was not his own son's childhood, that he was missing out on.

"I guess Evie was playing it safe by refusing to accept my proposal, before I left," he thought. He then relived the time he tried to persuade her, "Let's marry before I have to leave, we would have some time to be together."

He also recalled her quick response. "We don't know how long you will be gone. I could have a child that may never know a father." She continued reasoning, "I am only eighteen, the two of us may change, and we haven't known each other long enough." The case was closed.

For a time all was quiet in the fox hole. It was damp and dark. The greatest comfort was memories. Their whispered conversation recollected the past, and future dreams.

"Do you think she will say no when you get home?" Cleveland asked. " No!" Ray piped back. "The last letter I received she accepted the money I sent for a ring and selected it herself."

"I will replace it on her finger the minute I see her." With that happy thought he fell asleep.

It was raining when there was the early call to get moving. It was back to the real world of facing the heat, the elements, and the bullets.

"I feel like an old man," Cleveland admitted. "Oh! to sleep where I could stretch out my body once more." His wishes were muffled; he knew he should be content that he had not fallen with his comrades.

The battle that day was for real. It was the largest battle they had encountered. Ray was now Corporal Miller. The natives were fleeing their straw huts. The Japanese hid in the huts. A brave Chaplain stuck closely to the battle front and quietly suggested, "Why not light a match to the huts?" No sooner said than done. The enemy thinking they had a perfect place to fire while not being seen, ran for their lives. They now faced the bullets, head on. Surrendering was not an alternative; not for a Japanese soldier. They preferred being dead heroes.

Luzon was finally cleared of the enemy. There was not one hut left on the island. The natives could return and rebuild their homes. They could make the blueprints while waiting for the American soldiers to make their exit. "Let's have a picket fence with a flower garden just like the picture we found of a G.I. home, and let's build it on a coral foundation."

The headlines in the Fergus Falls Daily Journal described the battle as follows. "American Soldiers kissed the guns that swept Mundas jungles, and saved their lives". In one such attack, they would have succeeded in surrounding and wiping out the 43rd Division command post, if a recklessly close covering barrage of howitzer fire had not stopped them.

A short rest and hot meals were overdue. Ray had time to write letters, play ball, see movies, and *dream.* The nightmare of the past weeks, the rationed diet, the loss of close buddies, and the hopeless feeling of an endless war, created depressed soldiers. Many including Ray were fighting the malaria bug. The evidence was strong in the letters Evie read and reread. Here is an excerpt from one:

Dearest Evie;

I don't have much time to write, and no letter from you to answer. Mail has been scarce . . . This is such a lonesome day, and everybody feels the same way. More training starts tomorrow. I guess it is just rotation blues . . . Every letter I get is the same. "You'll be home soon I know," or "don't you have enough points for a discharge yet?" or "the war will be over before you know it." Things are different over here . . . They tell us there is no transportation back to the states if we did qualify for a furlough. Hope to get mail soon.

All my Love, Ray

Little did he realize that within one month he would actually be packing his bags.

The war-worn soldiers breathed a sigh when an officer informed them "Number 37322636 along with many other numbers will be sent back for a rest, and await further orders. It was August 1945. Thirty-four long torturous months were unforgettable history. "I hope I am not dreaming," Cleveland screamed, as he waved his hands skyward and grabbed Ray on the shoulder. They did not waste time getting back to the training area. The Sergeant informed them they would be having a forty-five day leave. A week passed and they were still waiting for an American Merchant Ship to carry them back to old Virginia, Texas, Minnesota, and the good old USA. The merchant ship was manned with an English speaking crew. The tired, hot, but happy soldiers marched from trucks to landing craft and then into the large ship. It was a straight shot toward San Francisco. Japanese submarines were no longer a threat. The days of the return trip were drawn out. It was a time of rest and wondrous anticipation of being home.

On August sixth word quickly spread throughout the ship of the bombing of Hiroshima.

"Why do we have to land on an Island off the coast of San Francisco?" The question was not verbalized, but weighed heavily on the heart of each man.

As though reading the minds of his soldiers the Staff Sergeant answered the question. "We all have to be checked for native diseases." New clothes were then issued and at last they were in sight of the golden bridge. What a glorious picture. Life was as beautiful as the sky above the shore lighted city. A troop train awaited them, and the following day they were enroute to camp McCoy. It was a Pullman at that.

"Real white sheets!" Ray almost shouted, and then recalled as a Corporal he had better set an orderly example for his fellow comrades. The train could not speed fast enough for all concerned. The porter even made their beds every day. "Will I wake up and discover this is all a dream?" Ray questioned.

An announcement of the bombing of Nagasaki came just as they neared Camp McCoy. August ninth bunks were again assigned to the travelers. "We are going home. We are going home." On August fourteenth Emperor Hirohito accepted the terms offered at Potsdam.

Reality set in and Ray realized that he would not be carrying out his next assignment to invade Japan. He was not debriefed as soldiers of future wars. He boarded a train for Minneapolis, arriving at night with no one to meet him. He met another soldier on the train and they stayed in a hotel on Washington Avenue. There was no cheering welcome committee. No one knew a soldier that had been gone for nearly three years was arriving home. The next morning he called his Aunt Anna and boarded a city bus. His sister Lou and Aunt Anna met him at the bus line.

Two days later he was on a Greyhound Bus for the final lap of his thirty five month journey. Would Evie meet him? Would her love for him have grown stale with only letters to cultivate their courtship? "How can I support a wife? Can I *ever wipe the cruel memories of the past three years from my memory, and get on with my life?*" These and other thoughts brought mixed emotions as the bus sped toward his destiny.

His shoes were polished to a spit shine. He was freshly shaved, and his short hair was groomed beneath his soldier's cap. He drifted back over his entire life. "Next stop: Bertha," the driver called out. Ray jumped as though a hand grenade had just been thrown in his fox hole.

10
The Long Night Has Past

It was July 1945. Letters were sporadic. Weeks slipped into history with no encouraging word of the war ending in the South Pacific. The letters that did make it to the Branstner mail box were filled between the lines with deep depression. The fact that Ray was on Luzon was overlooked by the censor. Evie read every article in the *Fergus Falls Journal* about the battles in that area, and when the war news was broadcast, every member of the family lent an ear to the battery powered radio.

Evie, too, was getting restless. She had waited patiently for nearly three years. There were few young men around. She was writing to other service men who were requesting pictures, and wanting to know her plans for the future. Attempts were made to get beyond the friendly stage. Some were in the states and wanted to spend their furlough in Minnesota. Evie saw her young dating years fleeting past, with only a stroll through the park or a walk to church together with a few young friends in three years.

She knew in her heart she could never give up on

Ray's return. Besides, she secretly concluded, she was sure if Ray ever received a Dear John letter he would purposely stand in the line of a bullet, as low as his moral had sunk. The decision was made to break off writing to two or three friends that made her acquaintance during her stay in Montana and Michigan. A few old school mates could also get along without her letters.

One neighbor informed Evie that an old school friend was planning to marry Evie as soon as he returned. She had never given him any reason to assume she was up for grabs or waiting for him. He wrote to the neighbor stating, "I will do and be anything Evie wants just to marry her." That was another friend Evie quit writing to, pronto! She settled it in her mind she would just continue to pray for Ray's safety each day, and for an end to the war. She could not deny that she really loved that man.

The content of a letter from Luzon written on July 9, 1945 was brief:

"This is our first day of freedom for some time. My mail has also been scarce. No letter from you to answer. Everyone writes that I should be discharged by now or "you'll be home soon." It doesn't help to hear that. When they still tell us there is no transportation home and we are still training everyday. Life is quite different across the Atlantic. We are stranded here for now."

Evie tried to boost Ray's morale in her reply. The week's wait for the next letter was long. Evie kept busy and yellow jaundice had taken its toll, but she met the mailman daily. A welcomed letter was postmarked July 28th, 1945.

Dearest Darling,

Hopes have skyrocketed. I was just informed that I will be the first to have a furlough. It will take time to cross the ocean on a slow boat. Don't expect me much before Oct.

All My Love, Ray

Ray would soon be on his way home! The Branstner home did not have the luxury of a telephone, so Ray could not call on his arrival in Minneapolis. During the war years the phone lines were not repaired. Each farmer was in charge of a portion of the line. Most of the boys that were brave enough to crawl the height of a telephone pole were either in Europe or the South Pacific. The farmers were busy trying to manage the farm without the help of their sons. There were usually eight or ten parties on one line and most lines were out of order.

Evie wondered why the mail box was empty for so many days. Ray's cousins, Russell and Louise came over often. "We would like to take you out for a ride tomorrow evening," Louise tried to conceal a sneaky grin as she made the remark. "Of course! I would like to go for a ride, and if I don't have a letter from Ray soon I am going to the South Pacific." Evie continued rather puzzled, "But where are we going?" There was not much going on in Hewitt or Bertha after the sidewalks were rolled up during the week.

Evie was ready and waiting when Russel and Louise arrived. They could barely contain themselves. "I suppose things would look that rosy to me," Evie secretly mused, "If I were that happily married and had a cozy home, like those two." To top it off they had cute little Duane, a two year old, and a baby boy in the Mother's arms. "Well, it was nice of them to think of me," she thought to herself. Louise was relating the progress of the eldest in conquering the English language. Evie sat in the back seat and broke what silence there happened to be with, "Where are we going?"

"You just wait and see."

"I know we are heading toward Bertha," Evie assured them. It was a beautiful fall evening, and Evie sat back and decided to enjoy the ride. Just then they pulled up in front of a closed gas station. Russell looked at his watch several times before he stepped out of the car, always with his eyes on the highway staring south.

Louise chatted on while feeding her baby, "I hope it doesn't rain before we get home; I left diapers on the line".

A Greyhound bus pulled up at the station. Three people stepped off the bus. The driver opened the side door to give them their luggage.

Russell crawled back in the car with such a puzzled look on his face. "He didn't come," the smirk he carried on the ride had vanished.

"Oh no! we were going to surprise you," Louise confessed. "Ray was supposed to be on this bus. Aunt Anna called us and told us he came into the cities late last night. We were sure he would be on this bus. Evie was in shock. Is Ray really that close to home? She, too, was disappointed that the surprise had not work as planned.

Evie thanked them for the ride, with mixed emotions. What was twenty-four more hours of waiting after thirty-five months. "I know he will be on the bus tomorrow night," Russ promised. Evie went to bed, but sleep forsook her hopeful eyes. "Will we recognize each other? Will Ray want to marry as soon as we see each other? Where would we live? How will we make a living?" Finally she drifted off, to leave tomorrow's joys and worries for that day.

It was with an excitement that was beyond expression that she faced this wonderful day. The mailbox contained a returned letter that Evie had written to Ray but none from Ray. Evie was now aware that Ray planned to surprise her. "What shall I wear to meet Ray?" Evie asked the opinion of all her younger sisters. Supper was served, but Evie could barely swallow a bite. Her hair was washed in some fresh rain water from the barrel. It did not have to be curled, God knew how busy she would be all her life. He gave her a permanent that was just that. Every brunette hair was in place. She glanced once more in the kitchen mirror as she dashed to the car. Her black and white saddle shoes were spotless. She wore her favorite flowered flair-frock. Ray's mother (Christina), his baby brother, his sisters, and Evie were at the bus stop, along with a few cousins. The moment arrived. Evie was wishing she could ask Emily Post, "Should the engaged girl or the mother be the first to greet the worn soldier?" Not having time for an answer from Emily, Evie decided to play it safe and allow the mother to greet her son first. After all he would not be coming home, without a mother.

She hesitated in the background. Ray stepped off the bus with a smile, but with the appearance of a tired, sick man. Not at all like the carefree young man that Evie bade good bye at the St Paul Depot three years before. He was as yellow as the Japanese he had just encountered. His face was thin and gaunt. Evie's turn came for the long awaited embrace as three little sisters waited impatiently.

"My, how you girls have grown in three years. Where is Pa and Harry?" Ray asked.

"They are in the harvest field somewhere in North Dakota. They did not realize you would be home this soon." His cousins finally had their chance to greet him. Ray wasted no time in getting behind the wheel to drive a car again. He was HOME.

"I hope this is not another dream. I awoke so many times and discovered I was still in a foxhole. Where shall we go first?" Ray questioned."

"I must get Jimmy to bed. He didn't get a nap today, and a meal awaits you. We live in a different house now," Ray's mother reminded him. Ray's father quit farming while five of his sons were employed by Uncle Sam. The children nearly smothered the uniformed brother. Marilyn and Pucky were soon having a heated discussion over who was going to sleep with him the first night.

Evie thought to herself, "If we had our marriage certificate neither one of you would get a chance." But Evie knew it would be a long time before that would transpire, and she intended to begin her honeymoon as a virgin. She must first reacquaint herself with this stranger. Should she have accepted a ring from him when life was so uncertain? After the long night of waiting there were times she felt so distant from him, as though she was writing to a phantom.

"I am really not hungry," he told his mother when they arrived home. He ate enough to satisfy her. Then taking Evie by the hand he said, "Let me take you home." They could hardly contain themselves, at last they were alone, traveling over the old familiar trail between the Miller's and Branstners'. "It's so wonderful to be back in the Valley with you." And then the question came. "When can we get married?" Evie did not care to dampen his enthusiasm his first night at home. "We have to work out a few things before I can honestly answer that question," she thought her answer would suffice until later.

"Should we go in to see your Mom and Dad before they go to bed?" Ray asked.

"I know they are anxious to see you," Evie assured him. Most of the children were asleep by this time. Elizabeth and Gus had waited up to greet Ray.

"It's good to have you home," Gus said as he extended his strong farm hand. Elizabeth had played a part in this courtship and was so pleased to have Ray home again. They exchanged a few bits of news from the valley and politely were off to bed, but not before Gus asked, "Are you hungry?" Everyone that crossed the threshold was asked that question.

"No, thank you. My Mom fed me as soon as I entered the door," Ray patted his flat stomach as if it might denote a stuffed appearance. Ray was not interested in food. A bout with malaria fever, plus the excitement of being home had just spoiled his appetite.

Evie and Ray's evening evaporated as thin air. It had taken two months to return an answer to a question or a comment at times. Evie endeavored to talk about the the things he could not tell in censored letters. "Please don't ask me now. Maybe some day I will be ready to tell you more, for now I must try to forget. I would not spoil our first evening with any of the last three years. I lived only for this day." It was twelve o'clock; Ray stared in surprise. He attempted to start home several times. "I guess it is just so much fun to say good bye, when I know I will be seeing you early tomorrow." The third try, Ray made it to the car, with a light heart, as though he was floating through the cool evening air. It was August 29, 1945. Evie watched until the lights from the car were out of sight. All that lingered was the fragrance of the after shave that Ray left behind. It smelled heavenly. Evie sat by the lamp lighted dining room table in utter amazement, dreaming of the future and waiting for the tomorrow that held the secret to all her dreams and fears.

11

No Garden of Roses

The forty-five day furlough was a dream come true. Ray and Evie put down their pens and did not write one letter during that period of time. They found an excuse to do something together daily. It may have been only a trip to Wadena. Ray had many aunts, uncles, and cousins to visit. Evie was always proudly introduced as his future bride, having proposed to her from the edge of a foxhole via mail.

He could not begin a job until he was officially discharged from the army. He must remain in uniform. Besides, he did not possess one civilian outfit. The Corporal was tired of the drab clothes, but Evie loved to have him in his G.I. attire. She was proud to walk the streets of neighboring towns with her soldier. He had three stripes to represent the three endless years. Each combat infantry badge had given him points to grant the forty-five day furlough. Saying good bye grew more difficult every day.

"I will be over early tomorrow. Can we go on a picnic?" Ray plead convincingly. It was difficult to have time alone with so many younger siblings in both homes. They said good night, with Evie's promise, "I'll fill a basket with surprises for you."

Ray did not keep that date. Evie waited impatiently, and then asked if she could use the family car to investigate the delay. "Where is Ray?" Evie asked of Christina as she peeked out the door of the small country home.

"He is in our bed. He is so sick. I have been bathing him nearly all night. He says it is malaria." I have changed the sheets twice and they are soaked again." She proceeded out with a basket of clothes to put on the line.

Evie ran into the house and found Ray dripping with perspiration. He reached for Evie's hand and apologized for spoiling a picnic and not having a messenger home from school to send by pony express. With no electricity in that rural area, Evie went to pump the coldest water to put on his head. Ice cubes were unheard of, and little did she know how experienced she would become as his nurse, with that affliction. It was three days before he asked, "When are we going on our picnic?"

The fall days crept in as though to steal the picnic. Malaria had taken its cruel toll. Ray was not tempted to stay up late. He tightened his belt a couple of notches and his uniform hung loosely.

"Come over to our house and I will make you my best soup," Evie promised. Ray was not ready for a heavy meal. He came early in the afternoon and peeled vegetables as Evie cubed them and added them to the tender beef in the kettle. At intervals she added wood to the range.

"I spent hours in the foxhole dreaming of days like this." He put aside the knife, wiped his hands and kissed the hand of the cook.

It took a large kettle of soup, for in marched the troops from school. Supper was served promptly at five o'clock. The routine was strictly kept. Five thirty it was news time and six o'clock the milkers were on their way to the barn.

"Tomorrow I must leave for the cities and back to Camp McCoy," Ray said with mixed emotions. He was anxious for his discharge papers, but dreaded separation again. When he left Luzon he was scheduled to rejoin his outfit and invade Japan. The war ending while he was on furlough had changed all that. He missed out on his promotion to Sergeant, but was glad to forgo that. "Evie won't you please go as far as Minneapolis with me," Ray asked with such a sad expression. What could she say?

"I will go visit my sister, Joy." Joy, Howard and Evie's little niece and nephew lived in North Minneapolis. Ray's Aunt Anna and Uncle Gus lived near their Crystal shop in the southern part of the city. "How long will you be at Camp?" Evie asked.

"Perhaps a week. Who knows? This is still the military," Ray answered with a look of uncertainty. The decision to attend Ray as far as Minneapolis was made, and Evie and Ray took their first train ride together.

The train was filled to capacity. It was impossible to buy a car. All car manufacters were converted to war plants for the duration of the war. Returning soldiers used trains and buses. Evie and Ray were alone as far as they were concerned. There were no little interruptions from their homes to interfere with the long talk.

"This gives us three hours to make our wedding plans," were the first words from the Corporal's lips as soon as the train left Wadena. Evie was just as anxious for marriage, but wanted to make sure they had settled any complications of lifestyle. The haunting question arose: do we really know each other after the years of separation? Evie was just eighteen and Ray twenty one years old when the war interrupted their lives.

"Where are we going to live?" she asked. Every young war couple was searching for a home. Building had reached a standstill. There were no materials to build homes or apartments during the war. "I do not want to live with relatives," Evie made that point clear.

"I will look for an apartment as soon as I get my dis-

charge and start work at Twin City Rock Crystal when I
return," Ray pronounced with a tone of determination. It
was difficult to face the real issues that were staring
them in the face. "Let's just get married and trust we can
find a place. We have waited too long already," Ray confessed. "I thought we would be married as soon as we
could get our license. That kept my hopes up through the
toughest days."

"I want a well planned wedding," Evie continued. "I
just plan to marry once. I want it to be a treasured memory."

"But parting is getting more and more painful. I
can't take it much longer." The trip came to a halt long
before any concrete plans were laid. The conductor called
Minneapolis, St Paul. Ray took the street car to Joy's
house to make sure Evie arrived safely. Again they must
say good-bye. Ray faced the fact that wedding plans were
on hold. The pain of leaving was overpowered with
thoughts of an honorable discharge.

Camp McCoy was flooded with Yanks. Morale was
high. The conversation was packed with dreams, and
wedding bells were the theme of the song. The meals
were a change from the battlefield. One night Ray awoke
in the middle of the night with nightmares of gun shots
and battle scenes. "Please get me some ice for my head."
He begged his bunk buddies not to tell anyone he was
sick, lest it delay his discharge. He took more atabrine to
fight the horrible attack. His bunk mates went for an
issue of clothes for him. His greatest fear was to be hospitalized and not make it home for a month.

Two days later he was off, with his discharge paper
in hand. His duffel bag was packed with everything
except his fever blisters, he was on a train headed for
Minneapolis.

Evie waited for him at the train depot. "I don't know
if you want to kiss me with all these fever blisters," the
thin soldier commented. Evie was so thrilled over the discharge papers that nothing would have prevented that

special moment. It was early in the afternoon.

"Someone on the street handed me this coupon to have our picture taken," Evie stated with excitement. "Let's go find the studio."

"Do you think they can cover up these fever blisters?" Ray asked. Evie had on the suit that she planned to wear on her honeymoon, but what day could be more special than the day Ray was free. How great to have a portrait in her honeymoon attire and Ray in his army suit.

Walking around on Washington Avenue in front of a clothing store, a business man motioned for customers to come in. "We have suits for sale!" All of the wool had gone into military clothes during the war. In fact sheep farmers were given extra incentives to raise more sheep. With the shortage of wool to make suits, Ray and Evie walked in.

"I hope I am going to need a wedding suit soon." With that in mind, Ray tried on suits. He chose a grey pin stripe. Evie's eyes lit up when he tried the suit on. Ray just received his mustering out pay, and clothing was number one on his list.

"I love it, but you can't wear it with that army shirt." Ray put on his army suit, and they took off on the train back to the valley. Evie could predict the subject Ray would bring up.

"Now I have my suit and my discharge! What are we waiting for?"

"I don't have my dress, my shoes, our invitations, or the preacher to go with your suit. That is what we are waiting for. Did they issue you a tent for us to live in?" Evie questioned with a hint of sarcasm. They held hands in silence as they faced the reality of life, and the train sped them nearer home, and in the corner of hard fast decisions.

Ray's brother Murley, his wife Mary, and Ray's first little niece, Joyce came up to spend the weekend. Ray packed his bags to go back to his job at Twin City Rock Crystal.

"I have to get to work now or I will never be able to support you," Ray spoke softly with a note of sadness that he could not hide. "Can't you come with me and work in the cities? I don't want to be so far from you "

"I feel compelled to stay and help at home. I know you can't understand my position, but I need some time to think, and I have quilts I need to finish. I need to do some sewing." Evie rationalized until she convinced herself, but not quite to Ray's satisfaction. Saturday night they could only embrace. Words could never express the dread of separation and corresponding again. Ray left early on Sunday morning with Murley and Mary. On Wednesday Evie tore open a letter that said in part:

Dearest Darling   *November 13, 1945*

We were on our way for eight hours. We had icy roads to Little Falls. We broke two fan belts and had one blow out. The folks here all send their greetings. I have been here two hours and no one has asked when we are getting married. I don't know where I am going to sleep. I must bathe and get up at five thirty. I plan to work ten hours a day. I hope you are over your cold. I hope I don't have to make any more trips in Murleys' broken down jalopy. Thinking of you and Loving you Always

Ray

Dearest Darling;   *November 18, 1945*

My first Sunday here I don't know what to do with myself. I have been thinking of you all day and wondering if you recovered from the flu. I put your picture in a frame. You are just two feet away from me, smiling. I miss you more than I ever thought possible. You look like you could just walk out of that frame. I dream of that day. Your health is priceless. You need to be around another hundred years. Please take care of yourself. I hope to be shar-

ing some of those years with you. I suppose you are tear-
ing around getting the house spotless for Joy and
Howard's arrival.I hope that is not the reason you have
not written to me. We were all invited to Aunt Laura's for
a five course meal last night. My first pay check was only
twenty dollars. Must put in a longer week next week. I get
sixty cents an hour.

All My Love, Ray

The long letter was filled with personal admiration
and tidbits.

Dearest Evie;   *November 19,1945*

Your letter dated November15th came today. I wish I
could find a decent room and boarding house. This sleep-
ing on the couch isn't the best of things. I hope you don't
make the mistake of sending my letters to the Forty Third
Division. That would mean a few days without you. I miss
you and think of you constantly. I knew I would, but did-
n't think it would be quite like this. Call it home sickness,
or love sick. Whatever it is I have got it. The shop is behind
on orders. Are you interested in a job?

You are wondering why we are not coming home for
Thanksgiving instead of going to Murley's in Rochester. It
is twice as far. Haven't spent much time with Murley for
years. It almost as hard to quit writing as it was to say
good night.

Evie discovered later the real reason Ray did not
want to come home. On November, 22 1945 Ray penned a
short letter.

It is after midnight so this will be short. The turkey
and dinner were delicious. Buses were packed. I had to
hold my sister Lou. Now if it would have been you, I would
not have minded it. This is my seventh letter to you and I
have only received four from you. I haven't missed many

nights. I feel so lonesome until I write to you, and then I go to bed with a lighter heart. The radio is on. I can't stand it too quiet. Gets too lonesome. Guess I was used to too much noise the last three years. I will not be home for Christmas the buses and trains will be packed to the door. We would only be together a few hours.

Thanksgiving dinner was great. It was the first I have been able to eat that much at one setting without suffering from the effects of it.

Living on C rations for weeks, and having malaria every few weeks, had taken its toll. This letter left Evie wondering why he was not coming for Christmas, sensing crowded buses was not the real reason.

Dearest Evie,   *November 22, 1945*

I hope you have convinced yourself that I am here. Not only so I get letters. Maybe bring yourself down here. Your letters written 17th and 19th came today. You could stay longer. I have to stay on the job even though I am working for my uncle. Not only for myself but the one I love, and possibly a few others. I know it is not the best policy to be working for relatives, but I don't think I could find another job considering my experience. I wouldn't want to work for a farmer again. If you had your own farm it would be a different story. That would cost about five thousand dollars more than I have. I know you aren't in love with me working down here, but it has to be that way for now. Army life set me back three years. I hope you will be patient with me until I catch up with myself and continuing with our plans of working things out in the spring. I think you were using your head, in waiting til spring. Everything needed for a home is hard to get. The gravest shortage being the home. It is almost impossible to even rent a room. I hope it has changed when spring rolls around. Please don't be trying to turn back the time. I want to spend the rest of my life with you, not just a few hours now and then.

November 25,1945

I wish you were coming back with Howard and Joy. We could be together evenings. There are a lot of clothes and things I find myself short of. This isn't a Christmas hint, just a fact. Feel like cashing in bonds. I wear my army Khakis to work.They are OK for my job.

November 26, 1945

I had a wonderful welcome awaiting me. Two letters. They will never take the place of the individual. I will really be thrilled when I can come home to you greeting me. Then to sit down to a meal cooked by your sweet hands. I can see farther into the future since those two letters arrived. They were the tonic I needed.

I make between $35 to $40 per week. I just put $100 (from the Gov. check) in savings. That looks pretty small. I paid my insurance premium. So I don't have quite so many worries.

Last Christmas we were tearing up a camp and spent New Years on a boat. The others were spent in the tropics. It is hard for me to get in the spirit of Christmas. I do not plan to be home. I love you deeply and do not want anything to come between us. It's a nice night to walk over to Branstner's. I wish I was there to do just that. I wish we could be together always.

God bless you! Ray

Then the moment of truth in the long letter dated December 3, 1945 with its usual soft touch introductory paragraphs. It was in answer to Evie's November 30 letter.

You mentioned your duties at home. Just what do you consider your duty? You have spent your last twenty two years fulfilling those obligations. I don't know why

*you feel that way. Joy and May left young and now Irene
and Ruth will be gone most of the next four years. Do you
consider it your place to fill their place so they can make a
career for themselves? You have one, you know. I think you
have the notion that you have to be home to see that the
piano gets dusted, and the beds get made before breakfast.
Or that the weeds don't grow near the house! Ahem! or
that the corn wouldn't get picked. Please don't get mad at
me. I am writing just as I am thinking tonight. You also
said Lloyd's army career would not interfere with any
plans you might make. I take that to mean that you have
not planned for the future. You are doing all the worrying
about your family. Darling all I am trying to say is, it is
about time we do a little planning for ourselves. There is
no future for either of us this way, you know that. I am getting thoroughly disgusted with this kind of life, coming
home to a davenport. Now they have guests and I am back
on an army cot. I may as well reenlist. Finding a room is
easier said then done, so don't come back with that.*

*I don't mean that you should be working and mak-
ing money. That doesn't matter. I think it is a man's job to
make the living. It may not be the most luxurious com-
forts. I am just getting started now. We have never spent a
Christmas together. Maybe that is the reason I feel the
way I do. I hope and pray it will be different next year and
these dreadful days apart will soon end. I love you deeply.
Please answer this letter as frankly as you can.*

Loving you Always,
Ray

The letter was long and detailed. Evie began to
show empathy with how the war torn soldier felt. She
couldn't believe some of the content of the letter. (All letters are in part.)

December 5, 1945

Dearest Darling,

*I received your letter of the third today. Darling I
still feel the same as I did the past few nights. Instead of*

*your letters making me feel better, I find fault with them.
Darling something has to be done. I won't be able to go on
this way much longer. If you would only write and tell me
you have made definite plans that you are coming down.
You always sound uncertain. When you do come down I
know it will be on the spur of the moment. We cannot build
our lives that way. Being apart for no reason, will only
draw us apart. Something is trying to do just that now. It
is not right this way. Honey! why do you always say in
your letters, there are some things I wanted to write and
now I can't think of them, or you don't know how to
express them on paper? You don't think it is wrong to write
of love do you? You seldom write of it. You expressed yourself when I was with you, by things you did and not verbalized. This cannot pull us a part, I would rather die
than have to face life without you! Please say that you will
come down. It does not have to be until after Christmas.
Just give me something definite to live on until then. I
won't say any more until I start hearing from you on this
subject. Trusting you will understand my desires for us
and will come down. Howard did mention going to your
house. If they do as you said in your letter for Saturday
and Sunday, I could go along. That would be my
Christmas.*

*Christmas reminds me of last year, preparing for an
invasion of Luzon. I slept in the rain Christmas night, in
a pup tent and a tree fell down on the tent. I got up at four
thirty and marched to the boat. I think of those days, of
the ones that were left there. I took part in a dedication
ceremony for the boys that were killed. There is nothing
more stirring than the thought of a dead comrade. I have
never talked much about my experiences and I don't like to
talk about it, but I can't keep from thinking about them. I
will never be able to forget those boys. If everyone could
walk the rows of crosses and read the names, wondering if
the next one would be a relative or friend, there would be
more talk of peace and less of war.*

*Well Darling I must close. Honey, believe me when I
say my soul is craving for you. I need you and will always*

love you.

Ray

Ray's letter and the following letter of Evie's crossed in the mail.

Dear Sweetheart,

I really had a nice, long letter from you today. Don't know how far I will get writing before the school kids get home. [With about six children coming home to a six room house, it was difficult to find a quiet corner to think or write.] I will try to write a long letter to make up for the short ones you have been getting. Dad and Chuck are hauling wood today. Chuck says he has about six rows of corn left to pick and he will be through by Christmas. Incidentally I haven't helped him anymore. Did you mean you may come for Christmas, when you said to have it done by that time? Honey I have a difficult time keeping my promise, not to coax you to come home. I try to understand you not wanting to come home for Christmas. But this does not keep me from wishing things would work out for you to be here, our first Christmas ever. Just no harm done if I make a hint once in a while. I don't blame you for not caring to shop. I came home from Wadena and started looking at the Sears catalogue. The stores had so many items advertised that aren't to be seen in the stores. So I am going to try sending for the kid's gifts. They even have electric irons in the catalogue. I have been tempted to order one. They are advertised as prewar material. I did send for some material to finish my quilt that I started three years ago. I would have finished it before but there was really no place to store it in this small house.

You think it will be impossible to be content in the city. It does not make as much difference as you think. This place is not the secret of happiness. It is the person you share your home with.

So you were tempted to cash in your bonds. One of

these days we will combine our bonds, empty our penny banks and really go shopping. That will be a fun day! We will need so many things. If I write more it would be to about your coming for Christmas, so I must say good night to you now, My Love. With All My Love and Best Wishes.

Yours, Evie

Ray wrote on December 6, 1945:

Your letter of December 4, came today. It was not an answer to the two I wrote. Honey I am sort of scared to get an answer to those letters. I wrote you, just as I felt. I will feel better after I get a reply. I don't know what to say about your request for me to come home for Christmas. To add to the reasons I have already given to you I will tell you the main reason. I am quite disgusted with the way things are going at home. I mean my Dad and Harry. They only work part of the time and many other things. I am not trying to turn you against them. You will have to spend a few days down here after Christmas. I love you more than ever and miss you twice as much.

Later Evie read the letter that really spelled things out. It was written on December 9, 1945 by his mother. During Ray's overseas days, Ray had his checks sent to put directly in savings in care of his parents. The clause included that if under extreme circumstances they could borrow from it. She wrote the following letter:

Dear Ray and Lou;

Your letters greatly surprised us. I feel I must answer as I don't want you to think we swallowed all of that. You have cooked your goose. Neither Dad nor Harry would bother to meet you. So you and Lou cannot come home for Christmas. Your old Dad is sixty one years old next month, and if he feels like sitting by the fire, he is entitled

*to a little comfort. Anytime we take orders from you kids
the world will hear about it. You needn't worry about us at
all. As for gifts, we don't want any. Why throw it all up to
us about the money you sent home, while overseas. You
said we could use it, if we needed it. Dock said the same
thing. I don't have anything more to say except don't come
home, and Dad says he doesn't want to see you.   Mother.*
[The parts of this six page letter were copied verbatim
and saved along with letters from Evie.]

Ray was very disappointed to say the least. His pay
was never over $60 a month while overseas. He kept out
a few dollars to cover a few personal needs. The rest was
sent with plans of having some money to start married
life on his hopeful return. To discover not one cent was in
savings was most discouraging. The final blow came
when he found out his father learned the pattern of his
check arrival and met the mailman. He signed his checks
and wasted the same. Ray displayed righteous indigna-
tion in his letters home. To his surprise his Mother had
protected his Father.

At last Evie could understand Ray's down moods.
He did not have civilian clothes. His only blue suit was no
where to be found. He was living under crowded condi-
tions with an Uncle, Aunt, Sister, and another brother of
Uncle Gus', and Evie had not yet set a date for their marriage. His savings were nil, except for some war bonds,
and his family was rejecting him. No wonder he did not
want to come home for Christmas.

Evie did not bother to write a letter, she boarded
the train for Minneapolis. She was a girl of action. She
and Ray must spend time together. She wanted to clear a
few things up and make sure Ray felt welcome for
Christmas. She made up her mind they would begin more
definite plans. Ray was elated to have Evie surprise him
and to know they could start making some solid plans.
They spent every evening possible together. It was so convenient to have sister Joy in north Minneapolis. The two
phone lines had a busy signal every night, that they could
not make it across the big city to see each other. "To think

that you have not been home for four Christmas seasons and you weren't coming home again," Evie broke into a sob. Ray's spirit was lifted, and Evie went home with a light heart to make Christmas cookies, shop, wrap gifts, trim the tree and wait to spend her first Christmas ever with Ray. Truly there was no garden of blooming roses for either of them, but they would make tea of the rose hips and face the briars head on.

12
Wedding Plans
Are Made

Evie answered every letter that Ray wrote to her the weeks he was in Minneapolis. He was learning to hand-cut glass. His aunt was married to a native of Sweden. He brought his trade with him. Uncle Gus and his brother started a business registered as The Twin City Rock Crystal. They did deep cutting of lead crystal. It was mainly the wealthy that could afford such luxuries. After the war they made less expensive items that were not acid polished. Uncle Gustave had a secret formula to make the Crystal brilliant. He guarded this acid formula with his life. After the glass was cut it was dipped in this solution.

The glass factory was on a second floor building on University Avenue. It was a dusty old place with large pulleys hanging from the ceiling to the cutting machines and polishers. With a spinning whetstone the artist held the bowl or goblet on the stone and cut a pattern, usually by free hand with no pattern drawn on the glass. Earlier it had employed many cutters. It flourished until the depression and during the war the sale of fine cut glass declined.

Uncle Gus and Aunt Anna did not have a family of their own and borrowed sons from the large Miller family. While in high school, in his spare time, Ray was clean up boy. When his job was completed Ray would pick up broken pieces to practice cutting patterns. After the war he was skilled enough to cut glass for the stores, when he was not delivering the same.

By the time Ray returned from the South Pacific, Aunt Anna and Uncle Gus had moved to a beautiful home, and also purchased an old red brick building. It had four apartments on second floor and ample room for the business on main floor.

When Anna and Gus Carlson were first married, rich Aunt Laura lavished her with furnishings to fill her home. Evie could not imagine beginning her married life with a piano, over-stuffed furniture in every corner, a dining room set, lamps, side board, and knick-knacks to fill every table. The upstairs was also filled with luxuries of that era. The home was blessed with a sun room complete with wicker furniture. Two outside walls were entirely of windows. Aunt Anna was often in her favorite corner on a lounging chair, her paper fell to her side in a heap at times, as she caught up on a snooze after a hard day of socializing.

The kitchen was small, with a sink that hung from the wall, and had a splash back and drain attached. Aunt Anna could do up her dishes in jig time. She put on her rubber gloves and used a dish cloth attached to a long handle to protect her nails and dainty hands. Her hair was done weekly in an up sweep style. She wore a four-and-one-half size shoe, and her tiny little legs were slightly overloaded. Aunt Anna was a short person with dainty little hands to match her feet. Her sparkling brown eyes and curly auburn hair filled portraits of a lovely lady. Her hair was just losing some of its color, and sweet rolls, coffee parties, and rich foods had robbed her of that perfect figure. She was a social butterfly. Her heart was of gold when when it came to her nieces and nephews. Ray having lived four years with her before the war felt very much at home. Her heart was a wee bit larger than her home. There was no private room available for the returning Corporal, until the Swedish Uncle moved out. The Uncle had lost his wife and came to work at the glass factory. With a shortage of housing he also moved in the Carlson residence. Having graduated from high school, Ray's sister, Lou, sought employment as the secretary at Twin City Rock Crystal. The rich foods served at the Carlson Hotel were also conducive to giving Lou a head start to being a replica of the old Auntie.

Auntie was very critical of her foster son's choice of mates. Just no *one* could quite meet her criterion. Ray had proudly introduced Evie to Auntie at the time he left for the service and held his breath until he was alone with Auntie to hear her comments. To his surprise the verdict was quite favorable. She liked her curly brown hair, she was even a little taller than herself and the entire one hundred eighteen pounds passed inspection. The fact that she was very domestic also scored a point or two.

"You know, I think it is so important that every girl should attend a finishing school like I did," she said to Ray.

"Everyone did not have an Aunt Laura to pay for a finishing school," Ray murmured to himself. "Besides," his thoughts continued, "Evie has had some pretty valuable teachers, such as Mother Elizabeth, Grandma Bessie, Mrs. Hartung (the fussiest lady in Todd County), and Mrs. Enge, the rich lady she worked for in Wadena."

Uncle Gus was a true, tall, lanky Swede topped with thinning gray hair, sky blue eyes, and a Swedish brogue. Often while assisting Aunt Anna with her coat he would say, "Yump in Yenny." He was a soft spoken man and either quiet by nature or subjected to never getting a word in edge-wise; no one was ever quite sure which of the two applied.

Aunt Laura often came from Roseau to visit her

baby sister. The winding stair rail was of oak and Aunt
Laura had fully carpeted the stairway and all of the first
floor with a gorgeous rose carpet. One day the older sister stumbled and fell down the stairs to the spacious
landing. "You would have been killed were it not for the
carpeting," Aunt Anna gasped. "You saved your own life."
Evie and Ray heard the story again and again. The contrast from Evie's childhood home was like a dream house.
However Evie could smell a dusty odor that would not
have lasted long in the place she called home.

Evie's parents urged her to go to the cities and find
work. She thought the world would quit turning if she
was not at home to supervise the household. Irene and
Ruth were in high school. Every day had to be on a schedule to keep the large family home running smoothly.
Little Jane required so much care. Elizabeth, now nearly
fifty years old, kept busy, sewing and taking care of Jane.
She was tired and worn. Evie wondered how she kept
going. She persuaded Elizabeth to return with Joy to her
home for a few days before Evie finally made the break to
leave home.

The day after Christmas, Ray said good-bye. Evie
too realized that parting was more painful. Early in
January of 1946, Evie made her last break from home.
She packed her black suitcase and boarded the train for
Joy's house. Ray could hardly believe they would finally
at least be in the same city. Evie would be as close as
Aunt Anna's phone. After three-and-one-half years of
writing letters Ray's hand was tired.

Evie read the ads in the *Tribune*, then found her
way to Munsing Wear. "Sewing is something I like to do,"
she told Joy. She was hired the first day. Joining the tex-
tile union was the first requirement. It was a cold, cold
January. Evie started out by walking two blocks to board
a streetcar and then transferred to a bus to reach her destination. It was a nerve racking job. She would just learn
how to operate a machine well enough to start making
money on piece work when the supervisor would put her
on a more complicated machine. Some of the machines

made triple stitches. It took time to learn the mechanics of each machine. She worked on ladies' under-garments. Evie knew it was not a well paying job until she could gain speed and be paid for piece work. "Why do you change me from one machine to another?" Evie finally was brave enough to ask.

"We are training you for a supervisor and we want you to be able to run every machine on this long row," her boss stated. Evie was pleased they thought she was qualified for that position when she had just been working a few weeks. She had been fearful they wanted to hold back her progress.

The weeks disappeared into months. Every weekend Ray and Evie spent a few hours either at the Folkestad's or Carlson's. Weeknights found them on the phone making plans and checking every detail of the day. Evie searched the ads for a used sewing machine. "It is the most necessary item in a home," she informed her future room-mate. What she did not tell him was she was going to answer an ad the following night after work. Being unfamiliar with the big city did not prevent her from finding an address. Conductors were always helpful. "I am sure Joy will just think I'm working overtime. Besides, I don't want to miss the first bus or waste a nickel," she rationalized. Little did she know how long it would take at the end of a working day to travel. She did not know how far it was to her destination.

When she was ushered in to the dark living room by a sweet motherly lady, she felt the warmth of home. "It works beautifully," Evie examined both sides of the scrap of material to see if the stitching was tight. She looked in the drawers for attachments and bobbins and also sneaked a peek at the condition of the drawers. She hesitated to act overly excited, lest the price would increase. "How much are you asking for the machine?" The old lady thought thirty five dollars was a fair price. She was losing her eyesight and no longer had little ones to sew for. Evie sensed she really wanted her to have it. "I am just getting married and need a sewing machine," Evie continued. "Can I pay down and pick it up tomorrow?" Evie asked as she searched deep in her purse for a five dollar bill. Evie told her part of her life story and then glanced at the clock on the mantle." I can't believe it is after six o'clock!" Evie said frantically.

She then requested to use the phone. Joy answered, "Evie where are you? We've been worried sick, Ray has called us three times already."

"I am way out in south Minneapolis. I am just leaving, and I just purchased a sewing machine." She was like the three women that came to the tomb of Jesus, not once questioning who would roll away the stone. Evie was assuming her dear brother-in-law would pick up the sewing machine in a moment's notice. She entered the upstairs apartment weary and hungry, when she stopped to think about it. Joy was just tucking the children in and had kept some supper warm.

"Please tell us before you go on another goose chase," Joy begged. She couldn't say wild, as Evie thought it a very profitable evening. It did not prevent searching the for sale ads, she was still looking for a hideabed for the wee apartment Ray had rented. She found it with the same method.

The only apartments available were bedrooms that were converted into apartments by making a kitchenette out of a closet. A small commode held the two gas burners, and was also the only drawer space in the apartment. The shelves that were in the closet were left to store things on. The bathroom down the hall was shared with four neighbors. There was an old icebox in the hall leading to the bathroom.

"It won't be permanent," Ray reminded Evie when he described the lowly place he rented. "At least we will have a place to hang our hat," he assured Evie over the phone. Evie and Ray were promised a large duplex, just across the street from Joy. The friends that were now renting were building a new home. They expected to turn the keys over to the bride and groom by June.

"We can surely put up with crowded quarters for two months," they both agreed. Secretly Evie could hardly contain herself just dreaming of the prospect of living so close to Joy. She knew she would have to read a lot more ads to fill that large duplex and Ray would have to work a few more hours to pay the rent. It would also be a greater distance for Ray to go to work. Nothing of the likes could possibly dim their plans for the future. They would first live on Franklin Avenue.

"Evie I don't want you to work," Ray insisted. I want to make the living. I want you to be in a nice starched apron when I come home from work." They talked on and on until Joy was sure the telephone lines were red hot, making final plans for the wedding. Evie promised to write letters to the pianist, singer, former pastor, and to the trustee at the Alliance Church in making final plans.

"I will never make it up in the morning if I don't get to bed," Evie sighed.

Within a few days a letter was awaiting Evie, from her minister. I regret to tell you I have conflicting plans with your wedding date. If the date can be changed to two weeks earlier, or a later date I will love to perform the ceremony. Evie did not care to call Ray at work and tell him this news. Evie, Joy, and Howard took time out to deliver the message in person. Ray was at the wheel cutting glass. He looked up in sheer surprise at Evie coming over on a Saturday morning. She quickly greeted him and then gave the reason for her surprise call. "Reverend Foreman cannot come on the date we set for our wedding". Rays' countenance dropped as though he would faint.

He finally said, "You mean we have to wait again"?" Evie had already decided they would take the first suggested date.

"No dear! We have to set the date up two weeks earlier, do you think we can be ready?"

Ray jumped from his work and shouted, "Of course we can make it." Evie again made contact with all her wedding friends and sped up the procedure. March 30, 1946 would be the day. Three years to the day Ray had left on a ship for the South Pacific, not knowing what lie ahead. For now the horrible past was overshadowed with the future he had dreamed about since the day he met Evie.

Ray hurried to his quarters at Aunt Anna's, showered, and packed his overnight bag to spend the night at the boy's dorm in North Minneapolis. Howard and Joy lived in an apartment in the same building.

"I can't believe our date has been changed," Ray commented with the most excitement Evie had witnessed since the day his discharge papers were in his possession. He embraced his promised bride as though any minute he would wake up in a fox hole on Luzon.

"How can I write notes on my to-do list with you holding my writing hand" Evie questioned? "We will have to change the date to a month later if we don't get busy." Evie decided she must have ten days at home to make last minute preparations.

"We must resort to letters again for ten whole days," Ray groaned.

The next week Evie gave her employer notice that she would be leaving. March twenty-third Evie found herself once more on a bus alone. Alone with her thoughts of the long, long night, the darkness of World War II, and now the promise of a future with the man she loved and waited for. The question she asked herself, "Are you very sure of a life-time commitment?" was answered in the affirmative, and Evie fell in a peaceful sleep as the bus sped home.

Gus was at the station to meet Evie. He shook her hand and they hurried on to pick up her now battered old black suitcase.

"How is Ray?" Gus inquired rather seriously. "He didn't look well at Christmas time," he commented. "That war took several years off his life."

"He is very thin and has a bout with malaria every few weeks," Evie continued a detailed report. "The atabrine contributes to his oriental complexion, and I am not very conscious of it now. He looked Japanese when I first saw him."

Gus admired Ray, and was excited about the wedding. They continued catching up on news in the Valley as they traveled the country road. "Joy, Howard, Bobby, and Janet are coming a week from today," Evie informed the proud Grandpa, as they drove into the farm yard. Bum (the dog that had wandered in hungry) was on the welcome committee. "Sh! sh! don't wake up the wee ones," Evie repeated as she petted her old friend. Elizabeth was just tucking Jane in the over used crib. Some of the older children could not resist getting up for one more sip from the family dipper and to greet Evie.

The farm house was tidy. Evie noticed the cupboard in the other room. She always took pride in dishes being neatly stacked with the glass doors revealing the shelf paper. She concluded maybe, just maybe, they were surviving without her. The floor was a sparkling advertisement for Johnson Glo-Coat. (The product that kept Fibber Megee and Molly on the air.) The light colored kitchen inlaid was scrubbed just before Evie's arrival, without Evie's supervision (imagine that). Because of the large family's activities, it required scrubbing twice daily.

Elizabeth and Evie sat by the extended oak table, alone once again. It was a cool rainy evening. The aladdin lamp silhouetted mother and daughter. Evie laid open her plans for the week. The Folkestads and Foremans will arrive on Friday. The wedding rehearsal will be on Friday evening. "Let's count up our guests for supper on Friday," Evie suggested. There will be five of Foremans, four Folkestads, and thirteen of us. That makes twenty-two, if Irene and Ruthie make it back from school on time.

"I will make out the menu and get the supper," Evie volunteered, knowing full well that Elizabeth was tired of cooking. We will serve at five as usual. We must be in

Wadena at the church by seven thirty. Irene and Ruthie were in Wadena attending high school, but would be home for Evie's last supper as a single sister.

"I think we better go to bed," Elizabeth insisted ."We have a big week ahead of us". With that Evie prepared for the night and crawled beside two of her sisters. Sleep forsook her fitful eyes. How could she sleep with all the excitement in the country air? Letters were once again the only source of communication.

My Dear Husband To Be,

Here I am home once again. I will be counting the days til Thursday. I heard from Valerie today. She plans to play our wedding march. Her sister Verlie will sing. Went through my trunk today and sorted things over that I do not need at the present time. Mother is going to town for some new clothes when they go after Ruthie and Irene. I just discovered Irene's slip is too long tonight . Another last minute job. The kids wanted me to try on my wedding gown tonight. Billy said Evie makes it look like angel's clothes. Mother wants me to make her a dress. This setting our wedding day two weeks up has caused a little rush. I think Mother stayed up most of one night. Our wedding day cannot come too soon. The family members are as excited as anyone could possibly get, even Benny. Mother got him a navy blue sweater with matching short pants. Then he said "Won't they be nice for my wedding?" June thinks she needs a new dress. Mom told her she has lots of pretty dresses, but she said I need to keep up <u>with Dad's in his new teeth.</u>

I found the music today and saw the pastor about details of the church. Valerie may have the music to "O Perfect Love", and I have "The Lord's Prayer", and "At Dawning", the three songs that we decided on. I miss you so much. Yours in ten more days !!!

Evie

Letters once again crossed between the miles of separation. On March 21, Ray wrote:

My Darling Wife (Almost),

Time to let you know I am missing you and loving you oodles. I would be in North Minneaoplis if you were here. I am going to our apartment and do some work on Saturday. Just one week and I will be home and nine days we will be married. I love you more each day and will always be loving you. I am the happiest and luckiest man in the world.

All my Love, Ray

March 23,1946

It is only nine p.m. I am alone and dreaming of next Saturday. I managed to find an alarm clock. Bought the last one the jeweler had. I also found a locket for you to wear with your wedding dress. It is going to be wonderful to live my life for and with you. You won't have to write a letter after Tuesday, as I will leave on the noon bus on Thursday. Must press my pants, shine my shoes and a few odd jobs. Hope we can find a car by July. [Even used cars were almost impossible to find.] Good Night Darling. My last Saturday night as a bachelor!! Hooo, Ray!!!

Monday March 25, 1946. Evie sat by the lamp light with pen in hand.

Dearest Lover;

This should be my last letter to you before you come home. Just three more days, and I will be at the depot to meet you. I did not hear from you today. You must have house cleaned Aunt Anna's house. Ethel is planning a shower for us on Thursday night. Thought I should prepare you for it as men are also invited.

What a beautiful wash day. Washed all the curtains,

etc. Hope it is this nice on Saturday. Our country mansion is almost ready. I have invited Valerie and Verlie to stay in town with Irene and I on Friday after the rehearsal. I will press both of our gowns. It seems like a dream, that our day is really so near. Haven't finished our matching pajamas, but I will!! Promise! It does not seem real that OUR day is so near. It is the first thought that enters my mind in the morning, and the last thing I think of falling asleep.

Until Thursday I will be thinking of you. I love you more than this short letter can express. All My Love, Yours Evie

Ray was also writing on March 25.

Hello Darling,

This should be my last letter to you. Sister Lou decided to leave on Wednesday night. That would mean an extra trip to town, if I left on Thursday. I have decided to come the same time. So be in town about ten p.m. Aunt Anna got us a set of dishes. Just think in one hundred and thirty hours you will be mine. I picked up the license today and had my hair cut, and I am all set. All My Love To Mrs. Ray Miller. (Doesn't that look cute?)

At last the final plans were laid, and the long, long wait for the two was over. Evie did not have time to think until everyone was snug in bed. "Am I just dreaming?" she thought. She had often faced the reality that it may never come to pass; eight weeks would seem like eternity and still no letter from the fox hole in Luzon. Only her deep faith in God and his love gave her courage to keep letters on a steady stream to the South Pacific. "Why do I reflect on those days?" she asked herself. Perhaps it was to appreciate the wonders of God's providence.

13
The Wedding

Evie and her brother were early at the bus station (early was one of the traits drilled into their very beings by their father). The motor of the Greyhound vibrated to the depth of Evie's soul. One by one, tired travelers descended from the bus. There were mothers with sleepy, weepy children, soldiers, sailors, and Marines still in uniform arriving. After assisting an old lady with a cane, the bus driver opened the baggage compartment. Evie quickly edged through the crowd. "Are there other buses arriving tonight?" she asked breathlessly. Her question was answered by the braking of the next bus. Chuck and Evie waited on the sidelines. Again, weary travelers hopped off the bus; some with a sigh of relief, others with the tossing of a stub of their cigarette, many into the arms of tearful parents or rushing for their first glimpse of a child in the arms of a trembling wife. At last Lou came bubbling off, with her arms as full as her heart, with packages for her siblings for the wedding. Lou was the big sister of the family. Seven brothers in the family took part of the blame for making a tomboy of Lou. Her stay with Aunt Anna had mellowed her in a lady-like fashion. Alighting from the bus, as a calf out of a long winter pen she screamed, "Hello!" Ray stepped down, and Evie was in his arms. Baggage was claimed as the line shortened. Lou stepped in beside the driver, Evie and Ray were comfortably seated in the back seat. The Ford purred home as to complement the occasion, and Lou joked with the driver. Ray and Evie went over last minute plans, as they rode over the country roads, and were home before they could possibly catch up on all the news. Ray was tired. The long hours from five in the morning until eleven at night caused Ray to use his better judgement and go directly home as Lou rushed into the farm home.

"Tomorrow night is the shower," Evie reminded him as he bid her good-bye.

"I will see you before that," he promised.

Eighty people were at the Ross home to celebrate and prepare the newly established home with equipment. It was warm weather for the twenty-eighth of March. The home and large back porch were filled to overflowing. Children played games in the yard. Ethel was in the height of her glory entertaining the largest crowd that perhaps had ever graced her country home. Evie and Ray opened the generous gifts of life-long friends. Ray was only a short acquaintance of most of the guests. The packages contained pictures, linens, glassware and more glassware. It was too soon after the war for pots and pans to be available, or any products of metal.

To add to her collection for her "hope-against-war-tragedy chest", Evie had sewn one fan pattern quilt while Ray was at war. Embroidered pillow cases, and dresser scarfs were carefully tucked away during the uncertain wait. She had also made a sun bonnet quilt in her early teen years. Evie and her bosom pals, Grace and Edith met weekly and each worked on a Sunbonnet quilt every Tuesday evening. A lunch was carefully planned by the hostess of the evening. They laughed and joked of the children they would tuck warm and snug 'neath the sun bonnet quilts they were appliqueing. At the age of thirteen and fourteen, having a family seemed eons away.

Now she was actually on her way back to the old Chase home stead, from her bridal shower, with the soldier she had waited for over three years. The car was packed with passengers, with laps filled with boxes of glassware and linens. Evie could barely contain herself. The years Ray ate C rations and poor meals in the South Pacific inspired Evie to dream of serving him mouth-watering meals. "I will use tablecloths or luncheon sets for every meal," she boasted. She visualized Ray coming home to steaming roasts, vegetables, salads, and apple pie. Dreaming of the future was what kept hope alive. Evie's mind suddenly returned to the present. "My dreams are near reality."

Ray and Evie were grateful for the gifts. They were carefully packed for brother Carl (Dock, as he was best known to his brothers and sisters) to take to Minneapolis. Evie and Ray would be leaving by train and would travel with only personal luggage. "I wish we had a car, even if it was like the old thirty-one Chevrolet I sold before the war," Ray said for the enteenth time. Cars were still as scarce as hen's teeth. Dock was bringing their Uncle's car to use for the wedding and reception, and to carry them to the train depot.

"We will find a car," Evie assured him. "In the meantime we will make the best of what is available. You won't have to change buses to get to the Twin City Rock Crystal, and I will not be working if I carry out your wishes, so we can make it," Evie went on to make her point. Memorizing the prayer of serenity early in life was an influence at times like these. "Lord help us to change the things we can, accept the things we cannot change, and give us wisdom to know the difference." How many times would she have to utter that prayer was beyond her vision of coming years. Nothing, no nothing, could invade these wonderful moments.

Evie returned to the present after her silent prayer. It was early on Friday morning when Ray dropped by to tell Evie he would be busy helping his folks move to a larger country home. He told her what he would be doing the night before, but he just needed an excuse to see Evie for reassurance that he wasn't dreaming in a foxhole in the South Pacific.

It was convenient that at the end of the month, two big sons were at home to help move. "What a time to be moving," Christine said, "The day before your son's wedding". Lacking a refrigerator, piano, deep freeze, or entertainment center, and with four boys home to help, the move went quite fast.

Evie knew with Irene and Ruthie in high school and other older children in school she would be making the dinner. Jane was just recovering from pneumonia. Three weeks before, after having an extremely high temperature, Dr. Will predicated she would not live. With the new drug pennicillen the Doctor was amazed. Elizabeth's time was divided between tender care of her three year old child and getting ready for Evie's wedding.

Evie's dinner was in the oven; the dessert was made for the twenty-two guests that were due to arrive before five. Fresh bread was on the bread board, covered with a white dish towel. Two large pans of biscuits were spreading aroma throughout the kitchen. The first to arrive was the pastor, his wife and three children. Close behind was Dock and the Folkestads with Baby Janet and little Bobby.

"How can you cook supper when you are getting married tomorrow?" The question came from Mrs. Foreman. "I could not have made a sandwich for myself the day before my wedding," she added. Joy helped put the finishing touches to the meal. The dining room and kitchen table were filled with hungry guests and plenty of food to satisfy the cavities. A peach cobbler topped off the big roaster full of beef roast, with vegetables from the cellar. June and Ruthie were on the dish crew. Joy would now take complete charge of the reception and the meals. Evie and Irene were dismissed, with barely time to make it to Wadena by seven thirty for the rehearsal. The rehearsal went off as though the bride and groom had rehearsed it in their dreams. Verlie Harris needed no practice. Her voice was golden. Her sister Valerie played the familiar march, and Evie recalled marching at Joy's wedding as bridesmaid.

"Just think we should never have to say good-bye again," Ray said as he kissed her his last good-night as fiancé. Ray returned to the farm house that his parents had just moved into. Evie, Irene, Verlie and Valerie stayed at the room that Irene and Ruthie rented to attend school.

"I will press our dresses tonight," Evie informed Irene. "We will splurge and all go out for breakfast," she continued "I can't sleep for an hour or so after all this excitement".

The sun did rise on March 30, 1946, but it hid behind the clouds. It was a cold, bleak, rainy day. "I refuse to let the weather spoil my day," Evie said as they walked uptown. "We have waited too long, and in my heart the sun is shining." They were facing a weeping wind as Evie spoke those words.

Reservations were made for the five Foremans, the attendants, Dock and Irene, the singer, pianist, soloist and the bride and groom. Every one surrounded the white linen table at twelve noon. It was a very special dinner. Neither the bride or groom were in the habit of being so extravagant as dining in a fancy hotel. "This is the only groom's dinner we will ever plan," Evie persuaded Ray. Parents were never expected to pick up the tab. Paddling your own canoe was part of life, when born to large German families. Ray and Evie had that in common.

The thick air was bursting with excitement. Irene and Evie rushed up the stairs to dress, Irene with her pink polka dot, laced trimmed gown, and Evie into Joy's bridal gown. Evie had purchased material for her very own gown. Her nearly life-long friend Lois was to have made the gown. Stepping up the date two weeks to have Reverend Foreman officiate the ceremony changed those plans. Joy graciously offered her gown. Ray thought that a wonderful idea, causing Evie and Ray to disagree momentarily.

The girls did get dressed and to the church by one-thirty. The church was already filling. With all the relatives from two large families, filling the church was no problem. The small country church could not have contained the family members, so the Alliance church on Jefferson Avenue was where the memories were created, and knot forever twisted. There was ample room for all the church friends from Union Corners. Ray's brother, Dock, was by his side. How wonderful to see the two brothers after four years of separation. How gracious God had been to spare the lives of five brothers.

Waiting and watching, Irene looked beautiful. Her blonde hair was shoulder length, hanging in a natural curl. Evie peeked around the corner of the door, waiting for the loud note of Wagner's Wedding march, to begin her first step into the unknown but thrilling future. She skimmed over the large crowd, recognizing the hats and clothing of neighbors of a lifetime. "There is my first Sunday school teacher!" Bernice, Ruth and Harold, memories of cousins and friends flashed through her mind. "It's true, it's true! Ray is really home." No more separation! No anxious waiting for delayed letters. Evie thought her heart would burst with thanksgiving and anticipation. She endeavored to keep her steps slow and properly spaced, but inner desires were to run as though the sacred moments may vanish, as Cinderella experienced at midnight.

Pastor Foreman stood silently, waiting to perform his duties. He had baptized, nurtured, and witnessed a freckled little ten year old develop into now a twenty-two year old bride. "It is as though you are one of my own children," the pastor stated later. Miss Verlie Harris stood tall beside her sister Valerie at the piano. Her dress was floor length baby blue, with lace trim at the tip of the pointed long sleeves. Her laced trimmed collar was high on her neck, adding height to her slender frame. Her golden voice penetrated every corner of the beautiful sanctuary. Miss Harris added perfect volume, lest the message of the song be drowned. The music and words of "At Dawning", and "O' Perfect Love" would forever fill the church and heart of Evie.

Pastor Foreman read from the King James Version of the Bible. The most thought provoking verses were solemnly quoted. "For this reason shall a man leave his father and his mother." The prayer of a righteous man was carefully phrased. Evie and Ray knelt, while "The Lord,s Prayer" was echoing in their souls and the sanctuary. Vows were sincerely molded in history. "I now pronounce you man and wife," Irene lifted Evie's veil and Evie turned for the kiss for which she had made preparation for a life time. The pastor smiled as he introduced Mr. and Mrs. Ray Miller. Valerie played the organ as husband and wife gained momentum with each step. The minister followed closely behind and families filed in line. The bride and groom accepted each wish with thanks. It was now time to leave the church. The congregation was standing outside as though to make a living forest for them to pass by. Handfuls of rice rained from the crowd, and cameras clicked. The clouds parted momentarily. Evie thought to herself, "God is displaying His blessing in a very tangible way." The sun disappeared quickly behind the clouds, but Evie knew that in her heart the sun would always be shining behind the clouds that may pass their way.

14

The Honeymoon

The very chug of trains or buses was usually attended with thoughts of separation. Those memories remained fresh on the mind of both bride and groom. Today it was overpowered with the promise of "'til death do us part."

"It was a good thing you bought your tickets early," Dock commented. "Look at all those people, and you would not have time to stand in line."

"Hate to miss the train on our honeymoon," Ray was grabbing the two suitcases as he jokingly commented. The two brothers embraced as though they would be separated for the next four years, when in reality it was just a bride that may consume his brother's interests and time.

Their bags were checked, and the newlyweds were at last in line to board the train. The shortage of autos created a bumper business for transportation systems. At last they were settled on the train. Evie nearly laughed and cried simultaneously. Ray was introduced to the fact that, on occasions, wives cry when happiness extends beyond the power of expression. He pulled her tightly to

his side and asked, "How can you cry?" He was unaware
of the audience seated across from them. Every precious
moment of the wedding was relived. "It went off without
a hitch," Ray said, revealing his farm back ground. After
the last minute rush of preparation, they nearly fell
asleep on each other's shoulders. The conductor reminded them the next stop would be St. Cloud.

The choice of where to spend a honeymoon, was
made during a long telephone conversation early in
January. "I want you to see where I lived and worked in
St Cloud," Evie pleaded. "We can't afford to travel far."

The plans were finalized. "St Cloud it will be," Ray
was in complete agreement. "I am just content that we
are finally planning one, *and it will be with you.*" And
there they were alighting from a train in the town that
held a chapter of Evie's life.

Having never planned a honeymoon, nor ever
affording the pleasure of staying at a hotel before, reservations were not premeditated. "There are lots of hotels
in St.Cloud," Evie assured her husband earlier. "Let's go
to the hotel walking distance from the bus depot." Saving
the price of a cab appealed to Ray. It was after eight and
dark by the time they claimed their baggage.

"I think we better find a room and leave our suitcases, and then have our wedding dinner," Ray suggested. The nearest hotel was not at all like Evie dreamed. It
was not overly clean (putting it mildly), and very few
rooms were available, after the long exciting day. The
weary travelers mutually agreed to take the room that
they were ushered to. They dropped the suitcases with a
sigh of relief and departed to find the nearest, and hopefully the cleanest restaurant, for this very special dinner.
The entire city sparkled with soft flakes of snow, and a
bright sign beckoned them in.

"What would you like this evening?" the waitress
inquired. She then began listing "fillet mignon" and other
foreign ideas. Ray, having lived a more affluent life at
Aunt Anna's, recognized each entree. "Give us a little

time and we will decide." Ray carefully explained the menu to his country bride.

The dinner tasted wonderful and the moments alone were precious. "It may be a morbid thought, but may I express it anyway? I don't want to spend one day without you, I hope that after a long, long life together we die the same day," Ray confessed. Evie was touched even though it could have easily turned her stomach if she would not have sensed the deep meaning of Ray's desire.They decided to forego dessert when they recalled the wedding cake that Joy so thoughtfully wrapped and tucked in Evie's suitcase.

Ray pulled out his gold pocket watch. "It's nine thirty! What are we doing out on the street on our wedding night?" Hand in hand, Evie tried to keep step with Ray's military stride back to the hotel.

A private bath was included with the large room. "Allow me to draw your bath," the proud husband requested. Evie hung the clothes she would wear to the small church she attended while working in St. Cloud.

Ray removed a package from his suitcase. Evie unwrapped it in surprise. "What a beautiful gown! Did you choose this for me?" Evie asked. "No! I was too bashful to go to the lingerie department. Lou picked that out."

"I have never worn anything quite so beautiful in my life, especially to sleep in," Evie could barely complete her sentence.

"Who said anything about sleeping in it!" And then in all earnestness he added, "I know you always pray before your day is through Evie, and I want to join you." They knelt together to give thanks to a Heavenly Father. With grateful hearts they remembered God's protection and mercy in allowing this night to transpire.

Could the exercising of restraint and solid conviction through the years of courtship in anyway hinder this union? "How thrilling to know that we have reserved our lives for each other," was expressed by both. Though temptation was sometime strong, they mutually agreed.

"I am so glad we did not spoil this memorable night," Evie whispered. These sacred moments could only be shared with the God who designed them for each other.

The plan was to attend church the next morning. They would surprise the Pastor that helped Evie and her close friends with a place to live during the war. Apartments were scarce in St Cloud, with a war plant attracting workers from near and far.

"We should get our tickets and check these bags," Ray suggested "I would hate to carry them around." Evie tucked in her dainty nighty and closed her faithful black suitcase once more.

"I am anxious to pack this bag away. It has been a faithful companion, but I will be so happy to settle down," she said as the past three years flooded her memory.

"The church is in walking distance," Evie convinced Ray. "I have walked it many times from downtown." We can stop on the way for breakfast," she continued. It was most appropriate to wear their honeymoon attire. Evie had on her green and white plaid suit and with light hearts and much to dialogue about, they were at the church before they could believe it.

The pastor hurriedly dismissed his Bible Class and greeted Evie. "This is my husband, as of yesterday at two thirty," Evie explained.

"Congratulations! Evie, we did not know he was discharged." He gave the civilian groom a hearty hand shake. And then it was time for the worship service to begin. Evie and Ray joined in the familiar old hymns, but it is doubtful that they remembered one word or even the text of the sermon. Evie was looking over the small crowd. Missing some of the members that were there during the war, seeing a few new faces, and waiting patiently to proudly introduce her husband to war time friends.

It was then time to go see the upstairs apartment. "How wonderful that it is not raining, and walking will be great exercise before we get back on the train," they both agreed. Rena, Lois and Evie had lived in the upstairs of an old house, while working at a defense plant. The home was owned by a saintly old couple. There was only time for a short visit.

Evie clutched her husband's arm as they walked up the open stairway, recalling the miracle of this moment *ever* arriving. "I sat so many hours writing you letters in this place," Evie said, almost crying as she recalled the eight week periods that did not bring one letter. She verbalized her concern almost in tears, "I wondered if you were dead or alive while here in this apartment."

Ray drew her closely and assured her,"Remember I am very much alive, and we must go on and forget those nightmares." They embraced in silence, in the musty empty apartment, as the past months flashed through their minds. It was as though time stood still. Ray broke the sacred moment with reality. "We must go or we will miss our train." They slowly descended the stairs to bid the dear friends good-bye, not knowing it would be forever.

It was a brisk walk uptown, and time just for one more snack before departure. "This is the jewelry store where I picked out my ring," Evie leaned close to the window to catch a glimpse of the beautiful rings inside the closed store. During the long war, Ray was very concerned that Evie would forget to wait for him, and had sent a money order for her to choose a ring. They stood together peeking in the window as they recalled the circumstances, two years into history. Then it was time to rush to the station.

"We'll honeymoon the rest of our lives," Ray said as the train carried them to their destination and hopeful tomorrows.

15
Home Sweet Home

The train arrived back at Minneapolis on schedule, but none too soon for the anxious bride and groom. They gathered their bags and rushed off to catch the bus that would carry them to their first lowly home. It was a stately old brick home, that had been converted into several apartments. The closets were now called kitchenettes (a name invented during the war). The bedroom itself was a dining, and living room by day, and bedroom at night.

"I must carry you over the threshold," Ray insisted as he swept Evie off her feet just as they were entering the stairway to the apartment. "How much do you weigh?"

"I only weigh one hundred and eighteen pounds, and you really should not groan over that," Evie piped back. "I hope I only weigh that much on our fiftieth anniversary."

"That's so far away let's not worry about that," Ray added.

They passed by the bathroom that would be shared by three apartment neighbors, and unlocked the door to *home sweet home*. The couch and the sewing machine were filling two corners, but there was not a chair in sight. The old ice box was just outside the door. A two burner gas plate was in the "kitchenette". There was no phone, table, or curtains. "I am sorry this is all I could find, but when Gene and Judy finish their new house just think we will have a beautiful duplex, and you will be across the street from Joy," Ray tried to be so positive.

"I am not disappointed," Evie continued, "I will show you what I can do to our little nest."

There was not a thing to eat in Mother Hubbard's cupboard—rather shelf. "We either have to go to Aunt Anna's or to a restaurant," Evie suggested. "Our wedding gifts are at Aunt Anna's; let's go get them and perhaps Dock will bring us home." They were soon boarding the Franklin bus and heading for 2444 Seabury Avenue South.

"Ray and Evie, how good to have you back!" Aunt Anna spread her dining room table with goodies as they had anticipated. Aunt Anna had to hear every detail of the wedding. " Carl (Aunt Anna would never think of calling him Dock) told me we should have been there. How was the Honeymoon?" No mere hint would get them to share those intimate moments.

Evie washed the dishes and they were off. "Thank you for sending your car for us on our Big Day," Ray said as he bid Uncle and Auntie good-bye.

"I did not unload the gifts," Dock said. "I knew you would be anxious to unpack them, and that big wedding left me dog-tired." The trunk was filled with wedding and shower gifts. Dock helped carry them up the stairs into the wee home and then promptly excused himself.

"We can't sort this all out tonight," Ray convincingly stated.

"I have one more day off and we will have to go find a folding table and chairs and get some groceries." Evie placed one set of glassware on the shelf and stood back admiring it's beauty.

"If we don't go to bed soon, I will have to go out to eat," Ray admitted.

"And here I thought we could live on love, at least for the first week," Evie said. They made out the couch for the first night in their own little nest. The new blanket and the quilt that Evie had so carefully stitched while Ray was fighting for her freedom was cuddly and warm. "We don't need to set an alarm tonight, how wonderful! Tuesday will be my first day back to work," Ray added a serious thought to those exciting moments.

A new day dawned, and the newlyweds were off to buy some food before a breakfast could be made. Bread, milk, eggs and bacon were on the list. "Of course we need sugar," Evie added. "I have my sugar stamps along." "I am sorry there is not a grain of sugar in the store," the manager apologized. "It will be in tomorrow about ten o'clock. Then he whispered "There should be some butter in this afternoon, about two."

"I will be back," Evie assured him. Whoever heard of cooking without butter? They rushed home to fry the bacon and eggs. Evie peeled two oranges in a fancy flower by slicing the peeling half way down, and opening it partially . She used the very prettiest luncheon set on the new folding table.

"We shouldn't use these linen napkins," Ray half questioned.

"Oh yes, we may use them, or did you want to save them for our grandchildren?" Evie responded. Evie was determined to have set the finest table, in consideration of the time Ray spent in the foxholes with C rations

Earlier, Aunt Anna had given Ray a toaster. "It doesn't work, but if you can fix it you may have it," she promised.

"It looks like new," Ray thought to himself and promptly took it to the basement. By removing a raisin, and reassembling it, the toaster worked like new.

"It is wonderful to own a toaster" Evie reminded

Ray.

The cook vowed, "We will have butter for our bread tonight", not realizing she would remain in a line that was a half block long. "I want to bake bread," Evie continued. "I saw an oven at the hardware that fits over a gas burner, let's go buy it." Ray would certainly find a way or make one, if Evie wanted to bake homemade bread. I will get the butter while you go to the hardware," Evie suggested.

"Do we have to part so soon?" Ray questioned sadly. "I want you to help pick out the things we need at the hardware."

"I can't believe it is nearly two already and we have have just finished our breakfast dishes," Evie sighed. Ray wiped the dishes and admired the embroidered dish towels that Evie had worked on long before Ray came into her life. He also admired the dish washer and had a difficult time keeping his mind on his work.

Earlier Evie made a cover for the hide-a-bed. It had big flowers in the center of the three pillows on the back of the couch. Lining perfectly with the pillows were three flowers on the seat of the couch. It was a beautiful heavy material, rose in color, and pleated at the bottom. Ray looked at it quietly and then said in all sincerity,"I will never sit on it with my work clothes on." It had taken hours for Evie to decide on the fabric and the sewing machine had been humming for days.

Waiting in line for butter was a new experience for the newlyweds.

Back with the big family there were plenty of ration stamps for both butter and sugar. The butter was purchased through the creamery, or if the the road was blocked with snow, the churn was utilized and they had fresh buttermilk biscuits to top it all off.

"Did you ever imagine we would stand in a line this long for one pound of butter?" Ray asked

"We are the only ones enjoying it," Evie piped back

as she squeezed his hand. It was a bright, sunny day and his companion was a lot more fun than an army buddy. A mature lady with her hair in a pug did not take her eyes off the couple. Ray was in his army fatigues and it wasn't too difficult to see that the returned soldier preferred this line rather than one to a Mess Hall.

A little freckled boy looked up to Ray and asked, "Are you a soldier?"

"Yes, I was for three years, but now I came back and married this lady." The line moved ahead and with a golden pound of butter in their hand they said good-bye to the little red-head.

They rushed on to the hardware store for an oven, and home to fix their first dinner in the modest little place they called home. "We can even bake potatoes, and I will make some baking powder biscuits." And so Evie tried out her tiny little oven, over one of the burners. She fried two pork chops on the only burner left. "I will make the coffee while we are eating our salad," she added. She managed to open a can of peas to heat quickly after removing the oven from one burner. "It was just like playing house," Evie often remarked. It took a period of time to not think of large kettles of food.

Her work table was the folding table and then she cleared it, donned it with tablecloth, and set it with her beautiful luncheon cloths, flowered dishes from Aunt Anna, and the silverware exactly as Mrs. Hartung had taught her. "The knife should always be to the right of the plate, the spoon beside it and the forks on the left side of the plate." The napkin was as carefully folded as though a king was joining them. She had a variety of glassware to use, and a large selection of tablecloths.

Ray's appetite was slowly recovering from his last bout with malaria. His weight was down to one hundred forty pounds. "This pork gravy is such a great flavor, and I wonder how many brides can make such smooth gravy?" Ray said. Evie's long hours of cooking farm meals paid off. "I have never had so many complements on a meal," Evie confessed. "Will it always be this much fun to cook for my husband?" she wondered.

The dishes were done once more. The only place to draw water was the bathroom, and that was the only place to dispose of the used water. Evie soon learned to have drinking water in the icebox and to draw her dish water in advance. It did not dampen her enthusiasm, for back on the farm she did not even have running water, much less a bathroom. She was accustomed to six rooms and a *path*.

"Tomorrow morning it's back to work," Ray reminded Evie. "We will make use of our new alarm clock, and it will have to be set for six bells, I have to be at work at seven o'clock." Evie was informed she could remain in bed. "I can't do that! I want to prepare you a big breakfast," Evie said as she carefully wrapped some sandwiches. "I can't believe how fast our first day flew by," Evie said sadly, as if they would never have another day quite like it. "I will enjoy thinking about it the rest of my life," Evie assured Ray.

The alarm went off with a bang, bringing with it the reality of this new day. Evie and Ray had time to pray together, and Ray reluctantly kissed his bride good-bye. "I will see you at five-thirty," he promised and he embraced her one more time, as though he would wake up in a foxhole, only dreaming of the future.

Evie busied herself sorting out the gift boxes that were stacked in the corner. "I will have room for one more set of glassware and the rest will have to be stored until we move into the duplex," she said to herself. The linens would have to be placed in her old black suitcase for lack of linen closet or drawer space. "Oh dear, I must get at my supper," she thought as she glanced at the clock. The small ice box in the hall held only a day's supply of food. Meat was not easily available and would have to be purchased almost daily. "I am going to splurge today if I can talk the butcher out of a couple of steaks," she thought to herself as she walked briskly over the two blocks to the store. She also needed to stock up on spices, yeast, and vanilla. Jello was hard to find. Evie had figured out a way to over come that problem. She found some Kool aid and unflavored gelatin that she combined with sugar and had a wonderful jello salad prepared for the following day.

The table was spread as Ray returned . He looked tired, but burst inside and sniffed his way to the "big" kitchen. "I knew it would smell so good, and I think I married the best cook in this entire city," he elaborated. Evie had on the apron that Ray had given her for Christmas. The top half was in the shape of a heart. It was covered with small flowers in her favorite blue background.

"Dock was so envious of my neat lunch today, that I think he will rush to get married." Ray gave Evie a run down of the day before he asked about Evie's day. "I see you emptied a lot of boxes by the looks of that corner and it must have taken all afternoon to make this meal," he murmured between bites of apple pie. "It wouldn't hurt if you would add a few more grains of coffee to the pot though. My mom always made German coffee so strong, and that is how I learned to like coffee," Ray informed his bride. "Don't feel offended," he continued as he reached for the hand that brewed the cup he was drinking.

"I can't drink strong coffee," Evie replied, "And a pound of coffee is not always on the grocery shelf, but I'll add a few grains and also add water to my cup." The pledge was sealed with a kiss and the dishes were carried to the dish pan.

The cover was removed from the couch and again they retired to a bedroom for their third night as new bed partners. It was not difficult to call it a day. They did not possess a radio, nor had the word television even been coined. The alarm was set again. "It will be a long stretch before we retire, I hope this alarm holds up," Ray remarked jokingly.

"Can you believe we are finally married?" was repeated almost daily by one or the other. The first week went by as though life would always be *so perfect!*

16
When Bubbles Burst

April showers, intermingled with bright sunny days, created a beautiful green carpet in a nearby park, but Ray's nine or ten hour days did not allow much time for romantic eventide walks.

Joy asked Evie if she would have time to make Janet an Easter bonnet and coat to match. Evie accepted it as a challenge. Sewing was her favorite pastime during Ray's working hours.

She was so anxious to entertain, but missed her Mother's kitchen range. However, on Easter Sunday Evie and Ray invited Joy, Howard and two little ones to dinner. Though having limited cooking facilities they managed to serve a four course dinner. The ham roast and potato casserole were slowly baking during the hour of worship. The meal was topped with everyone's favorite blueberry pie that was baked on Saturday.

After the dishes were all tucked in place, Howard suggested, "Let's take a walk in the park." With camera in hand, they were glad to get out of the tiny quarters. It was a perfect day, with no need of a sweater. Howard captured the spring beauty and a picture of Janet's pink

Easter outfit.

The afternoon ended in a walk together after their guests took the children home for their afternoon nap. "Our first Easter together!" Evie repeated. How wonderful life could be. They laughed at their inconveniences as they transformed the room into a bedroom.

The days seemed to just evaporate. Evie and Ray had promised to return to their farm homes. Evie had never spent a night with her in-laws. The younger sisters had written for their big brother to return. They secretly were trying to arrange for a shiveree. What Ray did not bargain for was being exposed to the mumps. Two sisters were just beginning to feel sick, when the newlyweds arrived.

Two weeks later Ray awoke with a swollen jaw. With his weakened malaria condition he became very ill. Evie served him broth and soft foods. He remained in bed for two weeks. "I always wanted to be a nurse," Evie assured him.

Ray later admitted "The only positive thing about this affliction is all the attention I am getting."

Evie opened her sewing machine, and decided to sew a slack suit for each of the Miller sisters, and also all her little sisters. There was a fabric store in walking distance. Marilyn, Joan, Louise and Charlene's sets were all in boxes ready to send. Irene, Ruthie, June, Donna, Orpha, Pearl and Ruby's were in a box labeled Branstners at Hewitt, Minnesota.

Ray returned to work for five days. On Friday the thirteenth he trudged up the stairs very slowly. Supper was served but without his usual flattering comments. He ate very little and was anxious to call it a day.

"It's your birthday tomorrow," Evie tried to excite him about something. "It will be the first birthday we have been together in four years," Evie added. She reminded Ray that their first date was on his twenty first birthday.

The sun shone brightly on his twenty-fifth birthday. "I wish you would not go to work on your birthday," Evie begged.

"I have to," Ray responded. "We are so far behind on orders, and I have missed so many pay checks already, we close at noon on Saturdays." Ray ate so very little breakfast, and Evie reluctantly kissed him good bye. She busied herself cleaning her apartment.

"It's almost ten," she half said to herself. "I must fix a special lunch and get a cake baked before Ray gets home." She grabbed her purse and was just heading down the stairs, as Ray opened the stairway door.

"I am so sick," he murmured. Evie met him half way and placing her face next to her husband realized he was a very sick man. She helped him to bed and ran to the landlord's residence, to call a doctor.

She explained that they did not have a car and he was much too sick to take a bus or streetcar. The doctor consented to make a house call. "His temperature is very high and he needs to be in a hospital. I will call an ambulance from the Veterans Hospital," he assured Evie as she followed him to the end of the hall. Ray was carried out in a stretcher down the long stairway to the ambulance. Evie followed close behind him.

She stayed by his side whenever the nurses and doctors would allow her to, and then they informed her, "Visiting hours are over you must go home." Ray seemed too sick to realize she was leaving. She boarded a streetcar and transferred to a bus to take her home. She stopped by her landlady's home to ask if she could use her phone one more time.

Joy answered on the first ring. "I just returned from the Vets hospital," Evie blurted out with tears streaming down her face. "Ray is so sick. They are taking blood tests, and he is so anemic." She went on to tell of how many times they had to change his sheets. "He has malaria, of course, but that is not the reason for his low blood. I will go back in the morning," Evie said.

"Howard and I will take you," Joy comforted Evie with that news.

"When I stop to think of it, I haven't had a bite to eat since breakfast." Evie sat alone in the very empty apartment. She cried until some of the tightness in her chest was released, and decided she had better eat. "I can't get sick now," she thought, "I will have to find a job very soon. This is not at all what I planned for a birthday dinner." She slowly ate some leftovers. For the first time she did not make the hide-a-bed out. She never knew a bed could be so cold and lonely. She tossed the first part of the night,"What should I do? Ray always said he wanted to make the living, and I quit my job at Munsingwear. I would have to work five days a week and would not have time to visit Ray only one day a week." The hospital had given Evie a schedule of visiting days.

"You may only come every other day," the stern nurse reminded Evie. She finally fell asleep, not having solved one problem.

"Mrs. Miller! Mrs. Miller!" the voice came from the elderly maiden lady next door as she softly tapped on the kitchenette wall.

Evie tried to sort out why she was on the couch alone. "Is this a bad dream?" She was on her feet before she recalled the horrible birthday.

"What do you want Millie"?

"There is a man in the hallway, he has been there since midnight. Don't go to the bathroom, you will stumble right over him."

"Thanks for warning me," Evie was finally wide awake. She opened her window and watched for anyone on the street. At last, a lady was on her way to early mass. "Would you stop by the front door and tell our land lady that there is an intruder on our hall floor?" Evie yelled.

"I am already running late for mass," she said. There was an attic on a third level. The landlady's sister slept on third floor. Her window was open and she heard the frantic call. She flew down the stairs, and the door hit the drunk. She banged him again and again, and he ran down the stairs. By this time occupants of all four apartments were witnesses, and were soon standing in line for the only bathroom.

With only four hours of sleep Evie thought she could go back to sleep. She knew in her heart after this episode she would never stay in this apartment alone. Why did it happen the first night Ray was gone, and how long would her dear husband be away?

She dressed, ate a quick bite, and again bothered her land lady for the phone. "Joy, you wouldn't believe the wild night I've had," and then related every detail.

"Howard and I will be over as soon as we can and you are not staying alone in that apartment,"Joy assured her.

They entered the hospital to discover they had moved Evie's soldier to the area of the terminally ill. Ray was weak and tired after the long day and night of high temperatures. His pitcher of ice water was just being refilled. Evie followed the nurse to the hall. "Why did they move him to this wing?" Evie asked.

"You'll have to talk to the doctor. He should be in soon." She tossed her head and went to the next room.

Evie returned to Ray's bedside. Joy and Howard were not permitted to stay in the room. "I will stay for the day," Evie decided. Joy and Howard promised to keep in close touch. "We will call you when we get home." Evie remained calm on the outside. She was thinking, "What home? It is not a home without my soldier. "I have been so preoccupied I forgot to call Aunt Anna." She knew he left for work sick and she perhaps thought it was another malaria attack and could not call to check back. "Aunt Anna, Ray is at the Vet's Hospital. No! it is not just malaria. They will have more results on Monday." She went on to be as specific as she could be about his blood condition.

"You poor little widow," was as comforting as Aunt Anna could be. Evie hung up the phone and wondered, "Why did she have to call me a little widow?" She must not cry now, the doctor was just entering by Ray's bedside. Evie hurried on.

"I hear you had a rough night," the doctor commented, as he looked over the chart. "We are going to run some more tests on Monday and get to the bottom of this. You'll need lots of water after soaking up three sets of sheets," he added as he continued examining Ray. Evie stayed by Ray's side throughout the day. He was extremely tired and drifted to sleep for most of the day.

"You better go home soon Evie," he said as he drank some broth for supper. "I don't want you on the street after dark, after the wild night you had last night," he added. His lips were filled with fever blisters.

"I don't know where to kiss you good night," Evie said as she kissed his forehead. He was not ready to let go of her hand.

"Here we go again, saying good night. I will be home soon, I know," he assured her.

Evie looked over the streetcar schedule then to the clock and said, "If I hurry I will catch the next streetcar." She was alone with her thoughts, and did not care to share them with anyone except the Lord. "I cannot despair Lord when I have you," and then she remembered the prayer of serenity that had been her guide through the unknowns. She hurried up the stairs, looked carefully in the dim lit hall for a stray night owl, and hurriedly unlocked the apartment door. Somehow it did not seem like home. How could that sense of home sweet home be so fleeting. She was exhausted and hungry. She carefully peeked from her door before checking the icebox in the hall. The bits of food she had left over were not cold. Then she remembered Ray was not home to buy ice on his birthday. She put the quart of milk in the window as she reminded herself, "I am not going to buy any more ice, I am not staying here." She opened a can of soup, found some crackers, and ate slowly as she contemplated her future.

Removing the beautiful cover to the couch, she doubled a sheet, put on her quilt and knelt beside her bed. At last she found a sympathetic ear that she could honestly admit her fears and limitations to. She crawled in bed as though a load had been snatched from her shoulders. "Cast every care on Him, for He cares for you," echoed in her heart and mind. She looked at the pieces of material in the quilt, and it brought back memories of dresses of family members. She fell so soundly asleep, that not even a knock on her kitchen wall could awaken her.

It was eight thirty, when she awoke. When the truth hit her squarely, she said to herself, "I wish I was dreaming." Promptly she dressed and went to the phone. "I hate to bother you so often," she told dear old Mrs. Nelson. Mrs. Nelson had her own problems. Having a stroke victim for a husband was not all sunshine.

"That is OK. You just feel free to use the phone anytime. We are usually on duty day and night around here." She then reminded Evie, "Your husband is young, he will recover. There is not a chance my man will ever come back to me." She gasped for her breath as she bathed her lover's face and hands, and began trying to feed him. Evie began to count her blessings and called Joy.

"You better move your belongings over here," Joy insisted. "You won't have to pay rent or be alone."

Evie need not be invited twice. "I will see who I can get to move me," she answered. She grabbed the yellow pages and looked for movers.

Nothing caught her eye until she saw the ad that read "Let a Vet Move You". Without a moment hesitation she was dialing, to hear a pleasant voice on the end of the line. She briefly told him why she needed to move. "We'll move you today!" And within one hour Evie had packed her earthly possessions. She ran to the bathroom to cover her red nose and eyes, before the truck arrived. The hide-a-bed, sewing machine, folding table, chairs, and boxes were being carried down a flight of stairs, by two strong Vets. "What is the address you want this delivered to, and are you coming with us?" the driver asked. Evie had planned to take city transportation, but with a friendly invitation to accompany the precious cargo, she accepted; thus saving a streetcar token and changing from bus to streetcar on her way to Joy's.

"You are here already!" Joy was surprised. She was glad for more furniture in her sparsely filled living room. There is plenty of room for your sewing machine and a big closet for all your boxes.

The room had formerly been a large bedroom before the upstairs was converted into an apartment. Evie paid the two Veterans ten dollars and bade them good bye as dear friends.

"We cannot visit Ray until tomorrow," Evie commented as she stacked her prize possessions neatly in the big closet. She slowly passed over memory lane as she hung Ray's army uniform, wedding suit and his favorite sport jacket beside her best wardrobe. Joy sensed the sad look on Evie's face and tried to boost her morale.

"It is lunch time, and I hear Howard coming up the stairs." Howard worked two stories below in a dingy print shop. His pay was barely enough for a family to exist on and that with careful planning. "Evie, I have a job for you the first day you have available," Joy beamed. Faith has some house work and about twenty shirts for you to iron.

"I will take it," Evie did not blink an eye at hard work. "I will be available on Wednesday."

She tried to call Ray's station nurse, with no satisfaction. "His doctor will call you now that he has your telephone number," the nurse replied. Evie waited patiently for that call. Mid-dinner the phone rang. Evie jumped as though it was her phone.

"Mrs. Miller this is Doctor Pierce. We have the results in from blood work. I am sorry to inform you of the results. Ray has three different kinds of native amoeba. He will be hospitalized for some time. It will take severe treatments to rid his body of these and then we must rebuild his blood." He continued to explain the plan of attack. He will have threats of malaria continuously until we remedy these other problems." Evie thanked him for the call and wished she had never heard of the South Pacific. She sat back at the table, but somehow the food had lost its appeal. The dinner had looked so inviting before the call.

Every visiting day Evie was on her way to see Ray. She spent at least two hours per day on public transportation. Ray was very sick from the treatments to rid his body of uninvited guests. The days in between, Evie managed to find day work. She slept in her own bed, but missed her roommate most when she had time to think alone. She appreciated a roof over her head and moral support from her dear sister and brother, Howard. Baby Janet and little Robert were her inspiration each day.

Time did pass. The duplex that was promised them, was soon going to be ready. July was ending, and Ray had no chance of a discharge. In late August, Ray was granted a week to return home. He caught the first bus and headed to Joy's apartment. "We can take a trip up home," Ray suggested. They boarded a bus to visit both families and relatives near the valley. Ray tired easily, but was so elated to be with Evie and loved ones. They visited Uncle Bill. Aunt Lottie had passed away while Ray was overseas. Uncle Bill was lonely on his farm. "You two have to come and live with me," he begged.

"I must go back to the hospital," Ray said sadly, "and I don't know for how long, and Uncle Gus is waiting for me to return to work."

Ray and Evie returned to the city. Evie to Joy's home, and Ray checked in at the Vets. The shadows hung low over the uncertain future. The duplex was rented to some other happy couple. Evie continued her day work. With grateful heart she accepted every day of work offered her. It was the middle of October 1946 when Ray finally received his discharge from the Veterans Hospital.

"I don't think you will be able to work inside," the doctor cautioned.

"It is the only job I have," Ray replied. "I will work inside." He went back to work for three days and returned to Joy's house so sick he could barely make it to a bed.

"I knew he would not be able to work inside," the doctor was not at all surprised to get the call. Ray lived through another siege of malaria. He contributed a load of clothes for the washer every few hours. Evie was vigilant and kept drinking water within his reach.

In a few days he felt much improved. He was restless and unsure of what lie ahead. "I am so glad we have each other. I can face each day with you," Ray confessed. Life had never been a bed of roses, but being young at heart, life was still an adventure.

"I wish I could buy a farm, then I could get the fresh air the doctor prescribes," Ray told his bride. "Let's go back to Uncle Bill's and see what we can work out."

In sickness and health took on a deeper meaning. They packed their bags and were soon on their way to explore new horizons.

17
New Horizons

Ray recovered again from a bout with malaria. "It is what I imagine it must be like to face childbirth," Evie remarked when Ray faced another attack, knowing it would be several hours of extreme temperature and no way of escape. She knew childbirth would not necessarily cause a temperature, but there was truly no way of escaping the ordeal. She did not know how soon she would be subjected to the analogy that she was drawing. In just a few mornings, Evie lost her hearty appetite.

"Why aren't you eating Evie?" Joy questioned with a sparkle in her eye.

"Breakfast just does not appeal to me," Evie responded.

When lunch and dinner did not smell appetizing, Joy began to laugh. "Evie I am sure you are pregnant."

Having been married nearly six months, Evie had been content to think she was immune to becoming a mother, at least until they were more settled. Everyday that she visited at the Vets hospital there were mothers bringing children to see their fathers, and Ray would enjoy seeing them. "I will be so happy when we can settle down and have a baby," Ray said longingly.

But the twenty-four dollar question: was the timing perfect? No job, not even an apartment, and living with Joy and Howard temporarily, the answer was negative. Evie and Ray calculated that conception had been the blessed week they enjoyed their second honeymoon, when Ray was released from the hospital in late August.

"I guess you were stronger than I anticipated," Evie confessed. With separation so early in marriage, all precautions were thrown to the wind. "Besides," Evie thought to herself, "I am not as susceptible as my mother was to a male bed partner."

With the prospects of being a father without a home or job, Ray became very serious. "We must decide what we are going to do," Ray said.   "What do you think of Uncle Bill's offer?" he asked.

The summer had ended, not at all like it was planned. Evie and Ray were dependent on public transportation. They were again on the train.

"We have each other, and something is going to work out for us," Ray said as he squeezed his seasick bride, reassuringly.

It was past the peak of the fall season, and everything looked bleak.

Evie concluded, "I refuse to allow all the unknowns to cast a shadow on our precious time together today."

Gus and Elizabeth met them in Wadena. Gus remarked,"You have both lost so much weight."

"I am feeling much better," Ray quickly informed them. The farm meals tasted heavenly, and Evie could even enjoy the vegetables. She confided in Elizabeth, "I am sure I am pregnant." Elizabeth accepted that as a very natural part of everyday life, and Gus looked at Evie with a very suspicious grin on his face.

"You should be able to get a Veteran's loan on a farm," Gus suggested.

"We will have to investigate that," Ray responded.

In the afternoon they borrowed the car and visited Uncle Bill.

"It is so lonely without Aunt Lottie, I cannot stand it," he blurted almost before they entered the house. "I would do anything to have you two living here. "Evie would you get us a lunch if I make the coffee?" She found some cheese and crackers, rolls and butter. The food did not tempt Evie. In between the sips of coffee, Uncle Bill revealed his proposal. "I think if I put in six or seven more cows, that we would have income for both of us. I have always wanted time to see the country, and visit my children. I will probably spend a lot of time up at Roseau, with my son Gerald."

Uncle Bill was a jolly, congenial man. A little over-weight, thanks to lunching and no cook. His dear wife had been a tremendous influence on Ray. The last night before leaving for the service, she took Ray aside and asked him to promise her he would not submit to temptations. Ray actually resembled his uncle more than his own father.

Evie tried to visualize Ray at that same age. "I will cook good meals she determined, and he may escape that bay window.

With no other alternative at the moment, Ray and Evie decided to move in with Uncle Bill. "Will I be cooking for Uncle a lot?" Evie asked.

"No, not much if he does all the traveling he says he is going to do," Ray said. Evie had looked forward to living in the duplex across from Joy by this time, alone with her husband. It was with reluctance that she would move in with anyone. She loved Uncle Bill, but with so little time together in their marriage Evie longed for a private family life. Besides she did not enjoy cooking for even her husband at the moment.

Their earthly possessions were still stored at the Folkestads. "Aldrich makes a trip to the cities every week," Uncle Bill suggested. Evie was on the phone in minutes. "Would you bring our furniture back next week," she inquired.

"I would be glad to," the kind trucker then added, "Maybe you and Ray would ride down with me."

"I would like to purchase a bedroom set," Evie answered. Ray consented and they were soon riding back to Joy's in a semi-truck.

Aldrich waited patiently as Evie and Ray chose their bedroom set. It was carefully loaded in the freshly washed truck bed.

"Oh I love that waterfall front," Evie explained as they loaded the precious cargo. Evie had saved for furniture while working in Lansing, Michigan. The rest of their possessions were carried down the stairs from Joy's apartment.

"How are you feeling Evie?" Joy asked as Evie shoved boxes from the closet.

"I can hardly swallow water, and I have lost fifteen pounds," Evie confessed. "I have just visited Dr. Will and he confirmed your predictions. I am now getting vitamin shots every other day, and I weigh one hundred and three pounds. They could not expect a trucker to wait for Joy and Evie to catch up on news, so Evie promised to write as soon as she settled in the farm home.

The long round trip, in one day, sapped Evie of every ounce of strength. The thrill of her first set of totally new furniture renewed her strength to help move Uncle Bill's set upstairs. Evie could hardly wait to go to Wadena and pick out a new spread. The following day, she chose a beautiful rose chenille spread. The closet was lacking a door, so she also purchased a heavy blue material to make a beautiful full curtain to cover that eye sore. How wonderful to have drawer space, even for her linens. Finally the old black suitcase was emptied, and carried to the store room.

"I can't believe we are semi-settled down," Evie whispered to Ray as they folded the beautiful spread back. "Don't turn the light off yet, please. I want to just lay and look at the closet curtain. Isn't it gorgeous?" The bedroom set was dust-free and held their wedding picture and a few precious nick-knacks. Uncle Bill was snug in bed with a stairway between rooms. They whispered softly. It was the only time of day that they enjoyed complete privacy.

"Why do you go to bed so early?" the Uncle often asked. The lonely evenings of the past year made him crave some one to talk to. Evie and Ray were torn. They shared the day with him, but had so little privacy in their first seven months of marriage. Evie was physically exhausted at the set of sun, and she wanted nothing more than to be alone with Ray.

"The school teacher is in need of a place to board," Uncle Bill announced when he returned from the country store of Woodside. "Would you consider boarding her, Evie?" he asked. "You will get thirty dollars a month and you can keep that for your own," he promised.

Cooking was not Evie's favorite pastime, since even the smell of food made her sick. "Let me talk it over with Ray, and I will let you know in the morning," she scratched her forehead and thoughtfully answered.

"What do you think about taking in another boarder?"

Evie could hardly wait to get Rays' opinion.

"Well it doesn't seem like old Unc is going to take many trips, so how much longer does it take to cook for one more? He continued rationalizing. "It would give you some spending money, but it is up to you," he added.

The next day Evie was upstairs, cleaning and preparing a room for the country schoolteacher. She would be going home every weekend, weather permitting. Her sister was also teaching in a nearby school. She came to meet her new family. "What kind of food do you like?" Evie endeavored to see just what would be expected for a meal.

"I don't like any meat except wieners, bologna, and

sandwich meats," was her answer. I do like most vegetables and salads," she continued. Uncle Bill would not touch any processed meat, and salads were not his favorite. It wasn't a meal without potatoes, gravy, and meat. Every night Evie prepared separate foods to please her growing family.

The month of November flew by. Ray waited for the extra cattle that was part of the bargain of farming on shares. Evie began preparing for the new baby. She hemmed four dozen diapers, sewed and embroidried on wee nighties. How grateful she was for the sewing machine. It worked perfectly. "What do you think we will have, a boy or a girl?" she asked the daddy in waiting.

"It would be nice to have a little boy, but I *love* little girls," he said thoughtfully.

The sparkling snow on the evergreens reminded everyone of the fast approaching Christmas. "We must have the most beautiful tree in the forest," Evie insisted. It would be their first Christmas as a family. Evie was feeling a little better each day. She shopped for the decorations, and the tall full tree was as carefully trimmed. "I could just sit by the hour enjoying the tree," Evie commented one evening.

Uncle Bill was thrilled to have the bride and groom remain in the living room later in the evening. He finally began yawning and admitted staying up wasn't as much fun as he thought it would be. He said, "Good night!" Evie and Ray remained on the couch almost in silence. Ray was thinking of two years before, of his pup tent falling down, and trying to sleep in the rain. He remembered his fallen buddies his second Christmas in the South Pacific. Evie relived the past year.

Ray broke the silence. "We must enjoy tonight, and the blessings of a peaceful Christmas."

Ray was being very secretive, and on December twenty-fourth a Lane cedar chest was delivered to the farm. It matched their new bedroom set to a tee, waterfall front, stain and all. Earlier, Evie had confided in

Howard to choose the best camera on the market for Ray. Included in the gift box was a leather camera case. They spent Christmas Eve with Uncle Bill, and the following day with their parents. It was the most wonderful Christmas ever.

"Just think next year we will hang our baby's stockings," Ray beamed. Evie stared at the tree, recalling Ray's letter just one year before. The words stuck in her mind. *"It is hard to get into the mood for Christmas."*

"Two years ago we were tearing up camp and spent New Years on a boat, and last year we were preparing for the invasion of Luzon. I think of those days and the ones I left behind and cannot wipe them from my memory." Not knowing what his wife was thinking Ray asked, "Evie, why so serious? Merry Christmas!"

18

A New Address

It was with tears that Evie began to untrim the tree. She did not want the season to end. "Our first wonderful Christmas together is over," she thought to herself. Ray had left for the woods to cut trees. She recalled the woodsman that cut fuel for her father and the day she met Ray. She stared a minute or two at the perfect shape and straight trunk of the tree. All the trimmings were new and chosen carefully. She turned on the lights once more. Packing reminded her of a funeral and always made her sad. The multi-colored balls were tucked in their original boxes and every strand of icicle was taken off the tree. The dry tree was dragged out to a snow bank and stood up straight to enjoy as an extra shrub for awhile. She quickly followed the green brook trail of needles back to the house.

It was January 2, 1947. She wondered what would transpire before she unpacked the Christmas trimmings again. "For sure I am going to have a baby," she glanced down at her dress that was tightening. She wondered where she would spend Christmas of nineteen forty eight, as she packed the boxes upstairs.

Ray returned for dinner as Cousin Eleanora called to inform Evie that Uncle Bill would stay at her house for lunch. Ray's time alone in the cool brisk woods allowed him to make plans for the future. "I have been thinking about buying our own farm. It does not look like Unc is going to buy those extra cattle, nor travel any further than Bertha," he continued. "And your Dad is sure we would qualify for a G.I. loan." Gus had been watching every farm that was for sale.

"We must do something," Evie agreed, "but we won't alarm Unc until we are sure we are moving." They were both grateful that he had shared his home with them the past few months.

Every Sunday after attending the country church at Union Corners, Evie and Ray visited either the Branstner or Miller home for dinner, and then returned to help milk the six cows and have supper with Uncle Bill.

It was February when Gus announced, "Mr. Stearns plans to sell the Freedland farm." He could hardly wait for Evie and Ray to see it. Two maiden ladies had the house built. It reminded Evie of a doll house. Two small bedrooms, with closets in between, a large living room, a kitchen with a breakfast nook, a small room intended for a bath room and an enclosed front porch. The porch consisted of windows on three sides. The snow banks were small pyramids when the farm was first inspected.

The price of the one hundred acres was three thousand five hundred dollars. A small barn, large chicken coop, double garage, a path, and a white picket fence to match the buildings were included in the farm. The thought of a house of their very own outweighed any questions that could have been asked. There was an entrance to the basement from the back hall, then three steps up and you were in the kitchen. The kitchen floor was of brown and beige checker board tile. White cabinets were along one wall with a window in the center over the sink. There were french windows over the nook and in the bedrooms, "I don't like the small bedrooms," Evie complained, "but I love the rest of the house. If the farm suits you, Ray, let's apply for a loan. There is plenty of space to build on a large bedroom someday."

Gus knew the loan would not be approved in time for spring crops, and he agreed with the banker to finance the farm until the loan was approved. They both cashed the last bonds they saved during the war.

Five Jersey cows, a team of horses, a kitchen range and a few necessities were added to their purchases. "You'll have to take over the milking at once," Mr Stearns bargained. He was getting older and anxious to turn the milking burden over to the new owners. It was nearing Evie and Ray's first anniversary, and instead of living across from Joy in the big city they were now moving to their own farm.

There had not been much of a cream check to divide through part of the past months as most of the cows were dry before calving. Uncle Bill was informed of the move as soon as it was solidified.

The problem was that the Stearn's farm was too far from Uncle Bill's to travel twice a day to milk the cows. They could not move until the purchase was finalized. Ray was anxious to have his own milk check. He bought hay and feed for the cattle to last until he could put them out to green pastures. The next battle was to find a temporary place to live close to the farm.

They inquired of the Lyman Country store keeper, "Do you know of any place for rent?"

"Yes, I think Mrs. Horn has an apartment." The apartment joined her house. It had a large old range, and very worn linoleum on the kitchen floor. Black worn linoleum was most distasteful to Evie. Before her marriage, the first thing Evie replaced was a worn linoleum when she returned to her childhood home with extra money burning in her pocket. Either the other room, a bedroom or the kitchen had a trail of wear and she could not bear her mother putting up with an old worn floor.

"You can't buy a new linoleum when we are only

going to be here a few weeks," Ray saw the look on her face as she stared at the old black floor.

"I won't have any visitors as long as I am here," she stated emphatically. The weeks would not pass fast enough. She scrubbed and washed and starched the old dusty curtains, with some improvement, and the satisfaction of, "I can move in now."

On April Fool's day, they bade Uncle Bill good bye. "You can come to see us often, and I will bake a loaf of bread for you every time I bake," Evie promised. The school teacher discovered another farm wife willing to board her. To make the move more interesting, the teacher met and married the young son.

Again the furniture and boxes were loaded in a trailer and moved. Evie knew she could endure the next few weeks, as long as she concentrated and dreamed of her doll house.

She was just getting accustomed to maternity clothes and was now going once a week for shots. The unborn baby was not increasing in weight as much as Dr. Will desired. Day by day Evie's appetite improved. "It is so great to just have you to cook for," Evie told Ray. Every afternoon she could now close her eyes while mentally decorating her new home, and was soon in dreamland.

Mrs. Horn's father-in-law had lived in the apartment until his death. The old black range and worn floor did not affect him in the least, nor the lack of electricity. "I am spoiled now," Evie said as she ironed with the old, sadirons that had to be heated on the range. She glanced over at the door between Mrs. Horn's living room and her apartment. "I will be gone just a moment," leaving Ray in wonder.

Mrs. Horn responded to the knock on her kitchen door. "Hello, Evie! How are you getting along in your new home?" she questioned.

"Quite well, thank you, but I was wondering if you would permit us to have electricity?" She went on to say how she missed using the toaster, her new iron and her lamps.

"Well, I am afraid that is impossible to wire your apartment," Mrs. Horn said abruptly.

"Oh, no! I would not expect that!" Evie blurted. "I just noticed that there is a very large key hole between us, and I know if I take the plug end off of an extension cord until I thread it through that key hole, we would have electricity. We would only plug in one appliance at a time, and we would pay half of your electric bill," Evie promised.

"Are you sure you know how to do that?" asked Mrs Horn.

"Oh, yes! I added two extensions together at our last apartment." What she did not tell was she had a paring knife that could enlarge on that episode. It carried the scars. Within minutes Evie was threading a long extension through Mrs. Horns key hole.

"How did you muster the courage to ask for power?" Ray could not believe what Evie was doing.

"Desperation," Evie said as she plugged in her iron with a smirk on her face. The iron flowed over Ray's white shirt, and all the ironing. Evie plugged in the toaster and made creamed salmon over toast for lunch. The days were getting longer, and as soon as supper was finished, the hundred watt lamp was plugged in. They both sat reading without squinting.

Evie tried to make the most of the drab apartment. The waterfall bedroom set dressed up the multi-purpose room. The bed was made daily, as smooth and straight as though President and Bessie Truman would call any moment. Ray and Evie's wedding picture was on the dresser, the center of attraction.

Easter morning brought eight inches of snow. Ray was determined they would not miss the Easter service. With a shovel, determination, and a prayer by his side seat driver, they succeeded.

"Just think last Easter we were out in a park in our

shirt sleeves," Ray remarked, remembering their first Easter in contrast to mountains of snow. Ray gradually had something to reflect upon and replace the memories of the battle front on the previous holidays. After the worship service, Evie's parents insisted they grace their Easter table. The weather cleared, and it proved to be a day they would always remember as the Easter of the big storm.

19
The Grand Day

The weeks in the drab apartment, were offset with anticipation of a new baby and a home of their very own. The first check from the sale of the rich Jersey cream, also eased the pain of the dreary apartment. Occasionally Evie would accompany Ray on his milking trips. "Jersey cows are gentle, and I much prefer milking them to a Holstein cow," Evie commented, as she leaned over the bottom half of the closed barn door. They gathered the milk pails and took them to the apartment to wash. "Tomorrow I'll wash them in my own kitchen," Evie said.

Ray had ordered three hundred baby chicks to arrive on the first of May, the big day for the final move. The new farmer and his wife could hardly wait for morning to come. "Are you sleeping?" Evie asked as Ray tossed around.

"Not really!" They finally drifted off to catch a few hours rest before moving day finally arrived. They loaded the trailer and took one load on the milking trip. Most of the kitchen had been packed by the last of April.

Evie again held her breath until her bedroom set was carefully unloaded and set up. She ran through the empty house, as she surveyed the rooms. It was difficult to kneel and scrub the floors, with baby only a few weeks away, but there was no better way to wipe the baseboards and clean the corners. The windows were washed, until they sparkled. Only the waterfall bed and mirrored dresser fit in one bedroom. The tall matching chest was placed in the second bedroom. Evie opened the french windows and the pure country air smelled heavenly. The second bedroom was planned for the new baby. Lou was assigned the task of finding a second-hand buggy. Its like-new condition pleased the recipients. The floors were varnished and easily wiped clean. Evie then attacked the boxes of dishes, like there was no tomorrow. "Oh! I will have room to unpack all of our wedding dishes," Evie squealed, as she washed the shelves and placed new shelf paper on them.

The kitchen range was a dark beige. They paid Mr. Stearns the sum of thirty-five dollars for it. There was always a fire in it, so Evie did not examine the fire box before they bought it.

"The grates on this stove are nearly burned out," Evie informed Ray. She later flattened a coffee can to prevent the wood and coals from falling in the ash pan below. Earlier they had traded a desk for a small kitchen table and four chairs. It filled one end of the living room. The hide-a-bed was placed in front of the bay window. The sewing machine graced one corner and the new housewife draped a luncheon cloth on it at an angle and stood back and admired it as she traveled over memory lane.

The shops had been closed on the battle front, so Ray had sent money to his Mom to Christmas shop for him, and that small luncheon cloth was her first gift from Ray. The black heater stove was in the center of one wall. There was nothing to put in the enclosed porch, but mentally Evie pictured it fully draped and furnished.

At the close of the day, Ray and Evie sat leisurely over their empty tea cups, with hearts filled with gratitude. "Can you believe we actually have a home of our very own?" Ray beamed. They were realistic enough to know that it would not be without challenges, but for tonight they knelt together to say "thank you."

"Can we go to Wadena tomorrow?" Evie asked as they crawled into bed.

"Now what do you have in mind?" Ray asked.

"I want to spend the last of my savings on curtains and a linoleum for the living room," Evie piped back.

By the end of day the the bay window and the three windows dividing the porch and living room were covered with gorgeous ecru lace curtains. The floor was adorned with a patterned linoleum until Evie could cover it with a *dream carpet*. The sewing machine was soon engaged in making curtains for all of the french windows.

The timing seemed perfect. Evie's house was taking shape before the arrival of the wee one. Ray plowed and prepared the garden plot. They carefully planted the seeds. Rain came to soak the seeds, but a cold wind seemed to steal the joys of spring. A fire was built in the heater on May twenty first. Evie was extremely weary, but could not find a comfortable position. She tossed for a couple hours and envied her husband who could sleep in spite of his restless bed partner. Only the ticking of the clock, and the rain beating on the window broke the silence.

It was nearly twelve when Evie awoke her husband with, "I think this is it, Ray. I have never had pains like this before." Ray awoke, and with a bang was out of the bed.

"This is it?! Are you sure?"

"I've never had a baby before, but I am as sure as I know how to be," she said as she doubled over in pain. Her suitcase had been packed in advance, and they were off in the '36 Chevrolet that they had purchased from Uncle Bill.

The country roads were filled with ruts. "I think we will have to go back to Deer Creek to reach the pavement," Ray said seriously. "It is the long route to Bertha but it outweighs getting stuck in the mud." It was only a few miles to highway 29, and then they would have pavement all the way to Bertha, though it involved several extra miles.

"It is for real, I know," Evie had confirmation of that fact all along the way. The rain came down in torrents, and so did Evie's pain. Ray kept his eye on the white lines and concentrated on racing with the stork.

Neither one, having experienced childbirth only at arms length before, knew what to expect next. They did arrive intact and stood dripping on the steps of Miss Theil's Hospital. Hester (Evie's friend, Grace's sister) came to the door.

"Well, well Evie, is that you?" she questioned as she squinted through the darkness. They hurried on in, and handed Evie a shabby old nighty. It was none too soon as far as Evie was concerned. "This is your first baby, and this could go on for hours," Hester suggested.

"No!" Evie thought to herself. The one thing she did not want, was her husband to think she was a big baby.

"I think you should go home Ray, if this could take as long as Hester predicts," she tried to conceal a bearing down pain as she completed the sentence. Ray was not allowed in the delivery room, and staying in the hall would be no comfort to his wife. He requested to talk to his wife once more and tell her good bye. "I will have them call you when it's time to give birth," she promised. Ray took the long road home, stirred the flickering fire and once more slipped between the covers.

Before Ray was five miles away, Evie was down to serious work. In no time she was wishing he was just outside the door. By four o'clock a little seven pound six ounce boy was exercising his lungs, and Evie was put to sleep for repair work.

"Well we called the proud papa," Hester informed her, when she awoke. Not only the father, but everyone on the party line knew of the boy. When the phone rang with congratulatory messages everyone knew a phone call at four in the morning had to be an announcement. Ray threw another log on the fire, milked his Jerseys, and was on his way to see his firstborn. Evie's long dark curly hair was damp and snarled. It was with mixed emotion Ray embraced his wife. She was now moved to a room with three other mothers.

"I must go see our baby," he told her, "and then I will have to check the baby chicks."

It was now seven in the morning. Evie was sure it was her baby crying. "You cannot nurse your baby for twenty-four hours," the nurse stated. Evie wondered why? It seemed so unnatural to be separated from the one she carried so close to her heart for nine months. She was permitted to hold her baby and unwrap his tight blanket to count his tiny pink toes. Everything about him was so perfect. "I am not finished looking at him yet," she pleaded. The nurse informed her, "It is time for your breakfast now."

"To think there are atheists, when a single birth is such a miracle," she mused. Then her baby was snatched from her arms. An aide brought a pan of water and soap to her bedside. She washed her face and reached for a comb, before her tray with breakfast was delivered. She did not realize how hungry she was until the aroma of toast and cereal reached her. Then, how sleepy she felt. The other mothers wanted to know her life history and were busy feeding their babies. Evie craved to be in a dark room alone to sleep.

Early the next morning Evie and her son experienced the joy of his first warm juicy breakfast. "You will see him in four hours," the nurse promised. The cry of babies was almost constant. Evie was sure it was always her baby. "If only that nursery was not in ear shot," Evie thought to herself.

Ray came daily to visit Evie. He knew it was time to name the baby. He had often talked of his little brother who died of croup. His name was Morris. It was decided to name the baby Morris Alvin, in memory of his brother.

The day arrived for the new baby to go to the little cottage. The sun shone brightly. Home never looked more inviting. It was now really a necessity to carry Evie over the threshold, as the stitches were too painful to walk. Evie tucked her tiny son in the buggy and planned to enjoy her own bed. "I can't sleep a wink," she told Ray. "I am so afraid he may pull the blanket over his face and smother." Neither parent slept well, with another first in their life. It was with excitement and wonder that they softly conversed in the wee hours.

"I missed you so," Ray admitted, "and this bed was so cold without you." Evie was so involved in her baby boy, she perhaps did not entertain as many lonely moments.

The next night Cousin Louise and Russell came to welcome the newborn. Louise reassured Evie, "Have you ever heard of a baby smothering? Don't lie awake worrying about that." Louise offered her crib for sale. Evie did not hesitate to buy it.

"Aren't you going to have another baby?" Evie asked.

"Three is our limit."

"How can you be so sure?" Evie responded.

Evie was soon back in full swing of managing her household. She was up early to sew and bake while baby took his morning nap. "I hope that washer comes in soon." They had put their name on the list for it early in March at the Zosel Hardware. Evie was washing the baby's clothes daily on a wash board. The appliance shortage was an aftermath of war and the return and flood of military personnel. Patience was a very essential attribute for all newlyweds. It was June now, and Evie took the tubs outside, lest she spatter her freshly waxed kitchen. She carried rain water from the rain barrel to the boiler and heated her water.

A few surprises awaited Evie and Ray, including rusty water and water in the basement. All the water they had used in the valley was pure clear water. When

Evie first heated a boiler of water, she placed some lye in it and the top of the water was a bright rust. She skimmed the rusty foam off the top of the water. The rinse water still contained the rust. Evie's white linens were in shock. Evie prayed for a barrel of rain water every week. In the winter months she melted buckets of snow. This endless job created sufficient exercise.

When they purchased the farm it was under piles of snow. The Stearns family never once mentioned that in the spring you may have lots of water in the basement. The deal was all cut and dried by the time of the spring thaws. "We have learned a lot about purchasing a farm," they both decided. The cozy cottage, the new baby, and the togetherness outweighed the problems. Again Evie repeated the prayer of serenity. "We will dig around the house, and see what can be done about our basement problem, as soon as we have the time and funds," Ray promised.

Evie loved the garden. The fresh vegetables were luscious. The million dollar smile of the baby, and Ray's improving health gave them a new lease on life, though Ray did have regular bouts with malaria. Fresh milk from the Jerseys and young fryers for dinners, and no waiting in line for butter, were blessings that they counted daily. She canned string beans, peas, corn, pickles, wild raspberries and everything she could get her nimble fingers on. How proud they were of their little boy and the filled shelves. And now, because of no melting snow, the basement was dry as a bone.

20

Dimples

Baby Morris grew, as did the grass on the beautiful lawn, and the weeds in Evie's garden. Evie did not mind hoeing the weeds, the food was her reward, and she rationalized that the fresh air and exercise were just what she needed. It was a very productive year. By late fall the pullets were providing midget eggs.

The country air and food gave Ray a more healthy color, though attacks of malaria often interrupted his plans. "It is a good thing I am a farmer's daughter." Evie was bathing Ray's feverish brow as she endeavored to cheer him up. She changed the wet sheets once more. The hours of perspiring weakened him, body and spirit. "Do you need anything more before I take care of the chickens?" the nurse-maid asked.

"No, I'll be fine if you fill another pitcher with water," a weak voice stated. She changed to her chore clothes, and trotted off to care for the livestock. The hours that Evie was occupied gave the patient time to remember where he picked up this bug.

Bad memories surfaced during his high fever. In the process of transferring his records from Minneapolis to

Fargo Hospital, all of Ray's records were lost. In order to
get compensation for his illness they would have to test
his blood during the attack. Ray was too sick to take a bus
to Fargo and by the time he was well enough to make the
trip, the doctors would say, "Perhaps its just the flu." His
G.I. insurance was also lost. After thirty-five months in
the service for his country, many of those months in living nightmares, they never located his hospital records.
Without them, Ray could not prove the months he spent
in the Minneapolis hospital. His check from Uncle Sam
was then withheld.

Milking the Jersey herd twice a day continued while
Ray was gaining back his strength. Evie felt safe beside
the cows on a milk stool. She set the alarm for five in
order to get the chores done before her baby needed her.
The washer had not arrived, so every few weeks she took
her big wash, including every sheet she had in the house
to Elizabeth's. How she loved the pure crystal homestead
water, and wished for iron free water from her pump.

One day Evie set off with her bulging baskets, with
her baby at her side. She had never heard of a car seat.
She asked a neighbor boy to hold Morrie in the front seat
beside her. The car stalled near the home of Julia Krause.
Evie managed to drive it in her farm yard. "Julia, do you
suppose I can leave my passengers here until I walk back
to Lyman's store?"

"It's a hot day to walk," she answered, "but my team
is out in the pasture today." Julia never drove a car. Her
only means of transportation was a team and buggy .

"It's a broken fan belt, and I know the station would
have one."

"The lad and baby will be fine here," Julia assured
her.

Evie returned to the car and started off with the
broken fan belt. She walked only a fraction of the way,
when a kind neighbor stopped to give her a ride. "I am
just going to buy a few groceries, and then you may ride
back with me," the neighbor thoughtfully added. Luckily,

every station carried the bare necessities for Fords and Chevrolets. A grateful mother was back at the store to accept that offer. They sped over the dusty gravel road.

"I cannot thank you enough," Evie admitted. She wished her a happy day and ran to her car. Evie loved tools and made sure she had them in the trunk. The fan belt was soon replaced and the threesome were telling Julia farewell.

Julia was a hard working, thin woman that now lived alone. She combed her hair in a pug and lived in a house with a low slanting roof. Her children now lived in homes of their own. Having always loved horses, she continued to farm the land, with her team. As a child she was once kicked by a horse just above her eye. The mark of the hoof failed to change her love for horses.

Evie completed her wash, with Elizabeth's Idle Hour washer. Then she visited briefly with the family and loaded the wet clothes. "It's much too late to hang the clothes out on your lines, Ma. I'll take the clothes home to dry." She placed the baby on Roger's lap and started down the old familiar driveway. She recalled how many times she and Ray enjoyed riding down Lovers Lane. A tired, hungry, baby suggested in no uncertain terms that she must not loiter.

"You put that fan belt on?" Ray questioned in amazement. He discovered how little he really knew about his wife.

Evie busied herself every moment of the day and felt wonderful early in the fall. Ray, recovered from a bout of malaria in time to finish the fall plowing. The upturned furrows of black rich soil were now frozen solid.

"I don't feel well today," Evie confessed. Days went by and she only became more sick. When she could not satisfy her hungry baby, she was very suspicious. "I think I am pregnant," she revealed at the breakfast table. And if I am, I will never believe an old wives' tales again. They assured me I was 'fire proof', as long as I nursed my baby." Ray insisted she go at once to Dr. Will. Having very little food for several days, resulted in weakness and anxiety.

"Did the doctor confirm that you are not pregnant?" Ray asked hoping his predictions were true.

After the long wait at the doctor's office and driving miles over snow filled roads, Evie broke into tears. "It's not that I won't love a baby, it is just that I am wondering how I can take care of the five month old child I have when I am this weak," Evie said as soon as she could communicate.

Life did go on. The little son gulped the Jersey milk down, as though he was starved. Evie had continued to nurse until the moment of truth. The prayer of serenity was again uttered. The shock was over and Evie began to dream of a little girl. "The positive side of this is I am not as sick as I was during my first pregnancy." Evie admitted. She was able to eat much sooner.

Baby Morrie grew though Evie missed the convenience and closeness of breast feeding. Boiling bottles, heating and diluting the rich Jersey milk was not Mother's preference, but when Mother could only digest enough meals to supply the unborn baby, it had to be that way.

As Evie regained her strength. Her son grew into the large crib and the creeping stage. Christmas was also approaching. "You just never know what a year will bring forth," Evie said as baby slept, and she and Ray sat next to the cozy fire. Our second Christmas and we are going to have our second child," she continued. Ray was excited about the new baby.

"A little girl will be perfect, and just think how much fun she will have with a big brother," he added. They talked of their first Christmas, and Ray seemed to stare into Christmas past in the South Pacific. It was difficult to forget those days. Again he thought of the comrades that did not come home, this time of the year and perhaps everyday, though never revealing the incidents in detail. Evie learned more from letters that his Mother and

brother had saved. He could not talk of the battles on
Luzon or any of the South Pacific. The fire was dying
down, as Evie read from *The Farmers* magazine, and Ray
came back to the present. "Time to stoke up the fire and
get to bed. Morrie will be awake at five, and we will be too
sleepy to find the crib."

Evie loved her little cottage and took great pride in
it. She dreamed of the day she could furnish it more elaborately. In her mind she knew exactly how it would be
furnished, when her ship came in all loaded with extra
money. Her savings during the war were to be specifical-
ly for furnishings. Ray received a check when he was discharged from the Vet's hospital for the months he was
confined there. It was spent, along with his bonds on a
Ford tractor. When Uncle Bill decided to sell his thirty-
six Chevrolet, Evie cashed some of her bonds and purchased it. With cars as scarce as hen's teeth, what was a
body to do? Her living and dining room furniture were
put on hold, as well as a new stove and refrigerator. If
Evie would have known the length of the "hold," she
would have forgotten the car and walked. Having a comfortable home to enjoy was top priority as far as she was
concerned. "Home is where her heart is," she reiterated.

Soon it was time to trim a tree in their very own
home, and hang up the baby's stocking. Ray searched the
pasture for the perfect tree. There were beautiful evergreens in the front yard. "We could just trim one of those
trees," Ray suggested. There was not a shortage of empty
corners in the cottage. The forest green tree from the pasture, filled the house with its chloraphyl fragrance. Evie
did not possess a Christmas table cloth, but she did have
a red and white luncheon cloth that fit on her enamel top
table with painted white legs. There were four chairs that
came with the set, covered with red plastic seats. The legs
were bent chrome, not at all Evie's personal taste. Evie
called it an Early Salvation Army arrangement. Now, the
folding table they bought for their first apartment, the
white table, and the nook would seat twelve, plus Ray
and Evie. It was not difficult to find that many guests.

The good news Ray and Evie were waiting for came late in November. "The Rural Electric Association is coming through before Christmas!" Ray shouted as he looked up from his local paper. Plans were made to have cousin Richard to do some extra wiring. Evie trimmed the tree and in good faith put on the electric lights. Busy December days slipped by. At last the lines were completed and on December twenty fourth the *current* was finally set free.

What perfect timing. It was going to be a rather lean Christmas. The baby, being only seven months old, would not be disappointed. Ray and Evie agreed to smaller gifts than their first Christmas of a camera and a cedar chest. "We'll just enjoy the gifts we received last year and settle for a few necessities." The feeling was mutual. Paying for the wiring and hook up of electricity lit up their Christmas. "Just look at the pretty lights on the tree," Daddy pointed at the tree while holding his pride and joy. How wonderful not to depend on the temperamental motor for power.

They sat by the lighted tree on Christmas Eve and enumerated the blessings of the past year. "Our baby boy is number one, on the list!" The proud papa then added, "The chickens and cattle are productive."

"Our basement is filled with canned goods, potatoes, and a crock of carrots." The carrots were buried in crackling dry leaves. Evie had learned secrets from Elizabeth and other gardeners. She cut the top off the carrots, making sure no top was left to grow and spoil the whole crock. She then picked the driest October day to gather the leaves and smother the vegetables. While the second year of garden was growing, Evie still had sweet fresh carrots, and rutabagies to serve.

They divided Christmas day between both sets of grandparents. The younger Auntie and Uncles tossed the baby around like a teddy bear. He loved all the attention on his first Christmas.

Ray and Evie attended the country church of Evie's

childhood, and Ray was soon elected Sunday School Superintendent. He also taught the youth class.

The months past. Ray came in from his early spring field work as Evie hung up the phone. "We just had a call from Joy, and Howard has lead poisoning [caused from all the years he spent in the print shop], and the doctor gave him just a few days to live." The sad news seemed unbearable. Evie had been so close to Joy and Howard. Her farm style dinner, was not appealing. The babe in the high chair sensed the heavy emotions in his parent's faces. Prayers ascended from all parts of the United States as the news spread. Doctors confessed it was out of their hands and sent him home to spend his last days. They were the first to admit it was a miracle when he lived past a week. A letter arrived from Howard (In part):

Dear Evie and Ray;

My doctor suggests I get out in the country and never return to the print shop. Would it be possible to visit you for a length of time. I will not eat a thing, just breathe in God's fresh air! Perhaps Joy could help you in the home when you have your new baby. The children could sleep on the floor.

Love To All,
Howard & Joy

Within a few days the Folkestads arrived. Little Janet and Robert were excited to live in the country. In late June the peas were ready to feast on and can, the radishes were luscious and sweet. The fresh new onions added spice to every lunch and dinner. Joy was very helpful and made the suggestion, "If we have to wait many more days for that new baby, I think we will take a trip, back to the cities, for a few of our belongings." Evie agreed that that would be a good idea. A few days later on July 1, 1948 Evie was rudely awakened at five o'clock.

"Ray get up and do your milking, I think I am going

to have my baby today."

"Are you sure I have time to do the milking,?" Ray asked. His clothes were always methodically laid out. From day one of their marriage, Ray would never go to bed until he made preparation for the next day. Evie was sure Uncle Sam included this in the army training. However, it came in handy on this particular morning, for he was dressed in a flash. He looked questioningly at Evie as he gave her a squeeze, before rushing to the barn. Evie's bags had been packed for days. She dressed and took care of personal hygiene, and combed her hair. It was a must that the bed be made. She was carefully putting on the beautiful rose spread when suddenly she was struck with bearing down pains. She flopped on her bed and knew that she must take fast action. Her brother Chuck had spent the night on the enclosed porch. Evie ran to awaken him.

"Chuck get up and go to the barn and tell Ray not to even finish the cow he is milking. I must leave at once!" She managed to put the spread over the pillows, and go take a peek at her little boy sleeping so peacefully. She quickly wiped a tear from her eye as Ray marched in. They were off without any time to spare. The pains were for real. "If we have any delay, you will deliver your first baby," Evie said between contractions. Ray had witnessed the birth of many farm animals, had faced bullets in the South Pacific, but his foot was now heavy on the '36 Chevrolet. They were speeding over the rough side roads, the creek, and through the woods to Bertha.

How glad they were it was not raining and the workers had finished working on the pavement on highway 210. Evie tried to grasp the beauty of the early morning. She gasped a lot of the pure fresh air at intervals. Ray had called the hospital and old Doc Will was at his post of duty. There was not much time for the usual prep. Ray stayed just outside the delivery room. No husbands were allowed to witness their own child's birth. A six pound five ounce baby girl was soon exercising her lungs. It was now just a few minutes past the hour of seven. Two hours before, Evie had been sound asleep. She was put to sleep again for extensive stitching. She awoke with her baby lying next to her heart. The baby yawned, as though to tell Mother, "That ordeal made me tired too." A dimple spread deeply into her cheek as she yawned. She was dainty and precious. Evie explored all her little fingers and toes. She was petite and fragile.

Ray rushed to his wife's bedside. "Isn't she another little miracle?" Ray asked. "When shall we have another one?"

"Don't ask me that now," Evie groaned. Ray gently kissed Evie good-bye and peeked in the nursery for one more glimpse of his precious daughter. "I must go home to tell big brother that he has a sister."

Baby Morrie had the juice from a freshly squeezed orange daily, and his own special cereal, or a soft boiled egg. His mother always had his diaper ready to saddle him, and a bib laid out. Chuck came in from finishing the milking and found him hanging over the edge of his crib and crying his heart out. The first thing Chuck saw handy was a piece of chocolate cake on the counter. Morrie tasted his first sweets in his thirteen and one half months. He also ate his unusual breakfast in his soggy old diaper. Evie couldn't believe the report Ray brought on the evening of July first.

"I did not want him to taste a sweet," Evie declared. "I wish I had brought him with me."

Joy was informed of the baby, and they were soon speeding back to the country. Evie spent six days in the hospital. Joy returned in time to do up the accumulated house work and come with Ray to take Beverlie Joy home. Auntie Joy held Morrie in the back seat. He saw his mommie holding another baby and cried like his heart would break. Evie exchanged babies and his sobs changed to laughter.

Ray carried Evie over the threshold once more. This time it was because of Doctor's orders and the swift birth of the new baby.

21

Farm Life

The family adjusted to the new arrival in a very short time. The baby awakened to be nursed and changed, and was soon cradled in her little basket. Evie insisted, "I am sure that baby was premature, or she would not sleep twenty hours a day." Cousin Robert and Janet were playmates of Morrie every waking moment. With sister Joy to help with the washing, cooking and baking, the entire household ran quite smoothly, though it was a wee bit crowded, in the two bedroom home. The enclosed porch was perfect for a spare bedroom from spring through late fall. The fertile garden produced enough vegetables to satisfy the appetite of a king. Fresh eggs, milk and cream were added to favorite farm recipes. "It is so wonderful to cook and bake with cream," Joy often exclaimed. After living in the heart of a city on a very limited budget, she had not forgotten her creamed recipes. The milk containers had thick whipping cream that raised to the top each day. Whipped cream was now an every day extravagance.

Howard drank in the beauty of the country. Each day he became a little stronger. He kept the lawn groomed, helped in the garden, and entertained the three little ones. "I would like to paint your house and the farm buildings," he suggested one day. Can you afford to buy the paint and some good brushes?" Ray knew painting was a necessity soon. Evie and Ray managed to purchase white house paint the next trip to Wadena. The dear brother-in-law wanted to feel he was earning his board and room. Evie and Joy spent many hours canning peas, string beans, corn, and wild raspberries.

"Just look at the rows of canned goods on the shelf," Joy said, as the sisters put quarts of corn on the basement shelf. "It will come in handy when the garden is buried in snow," they both agreed.

Joy and Howard were not around to enjoy the fruits of their labor. Howard longed to return to the church he had pastored a few years in Montana. As his health improved, he felt the call of the mountains and the ministry, for which he had prepared so diligently. Whitefish, Montana was now calling him back to the church he had once pastored.

The little white cottage seemed rather empty the first few days. Morrie missed his playmates. He spent more time at Evie's side, as she fed his baby sister. The folding bed was removed from the bedroom, and in its place was a pink crib. Baby Beverlie napped in the morning, and in the afternoon her brother joined her. Evie discovered the best time to wash clothes was at four o'clock in the morning. With Joy gone, and with two babies in diapers, she had less interruptions in the wee hours. She would hang them on the line, while baby Bev took her morning nap. The big brother pulled his wagon or leaned over the basket, reaching for the clean clothes. The early hours were also the only time it paid to plug in the iron.

Ray adapted to rural farm life. Malaria attacks were not as often, although still severe when they caught up with him. His small farm, dairy cattle, and chickens kept him occupied. Morrie sat on his Daddy's lap on the tractor while he cultivated. He often fell asleep and would wake up in his crib.

"I will take care of Morrie, when he awakens in the night," Ray offered. "I can't nurse the baby," he smilingly remarked. This generous volunteer was given the first evening that Evie brought the new baby home. Evie was happy to share the night shift with the proud father. Just maybe he would not be as anxious to have another in 1949. "Isn't she another little miracle?" Evie heartily agreed with Ray's observations, but the idea of having another, while still in the delivery room, was still on Evie's mind.

Evie continued to fill the empty canning jars. Pickles, vegetables, peaches, apples and pears, were placed on the basement shelves, awaiting the long winter to be totally appreciated.

Preparing for Sundays began on Monday. The two little tykes each had two pair of shoes. The shoe strings were removed on Sunday night and by Monday the white shoes were spotless with clean shoe strings. It may have been extravagant to have two pair of shoe strings for each pair of white shoes, but one pair could always be in the wash. Evie recalled polishing shoes every Saturday night, at the old home stead. They were put on the shelf of the library table in chronological order. Her brothers and sisters were limited to one pair of shoes, and lucky to have those.

The season changed from summer to the colorful fall. The black hungry stove found work for Evie's woodsman for the short winter days.

Evie opened her sewing machine, now that canning season ended. She could never think of buying ready made clothes for her family. The seamstress created little dresses, nighties, shirts and pants. How thankful Evie was that she had learned to sew. First she made clothes for the dollies, then for her sisters and brothers. She was now making men's shirts and coats for the children. The months before marriage, while working at Munsing Wear she learned valuable lessons. While an employee, Evie purchased tubular material by the pound. She made Ray's under shirts. With the sewing machine open and all threaded to go, she could complete a shirt while dinner was cooking. Little interruptions, like tying a shoe, or stopping to change a diaper, could slow down progress, and occasionally the potatoes may boil over. There were eight shirt lengths in a pound. One length was used to bind the neck and sleeves. The net result was seven sleeveless summer undershirts. The regular white, short sleeved shirts were also sewn for late fall and winter. The neck was bound as she stretched the binding. The sleeves and bottom were hemmed by hand, in the long winter evenings. Flannel shirts were double seamed for Ray, and Evie decided to make her father a shirt as well for Christmas.

Evie loved to have her younger sisters stay over night and catch the school bus to Deer Creek the following morning. "You kids are so much help, someday I will repay you," Evie promised. Summer was just around the corner and that someday tagged along. "The four of us all have a job at a city camp," Ruthie announced. "We will need an apron for each work day. Penny's great fabric selection gave variety to the project. Soon twenty aprons were pressed and ready to pack for a most adventurous summer

Evie missed Ruthie, June, Donna, and Orpha Ann. There were always more sisters where they came from, with Ray and Evie's large families. A letter arrived shortly from Mother Miller.

Dear Ray and Evie,

Joan and Marilyn will be on the six o'clock bus, the first Saturday after school is out. I am working every day and do not want so many of the children at home, with nothing much for them to do during the summer. Jimmy and Charlene will remain at home.

The little dimpled baby was now to be two on July first. Her big brother was three in May. "Little girls are so easy to train," Evie often reminded the proud Daddy.

Her brother was much too busy to take a trip down the path to the "little house." Morrie would procrastinate to the very deadline and refused to take time to send an SOS to his parents. Instead, he would race to the outdoor bathroom and take off all his clothes. Evie would look out the back door to find her son running up the path in his birthday suit. "The neighbors will think we have a nudist colony in the center of civilization," Evie feared.

Everyday was a new adventure for the toddlers. A new batch of kittens entertained them day after day. Morrie would put them all in his little red wagon, with Bevie to follow behind and pick up any kitty that decided it wanted off the merry go round. It was pure torture for Morrie to have to take time to stop for a meal. Evie finally gave up. She took a basin of water, towel and a bar of soap to the front steps and proceeded to prepare him for his meal. Every sunny day he picnicked on the front steps.

His sister preferred her high chair and Mommie's undivided attention. By the time winter arrived, they both wanted to sit in the breakfast nook. It took both the Sears and Wards catalogues to boost them to reach their plates.

"It is great to be past the diaper stage," Evie often commented. It had been like having twins in diapers for over eighteen months. Little Bevie actually taught her big brother the advantage of using a potty chair.

The Jersey herd had now multiplied as the Miller family. Ray's milking time had lengthened. "I will help dress the tykes to go to the barn if you will help me with the milking," Ray bargained. Evie hurried with the supper dishes, while snow suits, boots and mittens were placed on the children. The children loved to be a part of the evening chores. It gave them one last chance to play with the half-grown kittens.

"I want some milk for the kittens," was their first request. They would squat down on a bed of straw and watch the little pink tongues lap up the rich Jersey milk.

With two human milking machines, the milk cans filled, leaving eight empty bags. The cow's evening treat was alfalfa salad. After feeding the baby calves, Pauper, the farm dog, was locked in the barn for the cold winter night. For lack of a name Mommy and Daddy called the dog puppy the first day of its arrival. Morrie coined the word "pauper" for puppy and Pauper it was.

Pauper grew up as a constant companion to his master. Spring came and now four year old Morrie would sneak off with his dog across the road to the eighty acreage. He would lay on his stomach for hours watching the Kill Deer's egg hatch. "Whatever do you have on your chest and arms?" Evie asked as she bathed him. It was her first experience with poison ivy. She decided she must guard her son more closely. Faithful Pauper would risk his life for his master, but did not realize the danger of poisonous plants.

Ray took his position of Sunday School Superintendent very seriously. Evie joined with him and began teaching the youth class. One cold winter Sunday the roads were impassable by car. Ray, remembering life in the South Pacific, decided he could not stay home. He hitched up the horses and they were on their way to worship the God that protected him those horrible years.

The farm, the church and visits from the many city relatives, kept the family occupied. The seasons ran into each other and still another year made history. The year was nineteen fifty.

22
Beyond The Call Of Motherhood

Ray worked his way through the seasons. When he wasn't chopping wood, helping the neighbors or doing chores, he may be out cutting logs for lumber for a new parsonage. Planting and harvesting kept him occupied the short summer months.

Evie's best friends were the Lahrman sisters. She first met them when her father was a town board member. Mr. Lahrman was the township clerk, and the meetings were often at his home. The close friendship began when Evie's family began to attend the country church. Two weeks after Ray and Evie were married, her dear friend Rena and Eldo were married in the same church. The friends married returned soldiers. Now the two families lived in the same community, attended the same church, and were both new parents. "Little Robert and Morrie are going to develop as close a friendship as their parents," Evie remarked to Rena. They were guests of one another almost weekly. The soldier friends attended a farm school one night each week. Evie and Rena usually spent the evening together exchanging recipes, or perhaps finishing a batch of pickles, or possibly cutting Bobby or Morrie's hair. Their husbands took turns driving to Henning for their agricultural education. Eldo lived on a farm most of his life, and Evie doubted they could teach him more than he already knew. He was a mechanic, a carpenter, and knew how to manage a farmer's income. Ray went to the cities for high school and then learned the trade of cutting designs on crystal from his Uncle Gus. He returned to the country for the summer months and worked for farmers. The GI farm training was excellent and the supplemental income saved the day for returned service men, until they got on their feet. (as Gus would say)

Ray and Eldo were self-appointed log cutters. Mr. Ross was generous enough to donate the tamarack logs, and also the plot of land directly across from Union Corners church to build the parsonage.

The snow was deeper every day that they waded out to cut more logs. The logs were carefully stacked to await curing, and then sawed into two by fours, two by sixes, and all the rough lumber they would need. The following year the two ex soldiers began digging the basement with the scoops on their Ford and Farmall tractors.

The noon meals, and afternoon lunches were planned by the busy housewives of the church. By fall, a cozy little two bedroom home was awaiting the two lady pastors, Miss Grandy and Miss Haugen.

"I think we need to put a basement under the church," Eldo suggested before they could catch their breath from the last project. It was soon in the minutes of the church records. Again the Ford and the Farmall tractors were employed, darting under the jacked-up church and coming up with loads of dirt. The Union Corners Church was then turned to face the south.

"Mommie, can I go to town with Daddy today?" Morrie asked one day. He was now four years old and was content if he could sit in the front seat with Daddy. Ray opened, then closed, the white gate at the end of the driveway and was just taking off when Morrie cried out "Daddy, I have to go back! We have to go back!" "Don't you want to go to the store with me? Why should we go back?" "I forgot to kiss Mommy good-bye" he answered tearfully. There was no other way than to back up a few rods , open the gate and back up the driveway to allow Morrie to run in the house and kiss Mommy good-bye. Daddy's influence was strong. Morrie was already in the car when Daddy bid Evie farewell. The lad was overly anxious to take off and had forgotten his most important duty.

Bevie was a little magpie when it came to conversation. There was never a dull waking moment. The family of four was in their favorite spot in the house, and that was sitting at the breakfast nook eating. Bev was talking and her plate was almost untouched. "Eat your plate," her Daddy commanded. Bev quickly picked up her plate and pretended to take huge bites around the edge of her dinner plate. Her ability to create humor in situations was unsurpassed. She loved foods, except the sweets that her Mommie made. She would not touch a piece of cake, and Evie baked one almost daily. Ray delighted in having desserts at every meal. The long siege in the South Pacific made sweets overly attractive. Evie aimed to please her returned soldier. Pies were served regularly. Ray retained his thirty-four waist line, so Evie did not think desserts were harming her busy farmer.

Life was busy, but not too busy to remember the years of separation and uncertainty of nineteen forty-three, four and five. Malaria was a continuous reminder. Civilian life was not a bed of roses "We must continue to count our blessings," they agreed. "We have food fit for a king," Ray would continue. His mind carried him back to his C rations.

He loved Sundays and preparing for his adult class. "If we do not take advantage of the privilege of worship, we will soon be facing another war," he added. "I never want to see our son go off to war," Evie almost cringed to even utter the thoughts. She hugged her son and gave him a big kiss on his dusty little face. He had just finished plowing his make-believe field. "I think that is the third little plow he has worn out," his daddy remarked.

Evie's life was so full, but she was not anxious for her two babies to grow away from her. Ray went to a North Dakota potato harvest field to make extra money in the fall. Evie set her alarm for five o'clock. The Jersey cows needed milking before the children awoke. She changed from her milking togs just in time to dress and feed her wee ones.

It was lonely in the evenings, and bedtime was early. With Bev on one side and Morrie on the other, Evie switched on the bed lamp and read one more chapter from *Winnie The Pooh*. The doors were securely locked, and Pauper the dog stood guard for the night. In the wee hours of the day, Evie carefully sneaked out of the warm bed to check on her farm animals. Each day was filled with taking care of the large flock of chickens, milking the cows and keeping the children fed and clean. Weekends were most welcome when Daddy arrived to share the work load. " I don't think I can stand more than one more week," Ray confessed. The promise of a bonus for staying for the potato season, and the long winter ahead, would outweigh his preference. Ray promised Evie her first new gas range for taking care of the home-front.

She could hardly wait. They chose a combination gas and wood range, from their faithful Zosel Hardware in Wadena. "It is so wonderful to have such immediate heat," Evie beamed, as she cooked her first meal on her early Christmas gift. In winter the fire would be blazing most of the time to heat the kitchen, and Evie would make use of the wood heat to conserve the bottled gas. She was as thrilled over their new stove as any child could possibly be over a new toy. She also enjoyed her first refrigerator. "It will be so great not to have to run out to the cooler every time I want cold milk." She felt an overwhelming sense of appreciation knowing how many bushels of potatoes were picked to earn the cash for the appliances. Evie knew the price, for she first spent a week in North Dakota trying to care for her wee ones at night and work in the field by day. She proved "where there is a will there is a woman." She was set on new appliances, and farm income would not stretch for any extras for the home. Everyone had to have a partner in the field. It took four hands to empty the bushel baskets in sacks. Evie's sisters that went with her worked together. The only one without a partner in the patch was a Mexican. His wife would not work with him. The policy was to divide the check, and the husband would never give her her share of the check. The foreman assigned Evie to be his partner and promised to pay in separate checks. He held the record as being the fastest picker of the entire crew. Evie determined that no man was going to get the best of her. By three o' clock in the afternoon they had filled over one hundred bushel basket with red potatoes and there were two hours left in the day.

Conveniently Joy and Howard were now pastoring a church at Ardoch, North Dakota. Evie and her sisters boarded with them. Joy also took care of Morrie and Bev along with her Bobby and Janet. Evie promised to compensate for her precious services. The week was difficult. Bevie cried every morning her Mommie left. The children were both sick during the night. Evie left for the patch on Friday morning, exhausted. She approached the foreman. "I think I will have to take the children home." "You should try to stay for your bonus. You will get an extra two cent per bushel if you stay for the season," he said convincingly. "How about if I send my husband back in my place?" she bargained. "He could be back by Monday morning at seven." Early Saturday morning Evie packed her bags and two wee ones and was buzzing down the homeward trail.

The feeling was mutual. Ray thought the children would be much more content at home and maybe it would be easier for Evie to handle the chicken and cattle chores.

There were two such episodes of Evie's search for the pot of gold at the end of the potato patch. Her sister Ruth had also married and located near the potato field. Ray boarded with Ruth. She could make the best food and her chicken gravy tasted heavenly at the close of the work day. Even mashed potatoes tasted great, after staring into the eyes of spuds all day. When Ray returned to the patch, he was promoted to the automatic picker the second year. He rode across the field in style. Throwing the dead vines from the potatoes

Meanwhile back at the ranch, Evie had a few problems. Milking the gentle Jerseys was fun. In the evening she took the children to the barn with her. The morning milking was in the eight gallon cans and cooling before the children awoke. Helping with the chores around the hen house was entertaining for the children. They loved to scatter grain and listen to and watch the grateful chickens. They each had to carry a little pail of water. Evie made sure the family had their breakfast first, lest they would be tempted to join the flock.

A long rainy season crept in. Evie decided to keep the cattle in at night. She maintained a tidy barn and hitched up the spreader daily. She knew all about this new spreader. Ray was busy working on the parsonage at the time he decided he needed a spreader. The first winter months he made stacks of the rich fertilizer. Spring came and a spreader was needed. "Would you mind, when you go to Deer Creek with the eggs, checking out the manure spreaders?" Ray asked as he left to go work on the new house. Evie loaded her little traveling companions, ninety dozen eggs, and carried out his wishes. Being a girl of action she not only looked, but bought a new spreader without rubber or any tires. "You will have to go find tires," the dealer told her. "That old war didn't spare us much rubber." "I think I will first go to Wadena and shop for tires and come back this way to close the deal" She stopped at every used dealer in Wadena, but no tires could be found. Not knowing how to even spell defeat, she went on to the next town. The first place she stopped had just the size Evie needed, and the tires had a lot of tread left. The man kindly packed the tires in the trunk of the car.

Evie always carried water for Morrie and Bevie. It

was a hot day for early spring. They had a little sandwich and quenched their thirst and headed back to Deer Creek. Evie wasn't positive she wanted to put the tires on the spreader, but it would not have been the first attempt to try. She left the tires for the dealer to battle with, and went to buy groceries and pick up some chicken feed. By now the eggs would have all been candled. The groceries were placed in the empty egg crates, and it was back to have the spreader attached to the trailer hitch.

Ray was astonished when his wife related every detail of the day. The conversation was interrupted several times with the children's own version of the day. "We had a picnic in Sebeka, by a pile of old tires."

And now Evie was going to make use of that purchase. It was evenly loaded, and she knew which field Ray was fertilizing. She enjoyed driving the Ford tractor and was buzzing right along when all of a sudden she discovered the sinking feeling that her load was not moving. The spreader was sinking as well. The low spots were soaked with the fall rain. Bevie and Morrie were promised a treat if they would sit on the front steps and watch as she crossed to the eighty. Evie could see them from her tractor seat. She hopped off her tractor and ran back to her children. Just then the milk man came to pick up the milk. He spotted the problem and offered to drive his truck out to rescue the machinery. Evie was eternally grateful, and completed the task. This time she only drove on the high land , around the low spots, and did not worry about picking up where Ray had left off.

Morrie and Bevie loved to help scatter the fresh straw in the clean barn." I wish I could use a fork" Morrie pleaded. " When you get a little bigger" was the promise. "Now you may just use your hands. The tines on the fork are not safe for little children."

The next week the country pastor decided he needed to make a little extra money. His roots were implanted in Ardoch. His wife, Gladys, refused to stay alone in the country. She packed clothing for her three children and moved in with Evie. "I can at least watch the children while you do chores," she promised, "and help with the cooking." The two ladies now had four that could toddle all over the farm, and a babe in diapers. Plus a large coop filled with laying hens, eight milking cows and a team of horses.

One evening Evie discovered her dear cow, Daisy, had mastitis in one fourth of her udder. Gladys finished the dishes and came to collect Evie's audience to bathe, and put put them in bed. "Gladys! Poor Daisy has an infection," Evie lamented. "Well what can you do about that?" she questioned. "I am going into Wadena to get a prescription," Evie responded in no uncertain terms. She called a veterinarian as soon as she completed her chores. Luckily, the widows had a car available. Off she sped to pick up the medication. She could not afford to have a vet make a house call. Time was of essence. She bathed Daisy's udder and shot the medication up the milk line. Evie had experienced the same problem when she was nursing her baby. She recalled how hot packs seemed to draw out the infection and relieve the pain. A full teakettle was heated and taken to the barn. Heavy hot towels were doubled and placed on a clean gunny sack. She tied all four corners and placed it over the cow's udder. It was anchored with twine over the cows back. Every half hour the packs were changed. "It is ten o'clock," Gladys announced, as she entered the barn with a fresh batch of steaming water. "Evie you cannot stay out here all night," and added, "I am going to call the men home!" Evie stayed by her post of duty until after twelve. She put one last hot pack on and called it a day. This time she added a filled hot water bottle to the poultice. The next morning at five she could still feel heat from the insulated pack. The swelling had gone down and she milked that section separately, before shooting more medication in the cavity. Daisy never kicked or fussed, even with the tender quarter. Within two days the cow returned to normal milking and no longer needed special attention. "I always wanted to be a nurse," she related to Gladys, who boasted that degree.

"I can't believe you saved that cow's complete udder," Ray said when he returned. They were mutually thankful that was the last of the fall harvest. She had witnessed many "three teaters" in her Uncle Fred's and father's barn, and recalled that they were soon on their way to the hamburger market. How could she have parted with her Daisy? She was so gentle, and it was natural to become attached after resting her brow on Daisy's tummy each time Daisy shared her rich milk.

23
And Baby Makes Three

The two little ones were growing as fast as the green front lawn. Evie confessed to their Daddy, "I really miss their babyhood." Being extremely busy, the years went by too quickly.

"Are you ready for another baby?" Ray asked. He often suggested, "Two children are not enough."

"That's easy for you to say," Evie piped back. The first two children would soon be four and five years old. It was a mutual agreement. They had learned a few secrets of actually planning a child.

By late April, Evie wondered. Morning, noon and evening sickness were her lot. "I wonder why we didn't leave well enough alone," she groaned, when she could not swallow a bite of breakfast. Ray was penitent, as though it was entirely his idea. There was not a question baby number three was on *its* way.

It was soon time to plant the garden. Evie managed to gain strength to carry out her motherly duties. Ray was in full charge of all farm chores. A few days of milking his growing herd alone found him calling the Surge Milker Company. The Surge milker was installed pronto.

Regardless of circumstances, the Millers had their usual amount of city company. They were the only couple at that time from two large families to live on a farm. The summer months did fly by. The canning was processed on schedule, harvest time was history. Fall found Evie with her white sewing machine humming. The growing children and unborn child were in need of clothes. Once again the tree was trimmed and the days were being counted.

Evie was uncomfortable. "It is so strange how God prepares you for delivery day. You are so uncomfortable you can hardly wait," Evie confessed. She would try to find a comfortable position in bed by propping pillows beneath the heavy load, get just about to sleep and have to relieve her crowded bladder. She crawled back in bed and envied her husband sleeping so peacefully.

On January first Evie could hardly wait for the baby that she carried so close to her heart. "I hope it will be the first baby of the year." She was wishing to make headlines in the *Minneapolis Star Journal*. Five more days past by. Evie was sure it was time when Ray went to the barn to do evening milking. She did not say a word all afternoon, not even to her sister Irene, who dropped by. Ray may get overly excited and insist on going in too early. By the time Ray washed up, Evie revealed her condition. The trip to Bertha was now old hat to Evie's soldier. To the surprise of both parents, Evie was in the delivery room through the long night. Ray sat vigil just outside the delivery room. The beautiful baby arrived at ten after six.

"It's a girl," the proud Dr. Will announced. Evie was thrilled to see the dark hair, and a precious, healthy baby. Jacalyn Rae was the name that was carefully chosen. As the nurse wheeled the tired Mommie to join another mother, Evie expressed her gratitude for such a beautiful baby girl.

Evie was just settled when Aunt Tamma came in to see her. "We heard about your new baby, and happened to be in town." Evie tried to be interested in local news, but after twenty-four hours with no sleep and the rough night, she failed to communicate in a very excited way. Twenty-four hours passed before the new babe was permitted to nurse. It seemed entirely unnatural not to feed that crying baby.

Ray came to tell Evie good-bye . "I saw three babies in the nursery. Why isn't the mother in that empty bed, he asked?"

A roommate answered his question. "The other mother is an unwed forty year old, that would not even look at her newborn." The baby was adopted and whisked from the nursery in a few days. Evie could not imagine carrying a child so close to her heart and never even seeing it. She clutched her baby and shuddered at the thought.

Finally, the day came for the nurse to dress her baby in the clothes that had been so carefully packed weeks before. Ray drove up to take Evie and Jacalyn Rae home. On her sixth day, she was introduced to her big brother and sister. "Can I hold her?" Morrie and Bev had to take turns holding baby sister. The new baby seemed to sense she would be in for a lot of "lovin'" from her siblings. For the next few months, everything seemed to revolve around the new family member.

"I can't believe it is time to plan the crops already," Ray said as he swallowed his last drop of German coffee. Evie had mastered his Mother's strength of coffee by now.

"Yes, and I must order the garden seed," Evie added. Her shelves still had ample supply of vegetables and fruits in the glass jar to tide them over until the new crop matured. Every year Evie purchased about two dozen canning jars to add to her filled basement shelf. It was not always easy to compete with the virtuous woman in Proverbs thirty one. But the early hours, when her candle (now light switch) was lit to work while her children slept, were the most productive hours. The epilogue of the wife of noble character had greatly influenced Evie's life. Pastor Foreman promoted Bible reading. He challenged his flock to read the Bible through each year. Evie followed his plan of five chapters on Sunday and three chapters each weekday. She confessed she did not fully understand all that she read in her early teens, and not even now in her mid-twenties. She did discover it to be the most profitable reading in the formation of character. How challenging to recall a Proverb. How thankful she was to have it in her memory bank.

Time no longer permitted three chapters per day. Verses came to her mind that had puzzled her, and now took on real meaning. "Sufficient unto the day is the evil thereof," was one such verse (The King James Version). She learned she could not borrow what may happen tomorrow, but God's grace would only supply on a daily basis, as the the manna was supplied for the Israelites.

There was seldom a Sunday without guests surrounding the dinner table. Evie had known an old bachelor that her parents often invited to join their extended table. He lived in a shack and conversed with himself (for lack of roommates). Rollie enjoyed the country church, and seldom went home alone for dinner. Ray made sure that if no other invitation surfaced, he would follow Ray and Evie home. He had only his horse and wagon for transportation. He was a large white-bearded man with an over-extended stomach. His hair was thick and course. Perhaps the only day it was combed was to attend church. Often Evie carefully asked, "Could I do some wash for you Rollie? I have a washer." They must put into practice Proverbs 31:20, "Open your arms to the poor and extended your hands to the needy."

His cleft palate made it difficult for him to annunciate his words. This of course did not hinder conversing. The children were most fascinated, and could imitate him to perfection on Monday. Evie did not worry about leftovers, after this guest left the table. The old bachelor devoured the home-cooked meal.

Opportunities soon vanished, for that very fall Rollie was taken for a leg amputation and then to a nursing home. "Shall we go visit Rollie this afternoon?" Ray asked at the breakfast table. How thrilled the old man was to see familiar faces.

"It was a good thing we went to see the dear old man," the family agreed, when they heard of his passing.

A few months later Ray announced, "The lilacs are blooming, shall we pick some and take to Rollie's grave?" Sunday afternoon they were on their way to visit the Inman township cemetery. They placed a water filled jar with lilacs and silently surrounded the grave of an old friend. Bevie and Morrie experienced death for the first time. He was not soon forgotten.

"What happens to him?" Morrie asked.

Ray answered that, "Someday he would have a new body." He had a simple faith in the risen Saviour. "Jesus promised to go and prepare a place for Rollie, and said, 'If I go away I will come again and receive you unto myself.'" The children were satisfied with that hope and were soon running to catch a baby rabbit.

Every year Ray's herd increased. "We have so many young heifers now, we have to have more barn space," Ray commented. His friend Eldo had just informed him that the Lahrman farm would be for rent. The large barn, silo and other farm buildings appealed to the young farmer.

One day he came home and announced that, "We are going to rent Lahrman's farm."

"What are we going to do with our farm?" Evie asked in amazement. Ray was from the old school that fathers are expected to make all decisions that pertain to farming. The prospects of building a larger barn on their small acreage did not make sense to Evie. Moving away from their first real home to an older farm house was not easy for Evie. But Ray was convinced they could not continue to make a living for his family of five.

It did not take long to sell the farm. Someone wanted to buy the land and move the buildings to higher ground.

By the middle of August, Evie was packing and Ray

was planning his fall plowing. The move was just a few miles over the township roads.

Ray put a load of alfalfa hay in the hay rack, allowed a few cattle to nibble on it, and started slowly down the road. The entire herd followed along. That evening Ray was putting them in new stalls. He left the cattle in for a day or so, until they were familiar with where they belonged. The flock of chickens were not quite so easy to move. They waited until dark and snatched the hens from their roosts, and placed them in crates. It created quite a squawk. Were they surprised to wake up in a much smaller coop!

The hay rack was also employed to move the furniture. "I am not worried about any furnishings except the bedroom set, our new stove and refrigerator," Evie stated.

"We'll use lots of padding, and be so careful," Ray assured her. Evie labeled all the boxes and designated which room to put the boxes in. She packed the dishes between folds in her dish towels, thus avoiding having to wash them all if they were packed in paper. She baked bread and sweets, and made hot dishes and salads for the busy unpacking days.

"How could we have accumulated so much in those few years?" Ray thought. Three young ones accounted for most of the increase, he reckoned. They loaded two cribs, a baby buggy, two more chests, and a box of toys. They had also purchased a couch and matching chair from Ray's brother Walter. It was a dark maroon with a wood trim. Evie was so happy to add this to her home. Morrie and Bev were taught that the only time they could put their feet on the couch was in their P.J.'s. Morrie would get on the couch, reach to his shoes and brush with his hands. Evie did not possess a vacuum at first and could only clean the furniture when she borrowed Elizabeth's equipment. Being careful was the most sensible approach. The comforting thing about the move was they would now be only one mile from Grandpa and Grandma Branstner. Ray's parents had now moved to Rochester.

Jacalyn Rae was now a bubbly little eight month old. Her memories of the Miller's first real home would not be as vivid as her brother and sister's. Jacalyn's crib was placed almost in arms' reach from the master bed. The older children were excited to have an upstairs to call their own.

"It is a good thing we were so busy," Evie told her farmer. "I did not have time for even a good cry when we left my doll house." It was a long time before she cared to drive by and see the house moved from its setting.

24
"It's A Boy"

The garden was harvested before the big move. The canned goods were carefully unpacked in the cellar of the older farm home. There was no stairway to the cellar. Once more, as in her childhood Evie was going up and down a ladder with her arms full of canned goods, potatoes, carrots and other vegetables. How she missed her full basement with a stairway, in spite of the fact that every spring they had waded to their knees in water. Ray had attempted to lick the water problem in their first home. He dug around the entire house, and then put pipes around and waterproofed the outside of the basement walls. A layer of thick water-proof material and cement was put over the floor. When spring came they waited to witness a dry basement. The floor actually heaved from pressure and then, as sure as Noah predicted, the floods came. Having purchased the farm in the winter, and with no truth in housing laws, Ray and Evie were faced with the water problem every spring.

They knew in their heart they could never sell with a clear conscience under these circumstances. Thus the farm was sold to someone that was willing to move the buildings and farm the land. It was such a beautiful setting with the smooth green lawn and white picket fence. Evie would have been willing to fill in the basement as deep as the water came in, and build on the house for more space, but that did not take care of the need for space for the growing herd.

Evie dismissed all this from her mind and decided she must again utter the serenity prayer, and get busy with the duties at hand.

It was time to get Morrie ready for his first day at school. The bus was due in a half hour. He and his best buddy, Bobby Kirchner, were out waiting long before the bus was due. Evie watched from the window. "My first baby going out to face the world without me." Evie relived the highlights of his entire six years. "I hope I never have to see him go off to war," she almost uttered out loud. The deeply buried thoughts would perhaps always surface, as long as she remembered the long separation from his Daddy.

She tried to dismiss the haunting memories, as she watched his little legs stretch to board the school bus that would take him to the small town of Hewitt. Evie's thoughts were interrupted by her five year old daughter. Bevie looked longingly at the bus. "I want to go, too," she pleaded.

"Next year you may go with him," Mommie assured her. Bev busied herself entertaining her baby sister, and was often trying to carry her around. She entertained both the baby and her parents with her quiet wit and comments. The piano was great entertainment, and she could play familiar tunes without knowing a note. "We have to start Bev on lessons next year," Evie insisted. Loving music herself, she vowed her children would have music and voice lessons, even if she herself had to go shoeless.

Evie took her two eldest for weekly piano lessons the following summer.

Rena and Eldo now conveniently lived just across the field from Ray and Evie. One day the close neighbors stopped by and Jacie said, "I want to go with Rena." It was her first complete sentence. There were no rural telephone lines but old wall phones were left in each house. A line was strung between the two farms. Evie and Rena could talk whenever the need arose. The need arose quite often, however. The blessings were that no phone bills arrived and you were never tempted to make long distance calls.

Spring came, and Evie discovered there was a fertile fenced garden spot. Again she had ample garden to share with the Pastor's wife, neighbors and friends. The farm table was always filled with the current crop. She canned peas, beans, corn, and had over one hundred heads of cabbage. Sauerkraut, pickles, jams and jellies were either in the cellar or frozen solid in the new freezer. Evie did miss her strawberries. Renting, and not knowing how long it would be before they bought a farm of their own Evie wasn't sure she cared to set out plants and have to walk away from the fruits of her labor again.

During the summer Grandma Miller sent her youngest son to the farm. Evie always managed to have a large family to wash and cook for. It gave Jimmy a definite taste of farm life, and he concluded he would not choose farming as a vocation.

Ray was extremely busy with his large milking herd, planting and harvesting. He continued to fill his duties as Sunday School Superintendent. In the fall the big silo was filled. The double corn crib was stuffed for the large batch of pigs that he raised. With just a small space for chickens, Ray gambled with the pork market. Evie continued to stick with her laying hens. "I have heard of someone with a green thumb, but you have an egg thumb," were the comments coming from Mr. Lahrman. He was standing near Evie as she cleaned, and packed eggs in the small, old house. He came back to visit his daughter, Rena and her family, and also did some repair on the living room ceiling for Evie. How wonderful not to worry about the old plaster ceiling crumbling.

Jacalyn toddled around chasing the little kitties

during the summer months. In the winter, she would pretend she was teaching a Sunday school class from a class-
room in the stairway. Every stuffed animal and dolly she
could find were her students. Closing the stairway door
gave the little teacher privacy. The older children loved to
eavesdrop on the scene. Bev and Morrie would open the
door a crack. She knew her lesson well, and taught the
Bible stories she had memorized over and over. Then she
would sing "The Birds Upon the Tree Top," and other
songs with great emotion. When and if she caught the
sneaky audience, she was very unhappy.

One cold day Evie decided Jacie's security blanket
had to be washed. She did not miss it for a spell, until she
looked out the kitchen window and spied her closest
friend, hanging on the line frozen stiff. "My blanky! My
blanky!" Evie had to go retrieve the blanket and fast dry
it over the range. Electric dryers were not yet popular in
the lowly country homes.

In the fall of 1955, Evie began to feel the old familiar sinking feeling of nausea. By this time she recognized
it as something besides the flu. One day she sat out in the
fall sunshine on an upturned metal basket. She wondered
why some mothers had to get so unbearably sick. She was
reminded of a Bible verse about the grain of wheat that
must die to bring forth more wheat The fact that she lived
to write the story, is strong proof that she did not die. By
the time supper was served, Evie was ready to put Jacie
to bed and crawl in for a rest herself. She was never in
the habit of leaving dishes stacked, but it was a must.
After two or three stories her little girl was sound asleep,
she would muster up enough energy to finish her kitchen
work and prepare the school clothes for the morrow. The
winter went slowly by. After the holiday season Evie
began to improve, and kept up her house work with less
effort.

Spring did come with all of its muddy little tracks.
Evie taught the children to remove their shoes. Their
bedroom slippers were just inside the door. Ray left his
coveralls in the wash house. Cooperation saved the day

for the pregnant mother. As soon as the weather permitted, Evie moved her washer to the wash house. She had an old converted oil range to heat her wash water. Monday and friday were her wash days. Diapers were hand washed on wednesday. Jacie had out grown diapers two years before and given Mommie a vacation from the Wednesday hand wash.

After the garden was planted, Evie made preparation for the new baby. "I hope my baby is a boy," Evie expressed her hearts desire. "Then our family will be evened out, and complete. Again she hated to think of leaving the other children for even a few days. It was difficult to prepare Jacalyn for the separation. Her life was so routine. Every night she had so many stories and songs. Her crib was still beside her mother's bed. Evie hired a neighbor girl for a week before she left. Bonnie assisted with the house work and the children learned to love her. It was on a Saturday, that Evie baked a couple batches of cookies, a large batch of bread, and washed everything in sight. When Ray finished his chores Evie again was ready to take off. They lived closer to Bertha than they did for the previous births. None other than old Doc Will could deliver her baby. Earlier Dr. Will informed Evie he was taking a vacation, but was going to be on call to deliver her fourth baby. Having delivered all of her brothers and sisters, and Evie's three previous babies, he did not want to break that record.

In the small town hospital, there was not always a registered nurse on duty. Evie was experienced with childbirth enough to know it would not be a drawn out affair. "Please call the Doctor now!" she requested. The woman on duty was quick to respond. "Dr. Will is getting old and we are not going to call him until the last minute." She went on to inform Evie that the RN was also expecting a baby very soon, and would not be awakened until later.

"Well my baby is coming soon, I know that, and you better call somebody." Evie was about ready to alert Ray by screaming. Just then the nurse on duty ran for help.

Ray heard her say, "Call the Doctor at once." The pregnant nurse was as awakened as though it was a bad
dream. She did not have time to comb her hair or dress.
She rushed in the room, and attempted to prevent the
birth, by holding Evie's legs together. Evie felt a strong
push, kicked her legs apart, and an eight pound two
ounce baby boy was crying. Evie was put to sleep.

The next morning the nurse said, "Yes! Doctor Will
delivered the baby." Ray was outside the door and heard
the baby cry long before the Doctor arrived. The baby was
as sweet and innocent as his brother and sisters. Evie
and Ray agreed, "It was worth it all."

Jacalyn could only come to the window to see
Mommie. She cried all the way home. Mervin Craig was
the name chosen after some debate. Evie so wanted Craig
for the first name. Evie and the new baby returned home,
on his sixth day. For the first time Evie had a baby with
colic. It would sometimes be three o'clock in the wee
hours of the morning before Evie could get him to sleep.
He was thin, but active. Little Merv was walking around
chairs by the time he was six months and walking alone
at eight months.

It was June and just past his first birthday. "Where
is the baby?" Evie panicked. He had opened the screen
door crawled down the steps and ran to the barn. Ray was
milking and did not see him enter the barn. He went to
the milker motor, caught his thumb on a pulley and
began to cry. Ray came rushing in the house with a bleed-
ing, screaming baby. "You are so fortunate he did not cut
the cord on that thumb!" Dr. Will was trying to get the
parents to look on the bright side.

His entire hand was bandaged to protect the thumb.
A few days later Evie peeked in the room, to see if her
baby was asleep. Buried in the bandages himself, and
examining his wound Evie knew there would never be a
dull moment with Merv around the house.

Time went by, and Ray tried to persuade Mr.
Lahrman to sell the farm, without much success. Evie

and Ray began to farm hunt. Mervin was just past two when they purchased a two hundred acre farm. It had solid farm buildings. The former owners never owned a screw driver or paint brush.

Ray and Evie accepted it as another challenge. The week before they moved in, Evie rented a floor sander. Every room downstairs was sanded, and varnished light, instead of the darkest varnish you could buy. The kitchen and bath floor were covered with a new light inlaid. New cabinets were installed. There was a full basement and Ray took the milkers directly down the basement stairs. Evie could wash them in her large tubs. "We finally have a bathroom!" was the theme of her song. Evie knew she had a big job before she would be satisfied with the interior. The large closet had never been painted. She painted the bedroom and closet to match.

There were four bedrooms upstairs, and a good size master bedroom downstairs. By the end of two weeks Evie had lost ten pounds. She gave the sander the credit for most of the loss. Ray was just as busy getting his livestock ready for winter and filling the silo and also had loads of hay and crops to move. Wood was needed for the furnace. Who had time to twiddle their thumbs?

According to the state laws that Evie had investigated, if you lived more miles from your district than other schools, you could go to the school of your choice. Ray and Evie were sure Morrie and Bev could go to Clarissa school on the bus. The bus came one fourth mile from their new home. To their dismay, they were expected to attend the closest, country school, even though it was not in their school district. The children were accustomed to a town school. Evie visited their district school board. Their land was as far away as you could be, and still be in a district. The other country school had a few students and insisted the children attend a school without a music program and one teacher for all eight grades. It was too far to walk. Evie took turns with the neighbors transporting the children daily. But not without first writing to the state departments to change the situation for that first year. "It is things like this that make a tiger out of a gentle woman," Evie declared. She would not hesitate facing a battle for her cubs. The state agreed with the small country school, stating as long as it was open, it needed more students.

"Next year these kids will go to a good school, if we have to sell this farm!" growled one mad tiger.

25
What's A Mother To Do?

Five year old Jacalyn wanted to attend school. There were no Kindergarten classes in the country schools. Evie was glad to have her home for one more year. She entertained herself and also her brother.

The everyday schedule and trying to concentrate on one area of the home at a time, kept Evie out of mischief. The enclosed front porch needed attention. All the shades hung in shreds. Evie took the shades down and cut out all the torn areas, cutting them nearly in half. She reglued the bottoms of the shades and inserted the slats. The shades hung evenly at least. "Now when someone drives by, it'll at least look like someone lives here, although the shades cannot be lowered," Evie said as she went outside to view the results. "It is definitely an improvement until the budget allows new shades."

Evie had moved the cabinets from the rented farm house. "With all this storage space we do not need that pantry," Evie informed Ray at the breakfast table. "The entrance is too small to be of much use. Do you care if I

knock that wall out?" Evie questioned. Ray had learned
in their early marriage that it did not pay to say, "It can't
be done."

"I don't have time to help you. We are filling the silo
today and tomorrow," he answered. Evie was very aware
of that fact. She had been busy baking cakes, pies, cookies, and planning meals for famished workers. The next
day she fed them their noon meal, hurried with her dishes and went to the shed for her tools. There was nothing
that a man put together that a woman could not take
apart. A good sledge hammer, saw and hammer, were her
main tools. One door way had to be closed. A piece of
sheet rock and a couple two by fours took care of that
problem. Morrie came home from school in time to help
carry the old plaster and lathe to the deep hole that Ray
had hired some one to dig for the sole purpose of throwing in junk.

"Every time you walk across the farm yard pick up
anything you stumble over, and throw it in that deep
hole," Ray instructed. Two year old Merv joined the clean-
up force. The family did have to examine the hole once in
awhile. If perchance Merv delayed going in the house to
the bathroom, you just may find his trousers and shorts
at the bottom of the hole.

With rich farm land, Ray had a bumper crop that
first year. Before he could plant the crop the entire family picked rock. It would not have been so important,
except rocks had not been picked since the barn was
painted, and the barn was nearly bare. Ray had a stone
boat (low flat box over two logs). Someone drove the tractor and the family threw on rocks. "You don't have to help
Evie," Ray said knowing she had a list of indoor projects.

"I want to wear off a few pounds I gained over the
winter, besides it will be fun to get out of the house," she
insisted.

Big brother Morrie made a small stone boat, for
Merv. He pulled it behind his pedal tractor and picked
rocks every day in the yard. Evie could never get him to

stop for dinner. He ended up with picnics quite often. He would be so hot and thirsty but went non-stop until nap time.

Ray plowed a strip for strawberries and help set out the plants. He also prepared a rich garden spot for Evie. Morrie and Bevie raked the front lawn, and picked up all the old bolts, rake teeth or anything that could break the lawn mower.

They purchased gallons and gallons of paint. They first insulated and then painted the house. The tall barn required two coats of paint. The neighbors could hardly believe their eyes. Evie and Ray were now ready to tell their old friends where they lived. Ray hired some landscaping around the house also.

With the pasture land across the road, the cattle had to be driven across that trail. Ray cut wood during the winter and made a large brush pile. He decided to burn it. Every evening Morrie and Bev went to get the cows. Bev loved to go barefoot and the ashes from the brush fire looked so soft, she decided to run through them. She ran half way through before she realized there were hot coals beneath that soft bed of ashes. Both feet were badly blistered before she could get to the other side. She was taken to the doctor and came home with both feet in thick bandages. It was many days before Bev could walk or wear shoes. The entire household had sympathetic pain. How could this happen to our sweet daughter and sister?

Jacalyn was also subject to accidents and hurt her foot, but the greatest blow came when her favorite white kitty was sneaking behind her as she entered the back door. The screen door slammed on the head of the kitty leaving it's glassy eyes wide open. Again the family mourned with the sobbing child and gave the pet an honorable burial. However, it was not difficult to find a rock to mark the grave site. Evie later had nightmares wondering if they rushed the funeral and maybe the cat was just knocked out.

The summer months flew by with loads of city guests, nearly every week. One week Evie baked a five gallon pail of oatmeal cookies, thinking to herself "I am going to get ahead of all those cookie monsters". They wore a path to the cookie jar, when ever Evie was in the laundry room or out hanging sheets and towels. Within three days the bottom of the large container appeared but some how they managed to devour every meal that was served. Evie tried to rescue the last batch of cookies by freezing them. The twenty-foot freezer was in the entrance. Evie discovered the door ajar, with no cookies for afternoon lunch for the workers in the field. Only a farmer's wife had time to make cookies. City cousins were in the habit of having cookies rationed out to them and took advantage of the cookie factory.

As another school year approached, Ray and Evie were very concerned about sending Morrie and Bev to the country school again. Evie had made friends with an elderly couple in Clarissa. She knew the risk of moving away from the farm would perhaps create ugly rumors. Some friends agreed to rent an upstairs apartment so Evie could establish residence in town. Every evening Evie would take the two older children to Clarrisa to stay overnight and would drop them off at school the next morning. Once the school discovered Evie meant business, they allowed the children to ride the bus from the farm. They received a bill for bus fare, because they were not in that school district.

"We were supposed to have the privilege of the school of our choice, being we are so far from our own district, I will never understand this situation," Evie murmured. Politics played a part, even in rural areas. No matter the taxes they paid on their two hundred acres, they paid bus fare for the two children. If the children had started in a country school, it perhaps would have been a smoother adjustment.

"It makes a tiger out of a mother," Evie repeated.

At last both of the children could now play an instrument again. Bev chose the bells, and Morrie the trumpet. Both Ray and Evie were determined to give their children opportunities that were sadly lacking in their childhoods.

It was a late fall morning, when the phone rang so early.

"Evie something terrible has happened," the distressed voice was that of Aunt Anna from Minneapolis. "Carl died," and then silence until she could talk between sobs.

Ray's brother Carl had remained in the cities after the war. He was married and also had a little girl that was his pride and joy. He had been hospitalized for two or three days. Ray was not informed of this.

"Thank you for calling Aunt Anna," Evie replied in shock. "Ray will perhaps call you back, he is milking now."

Evie ran to the barn. Ray was just removing the milker from the last cow. "Ray! Aunt Anna called," Evie said breathlessly.

"At this early hour?" Ray asked with a sense of fear. "Carl died." Carl, known as Dock to most of the family, was bestman at Ray and Evie's wedding.

Ray set the milker down and burst in tears. Evie laid her head on his shoulder to share the shock. Dockie, was only a year and half older than Ray. He left home to stay with Aunt Laura in Roseau, to attend high school. Soon after he left Roseau, Uncle Sam called him at the beginning of World War Two. The two brothers were thousands of miles apart for four years. Ray married before Dock, and Ray was in the Vet's hospital for his first summer at home. They were then separated by one hundred and sixty miles after marriage. "I have hardly seen him these last few years" Ray sobbed. It was the first adult death in the large family. Evie tried to comfort her grieving husband.

"Breakfast is, or was, all ready, and I better check on Merv and Jacie." Evie came back to the reality of the day. Ray was in a daze. He automatically picked up the milker and put the last can of milk in the cooler, and returned to the house.

"He was only thirty seven years old," Ray moaned.

Ray and Carl had traveled together to Aunt Laura's funeral, just a year before.

It was a sad day. To add to the sorrow, the family were informed that the oldest brother, Walter, could not attend the funeral because of a heart attack. Walt married Beulah before answering the call of Uncle Sam. He ended up in Europe to participate in the invasion of France. During that conflict he suffered leg wounds.

He purchased a hardware store in Warren, Minnesota shortly after his discharge. He was enjoying civilian life and the bride, that he had been separated from for so long.

Six weeks later Evie again had to inform Ray, " Your brother Walter is gone."

"The doctor had said he could go back to work in his office. The office was just three steps up. He fell over the first few steps as he returned to work.

Ray decided life was too short to just make a living. One day Evie went out to save milk for the household before the milk man came.

"I am going to quit farming" he informed Evie.

It was Evie's turn to be in shock. You have worked so hard on shaping up this farm.

"What do you plan to do?" Evie blurted.

Ray had often wished he would have purchased a Christian book store instead of a farm. After being a Sunday School Superintendent for thirteen years, his interest in providing material for churches was keen. Ray read the ads under book stores. There was one for sale in Duluth. He left for Duluth to investigate. The couple who owned the downtown book store were in their eighties, and the husband had cancer. They were anxious to sell the book store. He reviewed the last few years of business records and was convinced it would be a profitable business, and one he would enjoy as well. "We have to sell our farm before we will be able to purchase the store," Ray informed them.

The day for the sale of the livestock, machinery, and farm tools arrived. After farming for over thirteen years, the auction sale included over sixty cattle. Ray had filled the silo with corn. How it saddened the farmer's wife to see her favorite cows sold. Ray had gone heavy into raising pigs and then the price of pigs had hit a rock bottom low. They did not include the farm in the auction. Somehow Evie could not question the rationale of selling the farm, considering the school situation, the long hours, and just the fact that Ray desired a change in occupation. Shortly after the two funerals, plans began to jell for the move.

Ray opened a letter from the owners of the store in Duluth. We have decided to accept a small down payment, and not wait for your farm to sell. You may take over the book store as soon as you locate here. Ray was elated. The only income they had since selling the livestock was from Evie's sale of the set of books for the John Rudin Company. The challenge of selling began shortly after Merv invaded the family. She went to Brainerd for a few hours of training.The set of books was called The Book Of Life. The experiences could fill yet another book. Suffice to say, after the sale of over one hundred sets she was asked to supervise the sales in southern Minnesota. The books were to aid in training children and enriching lives.

"I cannot promote the training of children and sacrifice our own family" Evie confessed.

The matter was settled. Evie would continue to sell on a part-time basis in her own area. The John Rudin Company now offered a trip to the Holy Land, and many other coveted prizes.

"With you home to take care of things and the need for extra income, I am going all out," Evie told Ray, with determination.

26

Honesty Pays Dividends

"Leave something for me to do," was the powerful suggestion from Ray. It was late in the fall of 1959. Evie's interest in homemaking made it difficult to find a stopping point and get ready both mentally and physically to leave for her sales job.

She kissed her little three year old son, her five year old, Jacalyn, and gave their Daddy a big hug, as she reminded him to adjust the oven.

"The children will be very hungry when they hop off the bus," she continued, "so don't wait supper for me or the children will lunch and not eat their supper. I will not be home until I make a sale or two." That was always her goal. The green '54 Ford started right up. Evie checked over her sales kit as she waited for the motor to warm up. She planned the schedule for the day. She knew the prospect's address, name, and ages of the children. The town was twenty seven miles from the farm.

Driving did not demand all of her attention. Evie recalled how she became involved in selling *Book Of Life*.

Ray examined the set of books while visiting Evie's sister June's home. He was impressed and copied the address of the publishers of the books. The company responded with an apology. We are sorry we do not have a sales person in your area. Because of your appreciation of the books, we are hoping you will consider selling the set. Ray recommended his wife and enclosed a picture of Evie. Evie was unaware of this until she received a full packet, including an application.

"And so here I am on my own again," Evie reminded herself. How very necessary that she make sales now that there was no longer a milk check. She was extremely grateful she had already experienced over one hundred sales. She had only worked a few days each month. She began when Merv was a tiny baby.

Ray had just recovered from another attack of malaria, leaving him as weak and limp as the wet sheets on his bed. That was just before the auction. After doing the chores with the help of Morrie, Evie reminded herself not to regret the sale of the cows, and hopefully, the farm. "I refuse to be attached to any one home," she convinced herself. "Besides," she continued, "we can make a home wherever our hearts are."

She could not believe she was entering town and nearing her first prospect. She shifted her thoughts to the task at hand of meeting strangers, in hope that they would not be strangers long. Satisfied customers had given Evie the leads for the day. A lovely home in a new section of town housed a warm and friendly mother. The grandmother was invited to share the presentation. They were both impressed. "Would you please stop by our office and show these books to my husband?" the mother requested.

Evie realized she must not stop at half a sale and inquired the location. She quickly put on her coat and gloves and conversed as she did so. "It has been a pleasure introducing the *The Book Of Life* set to both of you, and I hope you have the privilege of using them," and was on her way.

Evie located the office and asked for the husband. The receptionist said, "It will be an hour before he is available."

"Is there a grocery store close by? I need to do a little shopping,"and then added, "I will be back in one hour."

Evie made her selection carefully, realizing she had five dollars in her purse. The young clerk slowly counted out her change, "Four eighty-seven, four ninety, five, and ten dollars." He quickly turned to another waiting customer.

"Sir I only gave you a five dollar bill," Evie handed a five back to the young man. He glanced at the owner's wife and quietly placed a picture of Abe Lincoln back in the till.

"That only took fifteen minutes," Evie thought to herself. "I have forty-five minutes to make another call." She uttered a prayer as she rang the door bell. A cheerful housewife was framed by the doorway and greeted Evie as though she was expecting her at that very moment. Twenty minutes later Evie was bidding her good-bye, with a promise to return at 5:30 to show her husband. She left a brochure for him to read.

Evie's watch confirmed the urgency. She had five minutes to keep her appointment. "Mrs. Miller," the receptionist called by the time Evie was seated in the waiting room. Evie tried to look as relaxed as if she had waited for the entire hour.

"Mr. Simons, your wife was impressed with some books I introduced to her this afternoon and asked me to take a few minutes of your time to get your opinion," she began as she shook his hand.

The first closing was all that was necessary. He was a man of quick decision with an appreciation for quality. "We want the deluxe set."

Evie buttoned her coat, put on her warm gloves, and was off to face the elements and another husband. She was confident that his values were that of his kind wife.

Having read the brochure and listened to his wife and the grandmother's positive comments, Evie was soon on her way with her second order.

It was turning bitter cold. Evie had one more call on her list for the afternoon. "I am so glad I told Ray not to wait supper for me," Evie almost uttered out loud. She was in her car and heading for the last call. She was invited in the home, though it was now after six. She had no idea how the family made a living, until she rang the door bell. The owner of the grocery store answered the door. Without a moment's hesitation Evie was welcomed in.

"You're the lady that returned the five dollars to our new employee today," the mother explained. She was welcomed into the living room before she revealed the nature of her call. The presentation was given to both parents as the children looked on. With only one closing, Evie was writing up her third order. It was a good batting average for the day. Evie thanked them again and added,"I have a family to get home to." She raced to the cold car as wind and snow gained momentum. "I can't believe I haven't had as much as a drink of water since noon," she thought. Her foot became heavy as she left the quiet little town. She had put over sixty miles on the green Ford in just over six hours and a little wear and tear on the sales lady.

Ray met her at the door, "We were just getting worried about you."

He gave her a warm thankful hug.

"I am so thirsty and hungry, but with my one track mind I did not know it until I started home."

The dishes were done, but there was a warm dinner awaiting Evie. How thankful they were for the three sales. Evie ate her meal and spent time with her four children before bedtime.

A daily report for John Rudin company was completed before she crawled into her flannel nighty and knelt by her bedside to give her Senior Companion thanks for his divine help in every sale.

"Three calls, three sales!" She went over every detail as she cuddled closely to her warm bed partner. How could she settle down without reliving the entire scene?

"You know Ray, if I could do this every afternoon I would qualify for a trip to the Holy Land."

Evie recalled the time she made two sales at one stop. The farm family had company. The guest listened in from the dining room. Evie was writing up the order when the visitor interrupted with, "We would also like a set of those books." She also called on the doctor in the small town of Clarissa. She was never quite sure if he was that impressed in a fifteen minute view of the books, or if it was urgent that he get on with his schedule for the day. Her experiences were varied. The scenes returned as though they were on a reel of a movie as she recalled the long list of sales. She called on a well-known business man in Wadena. He could not possibly afford the books. Evie's next call led her to a home that was in dire need of paint. She was invited inside of the very modest home by a friendly, but poorly dressed, farmer. Both parents appreciated the value of having good books for their children. The sale was made with the question, "How long before we receive the books?"

One pastor of a thriving church convinced Evie that he could not possibly afford the set of books. It was in the days that TV's were just making their debut. News spread fast of any family that could afford a TV. Through the grape vine, Evie heard that the pastor purchased a TV the following week. She questioned her ability to sell or wondered if some of her prospects fell heir to their inheritance overnight. "It really is not for me to decide, what people buy," Evie admitted. She did wish she would have gone for one more closing, for the sake of their children.

There were great lessons on human nature. It was Evie's crash course in sales. She had taken her training by correspondence and met the head salesman in both Brainerd and St. Cloud for a few hours of final instruction. She had to go through a complete sales presentation with Ray as her prospect. He was ready to buy a second set, by the time Evie completed her closing. Bashfield sent his recommendations and Evie was off on her new career. She discovered her little niche in life. Her mother Elizabeth said, "Evie, you were always trying to sell an idea or something all your life." When Joy heard the news she wrote a letter to Evie (In part):

Dear Evie,

Now you won't have to sell green sour apples. You would stand on top of the wood box and give a speech when you were little and always be selling something. We wish you much success

Love,

Joy and Howard

Evie continued to rush with her house work, to get out and make sales. Ray busied himself trying to master the art of household duties to give Evie more time to reach her goal.

27
Surprise Package

The incentives to be even a part time sales person were the most challenging that Evie had ever experienced. Her goals were high. The prize for the greatest increase in sales, was a trip to the Holy Land. "I have never traveled abroad." Evie admitted.

"We thought we were lucky to go to Woodside Store," Ray answered. Evie not only dreamed about the trip, she planned her days carefully. She met her quota every day. Ray kept his part of the bargain by developing skills around the house. Evie was surprised to see the basket of ironing empty one homecoming.

"You did a better job than the last maid I hired," Evie said, as she admired the clothes that were on hangers. She had visions of the time she came home to damp clothes piled on top of each other. She had to iron them all again.

It was a cold, brisk February day that Evie came home, having only made calls on half of her prospects. "What brings you home so early?" Ray asked in surprise

"I don't feel so great." She was feeling nauseated. Her energy and sales fell flat. The blizzard that followed

gave her an added excuse to take a few days off. She ago-
nized over the fact that she was ahead of her goal, and
now she was more sick every day.

She was feverish, cold and perplexed. "If I am pregnant, it is the first time I ran a temperature." Within a
few weeks she was awakened to the fact that she was
having a miscarriage. Ray rushed her to Wadena to
Doctor Ness.

"We will do all we can to save the baby," he said as
he prepared to examine her. Evie was silent, but was positive it was too late for that. Her thoughts were soon confirmed. "You have already lost your baby," the kind Dr
informed her. You have a choice of going home with some
strong medication or going into the hospital and complet-
ing the job." "We just gave up our insurance when we sold
our milking herd. If I have a choice, I am going home."
Precautions were carefully laid out. She purchased the
pills and returned home. She spent the entire night in the
bathroom, attempting to take more medication at the
specified hours. Her body rejected the medication.

The office opened the following morning with the
phone ringing. "I must talk to the doctor. I could not keep
those pills down."

"You must come in now!" the doctor said in no uncertain terms.

It was the very day the truck was coming to move
the household to Duluth. Through all the hub-bub Ray
and Evie had managed to get everything packed. Morrie
rode with the trucker, and the three younger children
were in the car. Evie was to go to the hospital and Ray
and the children would go on to Duluth later that day.
The doctor suggested that she first stop by his office for
another examination. The doctor had a very surprised
look on his face.

"Evie, I can't figure this out. I cannot carry out my
plan for you. You have definitely lost a baby, but the
womb has entirely closed and it against the law for me to
proceed. He gave her the name of a doctor in Duluth and

said, "Do not delay in going to this doctor within three days. In the meantime take these pills, or you could get an infection. Evie joined the family and traveled on to Duluth. Though exhausted by the end of the day, they unpacked enough dishes to prepare an evening meal and set up beds for everyone.

"You are still pregnant," the new doctor announced. "Your blood is very low." Evie was not surprised to hear that verdict. She had wondered how many pints she lost in the past few days. She found a drug store to fill her prescriptions and wondered if she knew her way home.

"I am still carrying a baby." Ray could not believe what he was hearing. Ray left to visit the store that he was to take over. "We have decided to try to manage the store until your farm sells," the old gent informed Ray, in contradiction to the letter that they had sent Ray and Evie. It was reason for a law suit. Ray's countenance fell in disbelief. How could he relate the news to Evie after they left the farm house empty and now would be paying rent for a duplex? Evie was physically exhausted. The blow of the news seemed to be the straw that would break any camel's back.

Life did go on. Ray sought work and prayed daily that the farm would sell before spring. He managed to find work a few days now and then. Evie decided to try selling books. After one evening without a sale,leaving her totally exhausted, she realized she could not contribute to the family budget.

Ray was soon involved in a local church. Their faith was tested, but not defeated. Evie longed for her farm house. The children missed their rural friends. To top that, Jacalyn and Merv made contact with measles. Evie wondered how she could make it up the stairs with one more glass of iced water, and down two long flights of stairs to launder another load of sheets. She remembered she would just be supplied with one day of strength and grace at a time. It was soon summer. "I don't really call this summer," Evie complained. Mark Twain said, "The coldest winter I recall was the summer I spent in

Duluth." With iron poor blood Evie could relate to that.

Along with the summer months came letters and phone calls from Aunt Anna. "Ray! Please come back and work for Uncle Gus." He is getting old and needs some help. Ray once more contacted the book store. They were undecided. "We cannot stay here and wait for the farm to sell," Ray declared. So again the trucker was engaged to move them. Aunt Anna found a house to rent just two blocks from her home. It was walking distance to the Twin City Rock Crystal Shop. Once more Ray was back where he and Evie began their married life, only now with the fifth child about to announce a birth date.

The move was just in time for the school children. Merv would start kindergarten, in spite of his promise a year or two before of, "I will never leave you alone, Mom."

It was now a few weeks before the baby was due. Evie found her third doctor for the delivery. "Your blood is so extremely low, I think you will need transfusions at the time of delivery," the new Doctor said. Evie had tried every iron prescription to no avail. With no insurance, Evie's faith was tested.

"Why do I have to feel like this and why do circumstances work out this way?"

Just before Evie's due date a letter came from the owners of the store in Duluth.

Dear Mr. and Mrs. Miller,

We are ready to sell. My husbands health is failing fast. Come as soon as you can, and possibly take over the first of October.

The new baby was due any day. There was no debate. Evie and Ray agreed, "There is no way will we put our family through another move." Evie had just unpacked the last box. Her sisters June and Donna spent one entire day helping to curtain the windows and get settled. The house they rented was for sale, with the renters given the first option to buy, or move if a buyer made an offer.

The farm had not sold, but was rented out to neighbors. Because the farm was over one hundred miles from the Cities, banks would not lend money on the farm.

The suitcase was packed, and Evie was sure her baby would be born on October sixth. She had hardly taken time to wish for a girl or boy. The fact that she threatened to lose the baby for the first seven months made it difficult to be be assured of either. Evie's mother, Elizabeth, went to the same clinic in Wadena that Evie had gone to. One day the Doctor asked Elizabeth, "How is Evie?"

"She will be having her baby any day now," Elizabeth responded.

"No! She lost a baby about six or seven months ago!" Evie knew she would have given birth to twins. Gus had twin sisters. Evie had always dreamed of twins but that was before she gave life to four single births. "I will now be grateful for one healthy child."

"It is time to register to vote," Ray announced at the supper table. When they returned from registering, Evie insisted that the car be parked close to the house.

She asked Ray to put the suitcase in the car. "It is D day!" There was no indication that this would be the day, and it was time to go to bed.

"Just leave the light on," Evie begged.

Finally Ray got up and put the hall light out. "You are not going to have that baby tonight." The light was not out five minutes and Evie was down stairs calling her doctor. There was no time to complete prepping. Evie was soon rushed to the delivery room. A baby girl was exercising her lungs in minutes. There was no need for a transfusion. Evie's prayers were granted. It was just after midnight. Her prediction of the sixth was missed by a few moments.

When Jacalyn was named Evie remarked, "If I ever

have another girl I will have a Jack and Jill." Jill Anna was written on the birth certificate that was dated October 7, 1960. The four children at home could hardly wait for their new sister. The thirteen and fourteen year olds raced to pick her up at the first whimper, when they came home for lunch each day.

"Why did you wake the baby?" Evie questioned.

"She was wet," was Morrie's quick reply.

On Saturdays Bev begged to bath the baby. It was a lot more fun than tiding up the kitchen. Evie discovered she could tenderly bathe the baby as well as a mother could. It became a weekend ritual. How Bev loved to dress the baby in her Sunday clothes! Little did the parents realize how much they would have missed in life without each one of their five children. Evie's desire was to gain the stamina and energy enough to now raise the five she gave birth to.

Ray was back cutting designs in the glassware and delivering to the stores. When the winter months had passed, Evie longed for her garden and empty farm home. "I would like to take the children back to our farm home for the summer," Evie suggested.

"I could only be there on weekends," said Ray.

"I could plant a garden, harvest the strawberries, and get the house ready to rent." It was decided that the minute school was out they would move enough furniture to batch. Weekends in advance they went to plant a garden. Morrie had a summer job promised to him by one of the neighbors. How happy he would be on the seat of a tractor again. Bev, Jacie, Merv, and Jill would enjoy the solitude of the farm.

Moving day came. An apartment size stove, refrigerator, enough everyday dishes, pots and pans were packed. Essentials only were moved. They had left a sofa and chair and also curtains to the windows on the farm house when they moved to Duluth. Evie recalled that move as a bad dream.

The first Friday evening they arrived back home the children piled out of the car to explore there favorite spots. Evie and Ray grabbed the suitcases and proceeded to the house, only to find the back door unlocked. Was someone in the house? They approached each room with caution. The beautiful wood trim on the sofa and chair had been whittled on for hours. The shavings were on the floor. They investigated further. For lack of a stove someone had roasted a chicken in the wood furnace. The feathers were on the basement floor. Tracks of an intruder were in every room. The neighbors reported that they noticed the garage doors open some days but closed another. They thought they saw smoke from the chimney. "It can only be our wishful thinking, Ray and Evie are in Minneapolis," the neighbor related. There were car tracks, but this also was a safe place for young people to park.

Evie was so anxious to move back to the farm. "I won't be afraid if I have a phone," she promised.

"You won't have a car," Ray said reluctantly.

Evie was not as courageous as she thought. What if the intruder returned? He perhaps was a fugitive from the law. He likely stole the chicken from the neighbors, and on and on her imagination rambled. They spent the day cleaning house, getting a week's supply of groceries for the "widow". On Sunday they went back to their first country church and back to Grandma and Grandpa Branstners for Sunday dinner. Grandma had not lost the knack of making a tender pork roast, mashed potatoes with creamy brown gravy, and of course homemade rolls.

All too soon it was time for Daddy to take off early on Monday morning, back to the grindstone. He did not like separations. Memories surfaced of the long, long three years snatched from family. He promised to return as early as possible on Friday night. Morrie went to his farm job and Evie made plans for the summer. She had plenty of time to think as she hoed the first crop of weeds from the thriving garden. Bev, now thirteen, was the greatest little baby sitter. Merv was back picking up stones and playing farmer. The wonderful country air was invigorating. The children were early risers, and Baby Jill was the built in alarm. She was now creeping and exploring every nook that she had missed out on.

28
All in a Summer

Like all of Minnesota's fleeting summers, 1961 was no exception. Gardening, canning, painting, yard work and company seemed to hasten the coming autumn days. Evie looked forward to Friday evenings when her helpmate would return from Minneapolis. She was glad to be busy in her favorite farm house. The strawberries had all been devoured or frozen. Every weekend Ray returned with empty jars and took back the jars filled with pickles, corn, string beans, peas, and everything Evie could get her hands on. "Let's pick choke cherries," Mommy suggested at the breakfast table. "Choke cherry jelly will taste great on our toast next winter."

Bev volunteered to stay with baby Jill. Mervin and Jacalyn gathered their pails and trudged along. The berries were large and juicy, and it did not take long to pick a milk pail full. They hurried on home to get them cleaned and boiled. Evie wanted to make one batch of jelly before the sun set. By mixing apple with the berries she would not have to buy pectin to thicken the jelly. She planned to can the remainder of the juice and make up the jelly in the winter months.

Evie had one major project: puttying and painting the storm windows. With two porches and all the other rooms to the two story house, it proved to be a tedious job. By dividing it up to several day's work, between canning days, Evie finally completed both the puttying and painting of the storms. One week Ray managed arranging a ride to the cities. "How handy to have a car this week," Evie said. She had many errands to run. When the last window was washed and storm window hung, she left for Clarissa. She posted a "For Rent" sign on the school bulletin and at every space available in town.

Evie had just returned home when the phone rang. A new teacher and family were looking for a home in the country. How proud Evie was to tell Ray, "The house is rented!"

"We'll take it," they said before they had even reached the stairway. Evie completed her summer projects just in time.

"It will be our last week apart, and I will be back to get you all next weekend," Ray said as he bade the children good-bye before they were tucked in bed. Bev had just returned from a trip with her cousins in Montana. It was a glorious surprise to visit with Robert and Janet. Aunt Joy and Uncle Howard added so much to her summer. Bev decided she would rather live in the big city and was anxious to return to Minneapolis. She did not share the interest in the farmlife of her siblings. Morrie loved the summer months. He finished his work in time to spend the last week helping his Mom.

To the surprise of the family Uncle Kenneth drove in. "I talked to Ray this morning, the house you are renting is sold," Ken informed Evie.

"It is time to get the children back to school, and I just rented this house out," Evie replied almost in tears. She was canning one more batch of the choke cherry juice. That afternoon she was just finishing the last piping hot jar that refused to seal with a Kerr lid. She noticed a nick in the jar, so she stretched a rubber over the filled jar. The jar tipped and before Evie could get the sticky slacks off her legs, second degree burns covered her hips to below her knees. Morrie was not old enough to have a driver's license. Evie called to see if a neighbor could take her to the doctor. There was no answer. "Morrie you have to drive. I cannot move my legs fast enough to use the brakes." The blisters were swelling fast. When Evie stood up the water would run beneath the blisters. Her burns were dressed by Doctor Will at the hospital. She did not want to worry Ray, but decided she must call him to cushion the shock before he arrived home the following night.

The night was long. Evie tried walking the floor. She walked like a cowboy that had been born on a horse—in a very bow legged manner. That only made matters worse, the gauze rubbed on the burns. Her legs were bandaged from her hips to below each knee. It was a sleepless night. She wondered how she would be able to move that weekend, where they would find another house to rent, and would the farm ever sell? Again she was made to realize she had problems enough to handle for one night. She could nurse the baby while lying down. She only allowed tears when she knew the children were sound asleep. The big sister and brother came to her rescue and took complete charge of the other children. Evie remained strong around the children. But by the time Ray came home on Friday evening Evie was a complete basket case. Ray was tired and in shock over the ordeal of the house being sold from under them and now with Evie incapacitated. "We will be unable to buy the house though we have the option, without the sale of the farm," Ray related. They had one month to move from the city home. The teacher and family were moving in the farm home the following week. By now the country school was closed so that was no longer a hindrance to living on the farm. Evie could not go back on her word, though the deal was only sealed with a handshake. The teacher's family could not wait to move in the big farm house.

Sunday afternoon the family, summer furnishings,

and canned goods, including all but one jar of choke cherry juice, were buzzing down the freeway. By the time they arrived in Minneapolis Evie's legs were in severe pain. She was sure infection was setting in. She called her doctor. "Just crawl in the tub and soak in a detergent," the Doctor advised. Soak in a detergent?! Evie couldn't believe her ears. She ran a tub with thick Fab suds and crawled in. The first few minutes were murder, but gradually the pain subsided and she could increase the water temperature. Relieved from pain, Evie slept like a baby back in her own bed, with all her family under one roof. Trusting in God's promises to provide their daily needs, she had a new sense of peace. "I will never leave you or forsake you," was a comforting promise from God's Word.

The children returned to school. The ten month old baby discovered that during their absence was the only peaceful time of the day to nap. Evie continued to soak the burns often. She had such relief that she could make it up and down the stairways without severe pain. It was wash day, and the late summer sun dried her clothes in the breeze.

She renewed her friendship with the dear next door neighbor, Mrs. Rush. She was so unfriendly when Evie first endeavored to make acquaintance. When she discovered the children would not trespass or invade her privacy she let her walls down. Fresh cinnamon rolls and cookies broke the ice. When the Millers moved away, she was sad. Evie learned much from the old gardener, including how to care for apple trees. She later had lunch at their new home. Thirty years later she is remembered every time an antique bowl is used. The bowl was purchased from her when she gave up her home. Evie would take her shopping and treasured the sandwiched time they spent visiting over the hedge . . . Rush had admired the line of white diapers and sheets and was relieved that a bunch of hillbillies did not move next door to her. But the time for good-byes came.

Evie settled in as much as she dare. Tuesday morning she spent calling on ads under rental property. "How many children do you have?" was the first question.

"We have five, ranging from a one year old to a four-teen year old," was the near apologetic reply. The line was severed, bluntly. This happened so often that Evie grew tired of calling. Every day she awoke with new courage. The day for moving was fast approaching. Every evening Ray's appetite decreased. "Did anything sound hopeful today?" Ray sounded like a broken record, and the negative answer could have been recorded.

In one week they had to be out of the house and still had not a place to call home. Aunt Anna called and suggested the apartments above the Crystal shop. Ray had known they were empty. In fact he had just painted two apartments. He did not want to move his family above the old red brick shop "I will take you back to the farm before I will ask you to live there," he told Evie.

"It would be a temporary parking spot," Evie stated in a positive tone. "Besides we won't always have to stay there, and I don't want to make our farm renters move."

"Its a long stairway for you to climb with your sore legs," Ray continued.

"The kids won't have to change schools," was still another plus. As moving neared, Evie packed and prepared food ahead for the busy day. She baked extra bread, several batches of cookies, and a few hot dishes. She was learning every trick of making the transition run smoothly. Meals were prepared without delay and hearty appetites were soon satisfied. The Millers rented two apartments. One kitchen doubled for storage and laundry.

"We have a boy's and girl's bathroom," Bev said. Evie purchased some cabinets to put in the kitchen. They ripped up the old linoleum in both kitchen and bath and put in new linoleum. She read her favorite section of the paper, and went shopping for carpet for the living room. She found twice as much padding and also the carpeting she needed. The price was right and she bought it all. The floors in the old apartment were three to four inches higher on one end than the other end. Ray and Evie doubled the thick waffle padding on the low end and doubled the carpet also. The room was then level. "Now the kids can't slide down hill in our living room," the parents agreed. Evie's drapes fit the windows perfectly. The walls were freshly painted. She had earlier found a desk and love seat for sale. A little elbow grease and some stain, and the pieces looked like new, along with the sofa and rocker that were new. The living room was now inviting.

The two older children did not want to tell their friends where they lived. Evie did not blame them. The outside of the building looked old and dirty. Evie took the carpet from her other living room and cut it to fit the hall leading to their front apartment. She scrubbed the long stairway. It was beginning to look more and more like someone may live behind those ugly red bricks.

Merv went to kindergarten in the afternoon. Jacayln missed her kitty the most but gave her dolly extra attention and loved to play school. Merv would have his breakfast and play in his pajamas until Evie dressed him for school and gave him his lunch. His large set of tinker toys occupied his entire mornings. His structures towered and were complicated and perfect. The family could never tear them apart, but when Merv ran out of tinker toys, a wrecking crew was called in. Construction began on a new creation. They were on display in the living room for the family to enjoy. "Some day you are going to be a great craftsman," his mother proudly encouraged him. Little did she know what a prophetess she was, as one may discover in later chapters.

29

Thirty Eight Twenty East Thirty Sixth Street

It was nearing Thanksgiving. All of Evie's sisters living in the city area planned to have dinner at Donna's home. Donna and Gary were also proud parents. Pearl, Bob, and their four children, June and Hugh with their two sons and daughter, also lived in Minneapolis. Evie's legs were slowly healing. She looked forward to getting out of the apartment. She had gone to church a few Sundays and walked a block to the nearest store. She prepared her rolls and salad to contribute to the dinner, but Thanksgiving greeted her with a stomach flu.

"Ray, please take the children, I have to stay in bed and see if I can nip this bug in the bud." Her legs had scabs only on the deepest burns. They were still painful, but keeping busy was the best way to ignore the pain. With Evie's one track mind, she would end the day crawling in bed wondering if they had been that painful all day, though too preoccupied to notice. Thanksgiving day did give her legs a day with no irritation.

She often looked forward to a quiet time, but not to spend it in bed. At the close of the day Ray returned with five tired children and a dinner for Evie, but she could not swallow a bite. The flu was a twenty four hour guest. By the following morning she was ready for her motherly duties.

It was soon time to get ready for Christmas. The tree was trimmed early to enjoy for the entire month. Aunt Till and her daughter, Ethel, lived in the Mark Twain Hotel. Ethyl was Aunt Till's only living offspring. Her two sons suffered premature deaths. Auntie and daughter always counted on Evie's invitation for Christmas. Aunt Anna and Uncle Gustave were childless, so Christmas and New Years were spent at the Millers'. Aunt Till (in her eighties) would join in the new games. She was a gracious lady. Her thin hair was in a short bob with waves. She walked straight and swift, as though she had a batch of bread going, a peck of diapers to wash and babies crying. Having lost her husband years before, she made her home into a delivery home for babies. She was capable of being midwife, serving the meals, and keeping the rooms and clothes clean, though there were no disposable diapers and no automatic washers. She often had six patients. Perhaps she was up all night with a delivery. An old doctor worked with her in Stanely, North Dakota.

The year of the Stanley, North Dakota centennial, she and the Doctor rode proudly in an old model T touring. Ray and Evie journeyed twelve hundred miles round trip to witness this parade. In her prime, Aunt Till's daughter Ethel married a rich man by the name of Heffelfinger. She lived with him for a year or so until he went on to greener pastures. She worked at a clothing store downtown. Her hair was dyed red and swooped to the top of her head, with a few strands falling down by the time she arrived. When Evie served peas and carrots the children knew what she would say, "Eat every carrot and pea on your plate." She always made the dinner lively. Some how the guests did not care if the dinner was served in a cottage, mansion, or in an old brick apartment on Riverside. They just enjoyed the home cooked meal with all its trimmings.

Baby Jill was now fifteen months. Every weekend that the weather permitted, Evie and Ray would house-hunt with faith that the farm would sell by the time they found a home. One day Evie called in answer to an ad. The salesman came to the address he had been given. He walked around several times thinking he had the wrong address. He finally came upstairs and cautiously knocked on the door. He later remarked as they were riding to a home. "I could not believe my eyes when I saw your neat home in that old building with the carpeted hall." Evie was glad someone noticed. The family appreciated it as well. Clean windows, curtains, second hand, refinished furniture, doubled carpet, the aroma of home-made breads, and nutritious food, along with faith and love converted the dreary apartment into a home.

Ray was the most dissatisfied. He felt so responsible. "If we don't sell the farm by spring, I am moving the family to the farm." Ray continued to have malaria while at Riverside. That fact was conducive also to his desire to get out where he could garden.

On a January day Merv went into the bathroom and locked the door but could not reverse his act. Evie ran franticly down to Ray. He sat patiently cutting an order of glassware. After removing the hinges, Ray rescued the five year old.

An affordable house was located. Evie did not like the size of the bedrooms. The living and dining room were large. The kitchen was fair size and bedrooms were all up the open stairs. Ray was so anxious to move the family and tired of looking at homes, that Evie consented to the purchase. A close friend offered to loan money until the farm sold.

Early in February Evie was shampooing the carpet at thirty eight twenty east thirty sixth street. How happy the family was to move from Riverside even though it meant changing schools. Bev could walk to Sanford

Junior High and also Merv and Jacalyn to Howe Elementary, and Morrie finished the year at South High.

The first day for Jacalyn was a bitter experience. She became lost on the way home for lunch. Some kind soul brought her home. Evie could not forgive herself for not walking with her the first day. It was an eight block walk each way and would have entailed taking the baby and Merv with her; Ray took the car to work. Merv went to an afternoon Kindergarten.

Ray was busy with yard and garden as soon as spring beckoned. He managed to raise enough vegetables for the summer and Evie prepared extra for the long winter ahead. She moved canned goods that were left from farm canning. Grandpa Branstner took two of the baby calves from the farm before the auction. It was now in the freezer in the form of steaks, roasts, hamburger, and soup bones. Evie found a mill selling flour in one hundred pound sacks for eight dollars, and also whole wheat in the fifty pound bags. She discovered a bakery would also sell her fresh yeast by the pound. She had never ceased baking bread. The large farm freezer preserved many a bargain. Ray had a steady job, but his old uncle had never raised a family and had no idea how far the small pay check had to stretch.

The following summer, the folks that rented the farm decided to buy it. That news was the best Ray had heard in months. "We can now pay Eldo back!" were the first words he uttered.

"We can remodel the kitchen," Evie added. The breakfast nook was torn out, new cabinets, and sink installed. Their friend Eldo built the cabinets. Evie recovered her round oak table from Ruthie's shed and removed the white paint. "If we could take that chimney out we would have about four more square feet of space," Evie pleaded.

"That will have to wait," Ray insisted. "We would have to put in a new ceiling if we do that now."

Everyone seemed quite content. Evie was restless if

there was not some area to dream of improving. The bedroom situation was far from ideal. The bathroom was small. The house was a story and a half. "If only the upstairs could be as large as the downstairs, this house would be fine," Evie commented. She did not want to sound ungrateful, but she did want the girls to have another room. Jill had outgrown her crib. There were eight years between the two boys.

Evie prayed about changing the arrangement. She also searched the houses for sale, thinking it may be wiser to buy a house that met their needs. The ceiling in the girl's room leaked no matter what Ray patched it with. "I could not honestly sell this house to anyone." The former owners had done a good job hiding some of the problems. The ceilings were painted nicely and all stains were properly treated. The first hard rain revealed a problem. Evie consulted their faithful carpenter friend. "You could remodel that upstairs and have four bedrooms, ample closets, and a large bathroom," he assured them. He took measurements of the foundation and worked on a blueprint.

Morrie was now beginning college. He worked part time at Sears. The war in Vietnam was on his mind. Unknown to his parents he and a friend decided they may as well enlist as wait to be drafted. Morrie felt a sense of guilt, with other friends leaving. When Evie heard the news she was in shock. Ray cringed in his boots. From the day of his birth Evie had fears of war and separations. It was in March that the sun rose for his departure. The three years of his Dad's service days surfaced. Evie spent intervals of the day in tears. She was alone most of the day and wanted to come to terms with the reality of it all, before the family returned.

The following day it stormed. The snow was so deep that even the trainload of young soldiers had to stop on its tracks for hours. Ray seldom missed work, but this was one day everyone was paralyzed. The entire family began to knock out walls in the upstairs.

"If you ever had the urge to write on a wall, now is

the time," Ray told the children. The three younger children did just that.

"We are putting the cart before the horse," Ray
explained. We are going to need a loan to remodel, and we
have not consulted our banker yet." But when would they
get another stormy day to work together to take out their
frustrations of their eldest son's departure? Evie waited
until Ray ate his supper and had read his sport page to
ask a question.

"When can we go down to the bank and apply for re-
financing?"

"I am working every banking hour," was his reply.
"You will have to go down."

So the "little red hen" gathered up her bus fare and
made an appointment downtown to see the banker that
held their mortgage. With Ray's wages and Evie just
starting a business, plus money very tight, it was difficult
to borrow. Evie had to cultivate all the courage she could,
as she gathered up her bus fare. The banker sensed her
determination and the blueprint met his approval and
then added, "We do not loan for remodeling; we will loan
after the project is completed." He advised her to get a
loan at her own bank until they were sure of the amount
needed for the total project. Evie thanked him kindly and
stopped off at her own bank. She borrowed money for two
months. This implied that the project had to be ready for
inspection within two months. Her carpenter accused her
of being a slave driver. She always had that dead line in
the back of her mind and acted accordingly.

Ray worked at a part-time job on Saturdays. Eldo
consented to be the foreman of the job. Ray and Evie
helped in every way they could. Every friday they rented
a truck and filled it with plaster and lathe. The new roof
was built over the old roof, extending over the entire
house. Soon all the old was torn out with the exception of
the bathroom. That stayed intact until the very last. Beds
were made up in the hall, in the little room that Evie
wanted for an office, the dining room and also the base-

ment. Everyone found a corner to call their room, including the carpenter. His home was much too far to travel daily. In the evening Evie and Ray would go to Knox Lumber to get supplies for the next day. Ray also helped put on the shingles after the supper hour. When the outside walls were complete Evie insulated them. Ray insulated the attic. During the day Eldo would help place the twelve-by-four sheet rock, and Evie would nail the sheet rock on. She used her fingers to do the walking over the yellow pages and dial. By purchasing the shingles from one company and the nails from another, and mixing the dry seam cement, the cost was defrayed. Then the taping began. Before the floor was in, a two-by-four fell through the hall ceiling. This necessitated a new ceiling in the hall. A strong beam had to be placed in the center of the living room. Before they finished the entire down stairs had a new ceiling. It was a perfect time to remove the chimney Evie wanted torn out. It just took one brick at a time starting at the top. Eldo and Ray helped tape the living room, kitchen and hall. Evie taped the four bedrooms, five closets and bathrooms. She was taping in her sleep. The washing for the family of seven and meals were done like clock work.

Then came the finishing of woodwork, windows and doors. One Saturday Evie wanted to complete the last coat. She finally called a friend at Forest Lake. "LaVonne, I am so in need of getting out of here. If I stay, I can't quit working and I am almost seeing stars."

"Come on out and spend the night and all day Sunday," was the invitation. Evie knew LaVonne could also call on her, under similar circumstances. Monday morning Evie felt refreshed and ready to tackle the varnish brush, and sand paper. They did not care to borrow money to carpet the floors. Bev was out working the summer months. She carpeted her own private room. How happy she was to have her very own room. It was furnished with a beautiful bedroom set. Jacalyn and Jill shared a room. They envied Bev's new furnishings. "I will buy you girls new furniture as soon as I possible can,"

Mom informed them. Merv was to have a private room at the end of the hall. However he was willing to give it up for a cousin who moved from the farm for eleven months. He slept in his soldier brother's room directly under his new room. Evie was patiently waiting for this space for an office. Her Shaklee business was growing in spite of her construction work.

It was time to visit the banker again. "Who shall I list as the foreman of this job he asked?"

Ray said, "I guess we would have to say Eldo, as I was away at work so much and Evie ordered all the materials."

The banker could not believe that all remodeling was done for less than ten thousand dollars. He commended them and added,"It would have cost some folk twice that much. So often folks start a project and wait ten years to finish it." The bank had inspected the job the day before, and the project met the banker's approval.

Carpeting had not been completed when they applied for re-financing. The carpet sales were watched with an eagle eye. One by one the floors, halls, and stairway were carpeted. The walls were all painted. Evie knew as time and money afforded the walls would be papered. How they appreciated the large bath, the five closets and large storage space above the stairway. The house from the outside looked like a new home. The outside was coated with a light tan stucco, and the trim was of shiny brown paint. They had about twenty two thousand dollars in the home at this time. Evie knew the refinishing of the basement would be the next project, but first she must build her Shaklee business. Besides, she would feel unfulfilled without a remodeling job to look forward to.

30
New Territory

Evie's neighbor, Ruth Eide, worked for NorthWest Airlines. She brought Evie an application to work nights. Family finances were tight, and Evie was in search of possibilities. She had no idea when she would sleep during the day with a three year old, but carefully filled out the application.

The night before she submitted it to the airlines her brother-in-law, Bob, called and spent an hour talking about a miracle cleaner he was now selling. He wanted to come over the next morning. Evie thought, "I don't know how you can possibly do all that with one cleaner," but consented to try it.

She knew that her sister Pearl had four small children and that Bob was out of work. Bob demonstrated Basic H and Evie became excited about it. She was now allergic to every detergent on the market. Rubber gloves were not always convenient to use. She had swollen, peeling hands and could no longer wear her wedding ring. There was no doubt she was married, with all the patter of little feet. At last she found something that was kind to her hands, that left no ring in the bathtub, and could be safely used to wash the oily sprays from the fruits and vegetables. Ray washed his car, and Evie her nylons. The first eight people she made contact with were given a baby food bottle of Basic H. Eight people called and requested a bottle of Basic H. She had no intentions of selling the products when she gave out the samples. She only wanted to share what she enjoyed. She made a phone call, "Bob I have eight orders for Basic H.

"Can I sell this stuff?"

Bob invited her to a sales meeting, held in a Supervisor's home. Evie emptied every piggy bank in the house to get her first order of a case of Basic H. She also purchased the gallon size for her own use, having given half of her quart size away.

She forgot about wanting to work for the airlines. "I can have a business in our home," she convinced Ray. "And I can still manage my house-work." She continued selling to every likely prospect, and gradually tried the other sixty products then on the market, and introduced a new product when she delivered her second order. If a salesman, or a political campaigner came to her door, she demonstrated her cleaners, and usually sold that person a product. She put all her profits in a separate account and began building. The handicap of no car did not dampen her spirits. The first two weeks she sold enough to get a minimum bonus. The first month over three hundred dollars of products were delivered. With very limited time and without a car she received a larger bonus. At the first sales meeting she learned you could earn a leased car. She set her goal for that carrot. They had never owned a brand new car in their married lives.

"I am going to get a new car," she told her family. It was indelible on her mind. She was certain it would not be a smooth road. The routine of every day life took most of Evie's time. She was coordinator of evening and afternoon women's missions, a Sunday school teacher, and Deaconess at Minnehaha Baptist church. The latter being extremely time consuming at times. One week there were two large funerals of past leaders. The deaconesses provided meals after the funerals. They also called on the elderly in the church and had anniversary parties for those who were fortunate to have held on to their mates. There were birthday celebrations for the Seniors that were alone. They provided flowers for the hospitalized and were trusted to encourage the girls that needed counseling. Evie loved it all. The days could not be stretched for all she enjoyed doing. Working with PTA was also consuming time.

While the children were having lunch she may be typing a poem for a senior's afternoon party or last minute reading for the day. Dishes were done and she was off to pick up some poor soul that had to permanently park her car, because of bad eye-sight or slow reflexes. She recalled two dear souls that you had to allow an extra ten minutes to get their coat on and shuffle to the car. It was so rewarding to make their day by taking them to spend the afternoon with old friends, and reminisce of bygone days.

Evie continued to use every spare moment to introduce Shaklee Products. She gave all her inferior products to her neighbors. One lady came back with a gallon of shampoo and said if it is not good enough for you, it is not for me either. She ordered a gallon of Basic R for rugs and later became a distributor. Evie began offering the opportunity to all her best customers. It was not many months before the volume qualified her for an assistant Supervisory position.

During this same time Evie was helping with the addition on the house. Her biggest obstacle now was that Mervin was using the one downstairs room for a bedroom. That was to be her office. A cousin was using the other bedroom. During those months of waiting for the cousin to find an apartment, Evie's business continued to grow. She then moved Merv upstairs and was on her way. She maintained the three thousand volume and then rose to four thousand for the qualifying months for a Company car.

She met a new friend while taking Billy Graham's

writing course, that lived near by. "Jane, would you mind picking me up on your way home from work?" The dealer had called and said, "Your Shaklee car is in." Evie wanted to surprise the family, so she did not breathe a word to anyone else.

After the table was set, the dinner in the oven and a salad ready, the cook took off. The family was in the middle of dinner when she parked by the back door, and announced her *new baby*. "We wondered what happened to our waitress," Ray said as Evie burst in the back door with a grin like the cat that ate the canary.

"I walked in and signed for delivery, and they handed me the keys."

Evie was thrilled when the entire family could go for a ride. In August of that year, Evie and Ray qualified for their first free trip to California. The Shaklee Corporation offered their plane fare or the cash in that amount.

"Let's take the cash and with our new car we can drive to California and take the entire family." Bev was now married and Morrie was in the service. Jacalyn had her driving permit. Merv and Jill were passengers with their back seat driver's license.

The first stop was a weekend with Aunt Till. Cousin Ethel had now aged her way out of the clothing store. Having never planned on getting old she failed to save for this time in her life. She moved back with her Mother in Stanley, North Dakota and was quite unsuccessful at "bringing mother up." Having lived separately for years, the merge was rather difficult to say the least. The Millers survived for one day, and then just had to get on with their trip. They traveled all night and had breakfast in the National forest in Montana. The next destination was Uncle Howard and Aunt Joy's. They were weary of traveling, but the next morning they were on their way to see the ocean. The next stop was to visit Aunt Irene and Uncle Earl and Uncle Chuck and Aunt Elvira. The children stayed with their cousins, while Evie and Ray continued their trip to the convention. Arriving at Doris Day's Hotel in Palo Alto, they were escorted to a beautiful room. Evie declared, "I only ordered one large bed and there are two." She soon discovered that she could not walk through a mirrored wall. "I feel like Cinderella," she repeated several times during the three day stay. "I keep thinking the clock will strike twelve any minute." New Supervisors were honored and Evie decided it was worth all the effort and sales. She and Ray had always looked forward to extending their short honeymoon. Now nearly twenty years later, they celebrated like a royal family. The final night was a banquet fit for a king. As with all good things, that happy weekend was not eternal.

Once more they joined with their family and picked figs, and fruit from Uncle Chuck's trees. It was soon time to journey home and prepare to earn another trip. They did just that for twenty-four more free trips. They were in New York, New Orleans, Disneyland, Canada and several other cities. Last but not least was a trip to Kansas City. Like Dorothy of Oz, Evie still says, "I want to go back to Kansas."

Their first Supervisory Group was developed in Hibbing. Shortly after, a group in Bloomington sprung up. The next was a second level in Bemidji. Evie treasured the friendships that were cultivated. She limited her out-of-town trips to one per month. The car, equipped with extra heavy shocks, was loaded with products and usually returned home empty. She met the area leaders for a dinner at Bridgeman's and a full display was set up. The merits of the products were presented along with the plan for company growth, and she was on her way home about ten-thirty. She arrived back home in the wee hours of the morning in time to help her children prepare for school. After a twenty hour day it was time to crawl between the sheets. Blessed quietness! However, it was usually her biggest day for orders that month. Evie would repeat what her mother Elizabeth often questioned, "Is there no rest for the wicked?"

Evie's greatest challenge was to speak at sales

meetings. She had taken an evening course in public speaking a few years back, and wasn't sure why. How she loved to write speeches and deliver them. Every year she was asked to speak at an area meeting. It was held at the University in Bemidji. Two months of her *spare time* were spent on those speeches.

They rented two large rooms at the Paul Bunyan Motel in Bemidji, and took the entire family. The daughters sang and Evie introduced her first grandchild Jonathan as a future Coordinator. He sported a red white and blue shirt that said Vote Shaklee, as did all the family shirts. It was a year for Presidential election.

The family was always afraid to stop for gas. Evie would demonstrate how to use Basic H on a wind shield, in the radiator, and for washing cars. "Mom are you going to demonstrate again?" was like a broken record. The answer returned in the form of another question. "Do you kids want to go to college, and did you enjoy the trip to California?"

Early in the business Evie went to Kentucky to help a friend, Ethel Ross, get started in Shaklee. Morrie was then stationed in Kentucky. She went back with him and returned on her first commercial plane trip. Her friend visited farms daily in her milk testing job. Evie traveled along with Ethel. They only bought a few gallons of gas at a time in order to introduce products to several stations. Evie sold a quart at the first three stops. They visited a world famous Gamble farm. She demonstrated to the office manager in the barn, while Ethel was testing milk. Before they departed Evie had a bon a fide order for one gallon of Basic H, to wash cows' bags, calf stations, and for cleaning windows. The sale of cleaners to the Proctor and Gamble Farm would make a humble person proud! The farm was visited by world travelers and was open every day. Later Evie shipped many five gallon pails to her new distributor for that customer.

Some of the largest companies offered Doctor Shaklee the moon for the formula for Basic H. He said, "You will never discover it in two thousand years."

A custodian and distributor in Wausau, Wisconsin worked at the court house. He sold them Basic H. A few drops of Basic H in water left the windows and doors spotless. One day a man broke his nose trying to walk through the glass doors. The custodian labeled the doors, from that day on. Evie was thrilled to see this news in the Shaklee Survey and published in their local paper. She was off on a career that she loved.

31
Why Worry

"It is hard to believe that we have two teenagers," Ray said as they waited for his two eldest to return from their very first night out with the family car. Morrie now possessed his driver's license. The State Fair was in full swing and what better place could he try out his wings.

"Do you want to take your friend Gail?" he asked Bev. Morrie also asked a friend to join them, and so the proud foursome took off.

"I am going to bed," Ray informed Evie, as he closed the daily paper. "Those kids are trustworthy, and smart enough to take care of themselves," he added with a note of *hoping so*, while marching up the open stairs. Evie slowly prepared for bed, stopping to listen at every car going by. She wrestled with her pillow as she observed that the father was sound asleep. The clock ticked slowly as Evie wondered if she would always be this anxious with four more of her offspring to be out their first night with a car. Her heart was finally quieted when she uttered a prayer for the safety of the precious cargo in the old family car. A motto from her childhood home stood out in her mind, "Why worry when you can pray?" It was nearly midnight when Mother heard the door to the one car garage close.

She met them at the door, " Mom, we got lost on the way home," they both explained at once. Evie was so thankful to have them home safely and quietly crept back beside her sleeping bed partner. She vowed she would at least leave half the worrying to him in the future.

Morrie was seven years old when his school friend invited him for a ride with his big brother, a pilot. He soared over the Lahrman farm, as the young pilot tipped the wing of the plane. The plane circled several times as the proud parents and sisters gazed and waved. Morrie would never be the same. "I want to be a missionary pilot," he reminded the family often.

Putting feet to his desires he went directly to work from school, and rose early to deliver the morning *Tribune*, which provided the funds to begin his ground training. He ate five whole wheat pancakes stuffed with wheat germ, powdered milk, and soy flour, before leaving for school and then walked to his job. The end result was he began looking like a bean pole and "light for his flight". Going to the Anoka airport for flight training and Flying Cloud for his ground training kept him extremely busy in the hours he was not in school or working. His job with his father at both the Twin City Rock Crystal Shop, delivering The Star and Tribune, and also as custodian of the church, paid for the lessons.

The day arrived for his solo flight. He donned a new shirt for the special occasion. Evie kept very busy the hour he was to be soloing. "To think I worried about you the first night out with the car!" she said at the breakfast table. Mileage was building fast on the car as well. Evie had long forgotten worrying about them coming home with the car.

Mom had to hear every detail of the solo flight. "They cut off the tail of my new shirt, and it is on display in the hanger." The evening scene was back at the airport. One by one every member of the family was escorted to the heavens by one proud pilot. "I'll be so careful, if you will go up with me Mom," he pleaded. Having never been beyond the one story farm home in the Valley or the hay mow, Evie was reluctant to go with a pilot with such few flying hours recorded in his log book. She must not dampen his enthusiasm or reveal her fears, she thought to herself as she boarded the Cesna. The sky and wind velocity were perfect to take a forty-one year old Mother on her first private plane ride. She soon tossed all fear on a cloud, and thought of Morrie as a young lad flying over the Lahrmann farm. The landing was perfect, and a proud mother stepped from the plane, to add a new chapter to her life.

Maintaining the home for the family of seven, washing, baking, and cleaning endlessly, the months flew by. Soon the first high school graduate was marching along with eight hundred other Roosevelt High students. In the fall Morrie started college. He was conscious of the possibility of being drafted for the Vietnam War. His old buddies were joining and without consulting his Veteran father, Morrie enlisted. When departure day arrived Evie and Ray were heart sick. Memories surfaced of long separations and World War II.

To his disappointment, he could not be a pilot without a degree, but trained for Crew Chief on a helicopter for two years. He was well trained to copilot the copter, and if circumstances necessitated, pilot the helicopter. He visited home once or twice a year before the day to leave for Vietnam. Ray said good-bye as he left for work. The children likewise, as they left for school. Morrie packed many of his personal things away, and spent part of the day so very quiet, secretly wondering if he would ever return to his treasured family and personal things. "Some of you will return with your dog-tag in your mouth," the tough old Sarg informed them in a very calloused way. It re-echoed in his thoughts as he placed his pictures, and civilian clothes in a box in the storage space.

The morning hours passed slowly. Evie called Ray at work, "Ray aren't you going to the airport with me?"

"No! I really don't care to. Aren't the kids going with you?"

"They will not be home from school in time," Evie said. Evie knew her husband well and was aware of the reason he could not bear to see his son embark to the unknowns. Visions of the two years in the South Pacific haunted his very being. As he thought of Evie going alone to say good-bye, Ray responded to her plea, "Please go with me." Morrie loaded his duffel bag, took one more look around the house and was off to pick up his Dad.

The plane was loading. good-byes were final and Morrie walked to the plane, never once looking back. Evie and Ray hurried home to unleash their heartache, each in their own way; knowing that tears are a method of washing the soul.

For the next thirteen months, letters and tapes were sent across the waters again. Evie buried herself in building her business. Morrie left his car for her to use. She made trips to Bemidji, Hibbing and other out of town places. Her goal was having a company car by the time Morrie returned for his car. (Mission accomplished.)

It was nearing the date of the birthday of Evie's first born, now in Vietnam, in 1968. Evie made cookies, angel food cake, and other goodies. She placed a package of frosting on the bottom of the parcel. Miracle of miracles, it arrived via air mail on the late afternoon of May twenty second. Morrie invited his close buddies to share the loot. They managed to get some ice cream from a friend on KP, and ate the cake before exploring further into the box. " Look what I found, a jar of frosting!" the birthday kid shouted in dismay. There was only one way to put the frosting on top of the cake. Selected members of the third company of the seventeenth Air Cavlier enjoyed a taste of home. "Like cleaning out the frosting pan," Specialist Five Morris A. Miller said as he licked the last spoonful. It had been a hard day and they were off to bed, dreaming of the day they would watch Mom bake the cake. They applied the medicated cream on the sores around their belt line. Evie was beginning to wonder if they ate that cream that Morrie had requested so often. Evie related how popular her medicated cream was at every sales meeting. Morrie shared it with every buddy. After all, it was *free!*

The party truly had ended for that very night—just a few hours after helping Morrie celebrate his 21st birthday—three of of the party were killed defending the Fort. They died in the same bunker in which Morrie had been on duty the night before. It would not be the first time Morrie escaped by the luck-of-the-draw!

On July 31, 1968, Morrie's flight had just returned from their day mission, but Morrie's day was not over. He had agreed to do extra-duty so his friend Steve could go on R & R (Rest and Relaxation). The helicopter had been fueled and loaded with ammunition for the rare night mission. Shortly after the pilot had started the engine, Morrie noticed someone with a flight helmet and machine gun running across the ramp toward his helicopter—it was Steve.

Officially, SP5 Steven Morris Hastings, CAPT. Williams (Command Pilot), and two others have been missing-in-action since August 1, 1968.

The thirteen months did pass and the soldier was at last on his way home. The family back home met every plane from San Francisco the day he was to arrive. Soldier after soldier arrived but no son or brother. They inquired about flight schedule for the next day. The answer was, "It will be in at five a.m." Evie and Ray thought it best to stay home, in the event their son should call. It was about five thirty when the five children arrived home. After the initial greetings, Bev was at the piano once again, with four sisters and brothers, singing old hymns. Evie and Ray listened to the most wonderful blend of five voices they had ever heard.

Evie killed the fatted calf. (She bought the best steaks available.) Every cookie jar was filled to the brim. Fresh bread was ready for him to sink his teeth into. "Aren't you going to eat steak?" Mom said as her soldier passed the platter by.

"No, I am really not hungry for meat," he said. After many days of this, he confessed he heard of people eating baby rats and it turned his stomach against meat. The fatted calf faced rejection. Many other memories spoiled his appetite.

Coming home was so exciting that sleeping was impossible on the plane and at the airport waiting for the later flight. It had been days of no sleep. He finally settled down to a long summer nap. Evie had to caution the family, "Don't wake up the soldier!"

Morrie had made every arrangement to complete his dream of being a pilot. Within one month he was on his way to Oklahoma to a flight school.

Mother and Father were reminded of how little time you have to spend with your children before they literally try their wings. He not only completed his instrument training but following graduation he married and made his home in that warm state. Little did his parents realize how final the good-bye would be the day he left for Basic Training. Many times Evie caught herself wishing she could turn back the reel and watch her children playing with the little red wagon and the kittens.

32
Changes In The Nest

Life did go on during Morrie's three years in the Army much to a Mother's surprise. Bev announced her engagement. It was not easy for the household to give her up with Morrie in Vietnam. Ray and Evie's nest was truly in for changes. Child rearing days were disappearing all too swiftly. The wedding was taped and pictures sent to big brother.

Two years later, shortly after Morrie's discharge, he was about to become an uncle. Evie did not care to know when her daughter delivered. "Please don't tell me, until it is all over," she told them. After all, her memories of the delivery room were quite fresh. It was September 8, 1969 at five in the morning. Morrie hopped out of bed to answer the phone. He burst into tears. No one would have guessed how he worried about his sister facing child birth. The entire family breathed a sigh of relief. Little Jonathan had no idea the anxiety at delivery time or the joy he would bring to the big family during his childhood. He was the center of attraction at every family gathering. The grandparents were now forty-five and forty-seven years young. In a few years Jonathan had to share the limelight with his sister Julia, and cousins Lance and

Michon.

When Jacalyn was sixteen she spent her summers working at Trout Lake Bible Camp. Special attractions were the young males that also worked there. Her parents were very concerned about the choices the offspring would make in seeking life partners. In the process of elimination, Jacalyn invited a fine young gentlemen to her sister's apartment to meet at a family dinner. Mother and Dad were very impressed. Both of the young people loved music and singing. They tried out for the Youth For Christ Choir.

One day Jacalyn's phone rang while she was in school. "Is Jacalyn there?"

"No, she should be home in a half hour," Evie replied.

"This is the Choir Director. Please tell her I called."

"Oh! did she make it?"

"Now wouldn't a mother like to know. I want to be the one to tell her," he continued.

As proud parents you can believe, they attended every concert that fit in their already filled schedule. Much to the parent's dismay, they were informed that Jacalyn and Dan had broken off their close friendship. It appeared that every girl in the choir had their cap set for Dan. It was natural for him to be friendly to all. Jacalyn allowed six weeks for him to make a serious decision. Evie suffered through the ordeal and prayed for divine guidance for the young singers. Within a few years, preparations were being made for six hundred guests at the wedding and reception of Dan and Jacie.

Yes there were changes in the old nest at Thirty Eight Twenty. Jill cried as though her heart would break, while restlessly parading around, as she waited for the wedding march to begin. Losing her last sister at home was a difficult adjustment. There was even a spare room now for all the relatives and friends.

Five weeks after the birth of the first grandchild,

Evie held a sales meeting at Wadena, Minnesota. She visited with a few relatives at the same time. It was always a must to go visit Aunt Maggie. Aunt Maggie now lived alone with all her memories, on second floor of the Humphrey Manor.

"What a switch for you to be living in town," Evie remarked as her mind reversed back to the tar paper covered home on a hill in the valley. Evie delighted in making Auntie laugh. Her memory was still sharp, though her earthly house was showing signs of deterioration.

"Remember the time I slept in the upstairs, and you were sure I would fall over the unprotected stairway, while sleep walking?" Aunt Maggie laughed her old familiar way and traveled down memory lane, as she made a pot of coffee and placed cookies on a plate.

Evie had a few new monologues that she had written for special occasions. "You have to pretend I am in an old ragged housecoat with big curlers in my hair." She put as much feeling in the delivery as though she had a large audience. It was worth it all. Aunt Maggie laughed until her side ached.

"How can you ever think of such crazy things and how can you remember all that?" she questioned when Evie completed her Christmas drama.

Evie glanced at the clock, reminding herself that she had many more stops to make, and the day was far spent. With a fairly new Shaklee car she did not anticipate a delay over the weekend. She was soon aware that a new car can cause problems. The repair shop could not get a part until Monday. Evie had all kinds of time to visit, but no wheels to carry her over her childhood trails. It was late on Monday evening when she arrived home with her family.

The first announcement was, "Morrie and Diane have decided to get married, and we have to be ready to leave by tomorrow afternoon." Evie's mind raced through the projects she had to catch up on. The washing machine was activated for most of the night. Sleep forsook her fitful eye. She would crawl in beside her sleeping giant and attempt to catch a wink.

"I can't understand how you can shut things off and sleep," was part of the breakfast conversation. Morrie returned after three years from the service to discover most of his old buddies married, and things were not the same. Having met the only single girl in his Flight Instruction Class, he was soon bringing her home to meet his lowly family. She found a good job and remained in Minnesota. Morrie was now a flight instructor at the University.

Diane had gone home earlier to make preparations for the big day. The wedding would be in Oklahoma. The Millers traveled all night and the next forenoon, arriving in time to dress and attend the evening wedding. Bev, the new Mommy, and her six week old baby arrived by plane and joined the family for the return trip. The wedding was in a small church with a cousin of the bride performing the marriage ceremony. It was as beautiful as though it had been planned for months. The following day the long trek home was in progress. "It is my turn to hold the baby," was the main theme. Bev, Jacie, Merv, Jill, the new Grandparents and baby Jonathan were the passengers in the red Buick, the second car that Evie had earned through Shaklee. It was a leased car, and her sales volume of five thousand per month had to be maintained or she would end up with the rental. Evie was determined not to allow the latter. It was always in the back of her mind, and that prompted her interest in sales.

Morrie had left for the service at the age of eighteen. At twenty-one he was home a very short time and left for the flight school. It would have been a sad trip home had the newly weds not planned to live in the city area. This eased the pain of losing their eldest son. "Life must go on."

"We were pretty young when we had to try our wings," Ray reminded Evie. "I left home at fifteen to live with Aunt Anna and go to high school." Evie admitted she left home to seek her fortune much too early, but with the large Branstner family and the need for clothing and dental work she faced reality, sometimes very much alone.

Merv was fifteen when he announced he wanted to be in the Youth For Christ band. "They need a trombonist, Mom."

"You don't have a trombone," his mother reminded him. I will earn half of the cost of one, if you and Dad will help me buy one," he added in his most confident voice and body language. And so it came to pass, two or three times a week Pa and Ma were in heavy traffic with a car full of young people and instruments rushing to a rehearsal or a concert. (Usually without time to eat supper.)

By the time Merv reached his sixteenth birthday he was able to drive the old Volkswagon. His friends in the Choir were all older by a year or two but were not trusted with the car. Sixteen year old Merv was elected the cabbie night after night. The body of the vehicle was in sad shape. However, it had a new motor. It had carried Jacie to and from Anoka Tech without failure. Locking the keys in the car necessitated an SOS to Father. It was very few times that the old Volkswagon let her down. Now with a wing and a prayer Merv traveled cross country and city roads, through ice and snow with a load of bubbling youth.

Though three had flown the coop, life did not come to a complete stand still, with only a sixteen year old son and his baby sister home. Evie hired Bev to work in her office while Grandma took care of her first grandson in the forenoon, granting Bev the privilege of closing shop and joining them for lunch. Speaking engagements, church, and PTA work kept things lively. Ray was working full-time at his own glass cutting business, plus his Stockade work with boys. However life continued on. There was a supper served at five thirty almost as sure as there would be four seasons.

33
The Empty Nest

Mervin was now a teenager and kept everyone busy trying to keep up with him. Often Merv would dash in the back door and inform his Mother, "I have to be on my way to a concert in fifteen minutes." It took years of practice to prepare a balanced diet in ten minutes. There was never a dull moment having a member of the family in Sounds Of Life, the musical group of Youth for Christ. Between bites Merv continued to catch Mom up on current events in his exciting life. "You should have heard us while recording, Mom. I can hardly wait for the record to come out! How many records do you want?"

Jacie had been with Sounds Of Life the year before. After returning from a two thousand mile tour with the group, her response was, "I wish the trip was just beginning," and then added, "It was the most rewarding two weeks of my life."

Earlier Merv was informed that Y.F.C. needed two brass players. It was the topic of conversation at every meal. "I will pay half on a trombone if you will pay the other half." How could any red blooded Father say no to that bargain? Merv had methodically tucked away his hard-earned money. Delivering The Minneapolis Star was his way of creating the savings. There was no peace on earth until the purchase was made

Evie's mind went back to the day Merv's junior high school band director called and wondered why Merv had quit the band three weeks earlier. When Mother confronted him on the subject he said, "It was so dull."

Evie put on her "sale's lady cap" and said, "I would love to exchange places with you. I would have cherished the opportunity to become bored." She continued, using every ounce of her sales experience, "It will soon be exciting. Take advantage of every privilege you have. I loved music and I would have welcomed music lessons on any instrument."

Merv consented to try again. How happy both Mother and son were that Merv learned the art of persevering. And now being part of the band in a recording studio, and having his picture on the jacket of a record, was the most exciting thing he could think about.

Music was not his sole interest, however. He came home talking about his latest girl friend quite often. One day he decided the very nicest girl he knew was Lesa. "Well, tomorrow it will be someone else," Evie said under her breath. This time it was for real. For two years Lesa was the theme of Merv's song. He played guitar and sang at Coffee houses at least once a week, and his latest heart throb usually joined him.

The house next door to the Miller home was rented after a neighbor lady passed away. The house was now a house of ill repute. Neighbors were up in arms about what was going on in the neighborhood. During the early morning hours there were noisy celebrations in the back yard. But no one knew how to solve the problem.

Evie called the court house and secured the name of the owner of the property. "The folks in this block are very unhappy about what is going on in our block."

The owner of the house replied, "So am I, and the only way I can persuade them to move is to sell the property, they have not paid rent for three months. Do you want to buy it?" Evie did not plan to go into real estate, having just purchased a commercial building for the glass shop.

"Well, let me ask my husband," she said, thinking she better be on the safe side. After Ray had his tummy full and had time to read the sports page, Evie made a soft approach. She related every word of the telephone conversation.

"The only way we can get new neighbors, is to buy the house." She had covered the price and the arrangements with the seller. I can buy it with very little down and take over the mortgage that is now on the house.

"I would not have any time to help clean or improve that house," Ray stated, "but if you can swing it and want to take the responsibility of the project, go ahead and buy it." Evie was soon up to her elbows in dirty water cleaning and remodeling that house.

She hired a neighbor lady to help wash down walls. They removed paint down to the bare wood in the bathroom, painted and re-papered every room in the house. New carpeting was laid in two bedrooms and the long living room. Six layers of linoleum were torn from the kitchen floor and a new covering installed. Cabinets were taken from the wall to the back yard to be scrubbed sunned and painted. It was now a doll house.

Merv and Lesa often checked on the progress. Lesa beamed and thought it would make a wonderful first home. Evie rented it for one year to the carpenter that helped with the project.

"Mom, we set our wedding date, and I have saved two thousand dollars to pay down on the house next door, are you ready to sell it?" There was nothing like picking your neighbors.

"Do you think Lesa will want to live next to her mother-in-law?" Evie asked. Evie wondered why she had felt so strongly about buying that house when she had been advised against it by two sons-in-law.

The wedding date was set and soon new neighbors moved in next door. Merv and Lisa moved into a house instead of an apartment. The value of homes increased and the equity from that home, made a sizable down payment on a larger home for Merv and Lisa a few years later. The new owners also made improvements.

It was the first year that Ray and Evie were once again alone in the big house. Though extremely busy during the years, Evie was building her business, and Ray launched out on being a self-employed glass cutter.

Yes, life had been filled with adjustments. One by one the children had tried their wings. Jill, the youngest, prepared for Bethel College. "I am going to room with one of my favorite friends," she said. Packing the car and helping her settle in was not traumatic. Mom and Dad knew she would be home on weekends, and only a phone call away. Evie decided she was going to bury herself in her business, to help pay tuition and adjust to an empty nest.

It was a Friday evening, Evie was sleeping when the phone rang. "Jill why are you calling so late?" Evie asked, though only half awake.

"I must talk to you and Dad. I have been getting calls from Europe to go and work as a Nanny." She continued to explain that her friend, Dawn, had recommended her.

"Mom, can I postpone college? I think it would be a wonderful experience, and I will be close to Dawn." Dawn had been Jill's bosom friend since childhood. The coldest day in February little Dawn and her family moved just one door away. The family was huddled in the car trying to keep warm until their furniture was moved in the house. Evie had gone downtown that morning but not before making a large kettle of soup for lunch. When Evie returned, Ray was dishing up the soup for the new neighbors. It was a permanent bonding for the three year old girls. Dawn was the beginning of Jill's adventure to far off places.

Needless to say, by the time the conversation was over, Evie was very wide awake. Even her sales experience had not allowed her to get to first base in discouraging this brainstorm.

"We will have to think about that. This is so sudden." Evie tossed all night, thinking of all the things that could happen to an eighteen year old. Just taking the trip and changing airplanes in New York would be a wild experience in itself. What would it be like living in the heart of Brussels with an English mother, and a Belgium father that spoke three different languages? She wondered how Jill would adjust.

"When the novelty wears off, she will get so homesick," she reiterated to her sleepy bed partner. What could a Mother say? She finally fell asleep like a top that spun all night. Jill came home for the weekend to plead her case.

When Christmas was history, the packing began, and by February Jill was speeding on her way to far off places, leaving her college and distraught mother behind.

The decision to live in Europe was a blessing in disguise. Jill grew into womanhood during her stay. The parent's trip to Europe was a highlight of that year. The travelers returned to their nest with new experiences that enriched their lives.

Evie was experiencing kidney infections and knowing that in spite of a healthful diet, her health seemed to be deteriorating. She had extreme allergic reactions to almost everything. Never having these problems before, she was completely baffled. After going to doctors, and specialists, trying one prescription after another, she finally called a chiropractor, Dr. Ameli. On the first appointment, he discovered her blood pressure was dangerously low. Blood tests were taken, a strict diet recommended. She would not have considered such a doctor,until she recalled two Shaklee distributors that had testimonials of successful treatment for asthma and help to over come alcohol and also discovering that medications only increased her problems. She was confined to her home for the entire fall.

Recovering was a slow process, but by Christmas she was able to spend it with her family at their daughters Bev's.

Evie's health improved when on strict diets. She was first told to go on a cleansing diet that reduced the severe allergies.

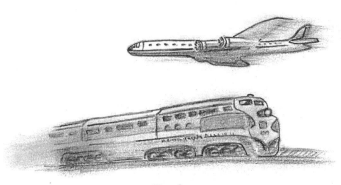

34
Travels Abroad

A letter arrived that was post marked from Brussels. The lines were filled with acute loneliness.

Dear Mom and Dad,

I miss you all so much. Could you make plans to visit Europe and stop off to see me?

When the invitation comes from your child rather than a travel agency, it seems so much more personal. Jill had been away for nearly six months. Neither Mother nor Father had even dreamed of going to Europe, but they were soon checking with Triple A Travel Agency and making preparations for their departure.

It had been a great learning experience for the eighteen year old *au pair* or governess. Her sisters had asked her, "Are you happy there?"

Her written reply was, "I didn't come in search of happiness. I came to grow up and learn. I have had more happiness in my short life than most people have in a life time."

The parallels of this trip and their journey through life were often drawn. First they had to make the decision as to when and where they were going.

"It will perhaps be the only trip we will take overseas," Ray stated.

Evie nodded in agreement. "So we must make the most of it."

"I have always wanted to see Scotland and seeing Holland is a must. It would be so thrilling to see the Corrie Ten Boom Clock Shop, "the Hiding Place." While Jill was attending Minnehaha Academy, she heard Corrie Ten Boom speak and bought her book. "Mom you just have to read *The Hiding Place*," Jill said as she tagged Evie from room to room, while reading portions of the book. Later the entire family went to a packed, large old church to hear the eighty year old saint speak.

The crowd endured the preliminaries and finally, young people from the balcony yelled, "On with Corrie! Where is Corrie?" Corrie was then ushered in. There was hush over the entire audience, and the extra policemen and firemen were idle. Corrie held the crowd spellbound. She told the story of hiding the Jewish people and the death of her sister and father in prison camp, and her miraculous escape, during World War II.

At the close of her speech, the crowd rose to their feet and cheered as Corrie pointed toward Heaven to give Jesus the glory. Later the entire family went to see the movie *The Hiding Place* and the movie of Corrie's eightieth birthday. They also read several other books by Corrie. She became one of the most influential people in Evie's life, and the desire to see her home was undying.

They landed in Prestwick, Scotland and then took a train to see the rolling countryside in Great Britain. They saw the palace in London, but missed seeing the Queen. They left their calling card and went on to catch the last ferry of the day to cross the English Channel. "We should try to call Jill to let her know when to meet us," Ray reminded Evie. The call was difficult to say the least. Trying to speak to someone that could barely understand English and speak it still less, made it impossible to make contact.

The train system was wonderful except, that very day, the chefs chose to go on strike. There were no meals served. By the time they reached the ferry the foreigners were famished. Food was plentiful on the Ferry. Evie made the mistake of drinking milk on a empty stomach. That fatal step led to seasickness for the remainder of the night.

It was early in the morning. Throngs of people were rushing to work in the stations. "They remind me of a herd of cattle rushing to the pasture". You just did not get in their path. The bathrooms in the station did not have doors. Evie blushed as she hurried past the men's room. She tried three phones that were out of order. The one phone that was working had a line of people several feet long, and the floor was wet from flooding bathrooms. "For Dear Ma Bell," Evie gasped, as she made one final attempt to call Jill.

"You're here! I will be right down to the station," Jill shouted.

"I never saw you with a beard before," Evie said as she stroked Al's chin while waiting for Jill at the Central Station. The meeting was mutually appreciated. How wonderful could familiar faces be?

A five-course French dinner had been planned for them and other American guests the first evening. Evie and Ray met the Depudyt family and had their first bowl of leek soup, before going to bed for the afternoon. Evie awoke so sick from the long trip and food on the ferry. She was unable to join the dinner party. Nor could she attend the family on a trip to Isper for a weekend at an expensive Hotel owned by the host's brother.

The next evening they were invited to the home of an American family that Jill's friend Dawn was working for.

"I think I feel well enough to go sightseeing. Let's visit Old Brussels," Evie ventured, after eating—and retaining—her Sunday dinner.

280 Life's Rugged Beauty

They visited The Grande Place, the city square, the trade Gild halls, a fifteenth century hotel with a three hundred sixty foot tower and the King's House, all in one afternoon.

They overheard an American conversation. It sounded heavenly.

"Where are you from?" was the question that followed closely after the introduction. A middle-aged man and his teenage daughter were in Brussells for their third year. Jill and her new friend were soon walking together as friends. The father was the afternoon guide. They were from St. Paul, Minnesota. Just across the Ford Plant bridge from the Miller home. A mouth watering Belgium Waffle hit the spot, and later a Pizza Place was just as great.

"Let's go to the International Baptist Church," Jill suggested.

Soon they were on the metro, and then they walked and walked before admitting they were lost. A kind man and his wife that spoke in broken English led them to the door of the church. It was like an oasis in the desert to hear a puppet show in English and to sing the familiar hymns. A kind American family took them back to their home away from home.

Monday, June eleventh found Ray, Evie and Jill riding the Metro to a station to catch a train to Brugge, the lace center of the world. Family and friends had requests to bring them doilies and gifts from this famous place. The day was filled and it was time to return to their home.

The following day they departed for Paris at six, arriving in Paris at ten where they remained for two days. Wanting a flexible schedule, no pre-arrangements were made for lodging. It was a walk by faith. While shopping around they were told by other travelers that a president from South America was visiting Paris and the hotels were booked to capacity. Checking out the tourist information,they were directed to the last room for three.

It was in the heart of the area they wanted to see. One man asked them, "How did you ever find a room without reservations?" I went to fourteen hotels to find a bed," he added. They visited the Eifil Tower before venturing to the fashion area where creations were designed. They should have allowed two years to see all the sights in Europe.

Mom awoke Jill on the seventh floor of Hotel Deloratoire and asked, "Do you know where are you Jill?"

Jill replied, "I am in Doo-Doo Ville." (*Do-do* was the term her French children used for a nap.) The following day they took a bus tour of Paris for about fifteen dollars per person, in American currency. After two days in Paris Evie asked, "Which way to Doo-Doo Ville?" They spent forty-five dollars on that nap and barely opened their eyes long enough to get a glimpse of the Eifel Tower.

Next they took the metro to a train station to board a train that would take them to Milan, Italy. By mistake they landed at the wrong station. Wandering around to get directions, they ran into an old friend from Minneapolis.

"What are you doing in Paris," was the question they fired at each other. The friend gave them tickets along with directions to the station that they should rush to in order to catch the train to Milan. Traveling at night was a great time-saver to stretch the three precious weeks.

Breathless, they sat down by a famous French doctor. They played charades and had free French lessons for the next two hours, and did not get to bed very early. Jill was invited to spend a weekend with the doctor's family.

They did reach Milan. Needless to say it was not of special interest, and they were soon on their way through the Alps. " I left my camera on that last train," Jill said in horror.

"That camera had our very best shots," Evie said. They reported the loss, and Ray was sure they were wasting their time. Jill's camera arrived in Belgium before she did, with pictures intact.

First Class Eurorail passengers could get on and off any time they pleased. The town of Basil looked so inviting. So the trio hopped off and found the last two beds in a quaint hotel with breakfast included in the price.

It was Ray's birthday. The hotel was so clean and perfect. Traveling light with one change of clothes, Evie washed clothes out each night before retiring. They dined at sidewalk cafes and drank in the scenery in a land where no one seemed to know the meaning of hurry. Having made plans to visit a family in Sweden, and a niece in Holland, they had to leave the most wonderful city of the entire trip. It was at an old Hotel in Meinz Germany, managed by the fourth generation that Ray enjoyed the black coffee served with a hot pitcher of milk, to dilute the coffee to your taste buds. Here in Hummel country, they looked high and low for Hummels, to no avail.

After a good night's rest Ray, Evie, and Jill were floating down the river for a five hour trip. It was not on a Sunday afternoon, nor in a canoe. They were on a large ship on the Rhine. The ship was packed with people from many places, including about thirty-five Japanese on the ship. Ray and Evie had to quietly bury their memories of encounters with the Japanese and enjoy the day. They landed at Koln and attended a service in the famous church of Cologne. It was cold and formal. Evie paused to thank God that life in His Son is abundant, and eternal life is free. They left the cold church for a hot sandwich at McDonalds.

"Does this taste good!" Jill was happy to have a taste of America.

They headed for Copenhagen, not realizing that weekend traffic was heavy.

There was no room on the first Class Coach, nor was there a bed to sleep on. Ray was separated from his companions for the night. They met some folks from Minnesota that gave them tips of good homes to stay at.

The lady phoned for a room for four, they had room for three, so she booked the rooms for the Millers. It was walking distance from the station and was priced at one hundred Krons per night. They went on two walking tours for the day (about ten miles). Walking along the canal where Hans Christian Anderson wrote his famous children's stories, *The Little Match Girl*, *Hansel and Gretel*, *The Ugly Duckling*, and other stories that are now translated in over eighty languages. Evie could hear Grandma Bessie reading these stories in a cracked, tired voice as she strained to see the words by the kerosene lamp.

Retracing their steps back to the square, they heard beautiful Danish Music. It was a Christian group telling the redemption story. They sat silently for one hour, understanding only a few words. Feeling the presence of the Holy Spirit, they silently worshiped in God's "open air cathedral" in the middle of the decadence they observed in that city.

At Fredrickshavn, Denmark there was only room for two people in room forty-one. Ray took a room on the fifth floor. "Now we can lay awake and talk," Jill told her Mom as she crawled into bed.

"Well what shall we talk about?"

"Let's plan my wedding."

Evie did her daily wash, as the entire wedding was planned. There was one catch, they had no idea who the groom would be! "Jill, talk about putting a cart before the horse," Evie said as she fell into bed.

Variety being the spice of life, the following day they took a ferry to Gottenberg, Sweden. "At least this time we have someone meeting us."

They had no idea what she looked like, but a young women that could speak English was there waiting and watching for a couple in their fifties with a teenage daughter.

"Are you and Miller?" Britta asked.

They were soon on their way by car to a Swedish home which was occupied by the same family for four generations. It was well preserved and beautifully furnished for the three grown children and their parents.

Britta was the sister, an old acquaintance of Erik Odingard. Erik was a salesman of cut crystal from Ray's shop. Britta's father had worked on Erik's father's farm in his youth. The Millers were introduced by Erik, via a letter.

The first evening, dinner guests included Erik's two sisters also living in Gottenberg. The best china, cut glass and linens were the setting for a delicious meal. The young people were interpreters for their parents. The following day found Evie and her hostess alone. Evie learned a few Swedish words. How very inconvenient to have a language barrier between two women.

The following day they took a boat all around the city, with Erik's sister as the guide. Quaint shops were visited before they toured the city. The next stop was at the home of Erik's sweet mother, and also to both of his sister's apartments and summer home. They drove by Erik's childhood farm home. Every stop was complete with sweets and breads and more sweets and breads.

"Wasn't it fun to see where Erik lived and to meet his Mother?" Ray and Evie agreed as they drifted off to sleep in anticipation of visiting glass factories (a must on the list) the next day.

To their chagrin, the glass factories were closed for three weeks in June. Everyone took their vacation simultaneously. They discovered one man at a factory, who was willing to demonstrate the art of glass making.

"Would you like to try blowing your own tumbler?" he asked the foreign couple. Evie was proud that her tumbler would be shipped to her along with the next shipment to New York. It was red hot when they departed, and would take hours to cool down. It is now proudly displayed as a vase, with other collector items.

Bidding their new friends good-bye was sad. "You

have treated us like a king, queen and princess and we are just everyday Americans. Please come to visit us one day." Dear Mrs. Nielson passed away a few months later. Several years later, Mr. Nielson and one son accepted the invitation.

The three-some were soon on their way to Amsterdam, Holland. A young woman was at the station, holding a sign "room for rent." They collected their baggage and accompanied her on public transportation, to her home.

"This is the city of Anne Frank," Jill said as she crawled in another strange bed on the fourth floor of an old flat. It was raining on Saturday morning and the line at the Secret Annex was a half block long, but it did not dampen the desire to see the place where Anne hid with her family and wrote her diary. They stood in silence as the scenes of World War II flooded their minds. Evie crawled the ladder to the attic and stood on the top rung in tears. They purchased Anne Frank's Diary before they left the famous place.

Evie's niece, Susan, (Chucks' oldest daughter) was now married to a man in the Air Force, that was stationed near Amsterdam. They picked their Auntie, Uncle, and cousin up by car. Susan now had three darling children. On Sunday they were on their way to find the Hiding Place. Younger Dutch people could speak English much more fluently than their elders. A lesson learned early on the trip was to seek out youth for directions.

"Do you know where *The Hiding Place* is?"

"No I never heard of it!" a young man answered. After all, World War II was history, before he was born. The Millers were not in the habit of giving up, so inquired of the older generation and were directed to "The Corrie Ten Boom Clock Shop." It looked like it did in the movie, except there was a "closed" sign hanging on the door as no stores were open on Sunday. They leaned closely to the window to capture a bit of the interior.

"I must see the back of the building," Evie said as

she began walking to the back. "This is the place the Jewish people were hid during the raids." They stood silently, in awe of the horrible things that transpired there. In their hearts they paid tribute to the dear saints that lived in peace at one time in the home behind the Clock Shop. "Now I can go home," Evie said. "I have fulfilled my heart's longing to visit Corrie's home."

It was soon time for Jill and her parents to part ways. They were on the train together and soon Evie and Ray would be getting off the train to board a ship to London. "I feel like getting off the train and going home with you," but Jill knew she must keep her one year commitment in Brussels. She quietly read *The Diary Of Anne Frank* until time for the painful separation. Many tears were shed, and Jill held up eight fingers out the window of the train as Mom and Dad got smaller and smaller. "Eight more months," she repeated. "Eight more months."

Evie and Ray were ready for their bed on the Ocean Liner for seven and one half hours. The motion of the ship soon lulled them to sleep. A knock on their door reminded them it was morning and they were near London. They hurriedly dressed to leave the ship. During their last train ride to Prestwick, Evie verbalized what Ray was thinking, "I wonder where we will find a bed tonight?"

By the time they gathered their baggage, her question was answered.

"There is a lovely Bed and Breakfast just a few blocks from here," a kind gentleman told them. What a dream place to stay! Flowers and shrubbery surrounded the two-story home. The home was elaborately furnished. The private bath and bedroom on second floor was in pink. The sheets were silky and pink. The kind lady directed them to a spotless unique restaurant. The table was covered with linens and the food was just as delectable.

"Let's take a walk. We've been sitting all day," Ray reminded Evie.

After returning to the home, they were taken into

the dining room to a table set for tea. Breakfast was served the next morning. "We have time to shop, and we'd like to look for Hummels," Evie told the kind lady. She directed them to stores that sold the treasured items. "It is unbelievable after all our hunting, we find Hummels on our last shopping spree. The Lord knew we would not want to carry them over land and sea," Evie remarked.

Saying good-bye to the kind lady was like bidding an old friend farewell. They were just waiting to check their luggage at the airport for the final lap of their journey, when a voice over the loud speaker said, "Everyone leave the terminal at once!"

Having not yet checked the baggage, Ray and Evie grabbed it and joined everyone else that was rushing out. "How far should we go?" Ray asked.

"As far as you can get. A bomb has been planted near the terminal," the man replied. They walked with their arms filled with suitcases, across a busy highway. It took several hours for the equipment to arrive to move the bomb. It gave the Millers a chance to get acquainted with the pilot and have their picture taken together. He later came back to visit on the plane, with a trusty copilot and the plane on automatic pilot, they dialogued far over the Atlantic Ocean.

Missing their connection in Boston, the honeymooners were soon on another flight, flying First Class, the only seats that were available. Safely home with a heart of gratitude and weary bodies, they knelt by there *own bed* and thanked God for the safe trip back to America; the home of the brave and the free, their family—except one—and friends.

35
Anniversary

"Mom, what shall we do to celebrate your Fortieth Anniversary?" questioned Jacalyn.

"We do not want you to duplicate the party we had on our Twenty-Fifth. You can do that when we reach the Fifty mark," Ray and Evie insisted. "We have always wanted to take a trip east and visit Washington, D.C., and Evie wants to visit her Chase roots at Newburyport, Massachusetts," Ray said.

Jill and her husband, Mark, had been with Youth With A Mission for nearly one year in Cambridge, Ontario." It was not difficult to convince Mark to be their guide. They, too, were ready for a much needed vacation.

Evie and Ray were packed to leave on August 20, 1986 and were at the mission on the following day. By August 22, they, along with their two new passengers, were on their way to Niagara Falls and on to Danville, New York the first night.

Touring Gettysburg was a day to be remembered. An old gentleman, who had lived his entire life at Gettysburg was an excellent guide. Spending most of an afternoon reliving the battles and seeing where the shots bounced off brick buildings was a sobering walk across the pages of history.

"Where shall we eat?" was the question, after the ugly memories faded. The guide said, "The Dutch Cupboard" serves excellent food, home-made rolls, and dinner with all its trimmings.

"I would love to stay a week in this historic town," Evie said as she looked longingly at the quaint Bed and Breakfast accommodations. Stories of the Civil War days were of great interest to the visitors. Trying to crowd so many places in one trip, they left for Fredericksburg, and Washington DC.

"We must see Mount Vernon," they all agreed. How thrilling to see the work of Martha's hands displayed on tables, the hooks she hung her clothes on, and the guarded tomb. The slave's quarters reminded them how the freed slave families were all given a portion of land to make a living on their own. It was a gorgeous day to walk the paths of President George Washington and Martha.

They continued their stroll through the pages of history by pausing at the boxed seats of the Ford Theater where they relived the scene of the great Statesman and the spot that President Lincoln was shot. Leaving to follow across the street, they stood by the bedside and his blood-stained pillow, where he took his last breath. "Since I first read the story, I have wanted to visit this spot and pay my respects," Evie said soberly.

The Smithsonian Institute captured their attention until the foursome were famished. They always managed to find a remedy for that affliction.

Nearly a week was spent in the Capitol area. It took two days to obtain tickets to see the White house. How very exciting to walk the path of the great leaders. After knocking on President Reagan's door, it was most disappointing to be informed that he was vacationing in California. Evie did do the white glove check, to see if Nancy dusted before she left.

As they stood by the undying flame, in memory of

President John Kennedy, memories surfaced, as though it were yesterday.

Arriving during the change of guard at the tomb of the unknown soldier was not planned, but an added bonus. They stood in silence before the wall with the names of the brave boys from the Vietnam War. The lines again were long. There were many cameras clicking and tears shed. It was Labor Day and Ray and Evie stood thinking, "It is only God's mercy that spared their son's name from that list. Their hearts were torn for the families that stared long and silent at the wall.

Vacation days were slipping by, and it was time to head for the New Jersey Turnpike and on Newburyport, Massachusetts. "Why do you want to go visit the graves of your ancestors?" Jill questioned.

"I want to see the port where my family landed in Newbury. Your Grandma Elizabeth would have loved to be with us today." The library and other public buildings were visited and the oldest cemeteries in West Newbury pointed out. They visited the Moses Chase house that was built before 1736, the Joseph Chase home built in 1755, and Samuel Chase's house, built in 1743.

"We must go to the the Park River Researchers and find the book of *Seven Generations of Aquila and Thomas Chase*," Evie insisted. They purchased one of two books that were left of the 1983 printing. The first printing was in 1928. "How thrilling to walk the streets of my ancestor's early settlement," Evie beamed.

There were many buildings that supported that fact including, "The Chase Insurance Company". Evie just had to walk in and inquire if there were any of the Chase family present. "No! We bought the Chases out about thirty years ago," the man replied. "All that is left is the name."

Evie was reminded that, "A good name is better than great riches." After purchasing the book on the history of Newburyport, Evie read of one "skeleton" from a Chase closet who was arrested for picking peas on the

Sabbath. "I hope they don't make an issue of that, and pray my grandchildren never get wind of that story," she joked.

Scanning the telephone directories, they discovered a host of Chase names in the area. With limited time, they decided they must move on to Albany, New York for an expensive nights lodging and then for one last glimpse of Niagara Falls.

It was time for farewells after one night of rest back at the mission, and Evie and Ray were again on their way to visit families from Germany, now living in Flint. Fred Branstner was a cousin of Gus Branstner. Fred's sisters and relatives met the Minnesota guests, for the first time.

"We certainly learned a lot about my Grandpa's family," Evie said as they left for sister Mae's home in Laingsburg, Michigan.

Filled with memories, Evie was back in the house that she hadn't seen since she lived with baby Grace and Russell, while Ray was in the South Pacific. Mae and Gene's children were also grown, leaving the large country home rather empty. Grandchildren visited often to fill that void.

How busy the two sisters had been during child-rearing days, leaving little time to visit in each other's home.

Visiting Amish settlements was a highlight of the trip home. "What a way to celebrate our Anniversary, our forty years together," was all the happy but tired travelers could say, as they drove in their own backyard.

36
Give Me Fresh Air

In the late seventies Evie developed severe allergy problems. Dr. Ameli urged her to get out of the city area where she could take walks in country air. Having been house bound for months, Evie could hardly stand the four walls that confined her. A chain of events, though totally unplanned, seemed to set their destiny.

"Mom could you and Dad come over for dinner today?" the soft spoken voice was that of their daughter Jackie. A quiet meal was enjoyed, before the two little ones were prepared for bed.

"Dad we want you to see some property for sale. It has four and three quarters acres of land, with a wooded area."

"It is just going on the market on Monday and it will sell the day it is made public," Dan went on to tell them. "There is very little land in the suburban area with acreage." Dan and Jackie continued with their enthusiastic approach.

Ray and Dan were soon on their way to survey the prospects. On their return, Evie and Jackie went to see it. Evie always loved an evergreen wind break. The spruce trees attracted her more than the little red brick home.

The negative arguments were, "We would not care to move nearly twenty miles from our work until we retire."

"You could rent it for the next four years and then move out to the *country*" was the answer for that argument.

Ray and Evie went back to their home of over twenty years and were about to take the "FOR SALE" sign down, that had been gracing their front lawn for some time. "Let's leave it up a day or two and see if any one notices it," Evie suggested. To their surprise, within two days a buyer called and knew it was the house for them. Evie and Ray had previously made an earnest payment with a contingency on a south Minneapolis home with a downstairs bedroom. The Miller home was listed but did not sell. The sellers of the other home became restless and did not care to wait for the Miller home to sell. They returned the earnest money.

Evie was now highly allergic to wool and slept in a chair or the couch for months because her upstairs bedroom hall and stairway carpet were freshly carpeted with wool. "We will need a bedroom downstairs in our senior years," Evie said. They continued to debate the pros and cons of moving.

"We both work at the same place and hours, we can commute for just a few years," they decided. They looked forward to long walks in the wooded pasture and they could cross country ski during the snowy season on their own property. Dr Ameli was pleased with the move. "Your health will improve, I am sure."

It happened as a flash. The old homestead was sold, and the decision to move to the suburbs was final. "I can't believe we have accumulated all this stuff since our last move," Ray lamented. "And I hope you don't move that box of our old love letters." Evie waited for an opportune time to drag the dusty box from the attic and hid it in a large box of blankets. She never had time to read them, but in her retirement she knew she would need them to write her memoirs. The children had opened the box a time or two. The letters of buried treasures would in no way be left in the attic!

There had to be some juggling of furniture, moving from a four to a two bedroom home. Luckily grandchild Julia, had just given up her crib and needed a bedroom set, and other family members made use of extra furnishings.

This time it was Ray's turn to cry on the last trip to the house. Evie was not sad. The long siege of illness in the house,being alone by the hours had caused an undescribable restlessness in her. She was anxious to move from the heavy city air. Planes passed over often. It became almost unbearable on foggy or cloudy days.

"I refuse to be too attached to a house, and I can take my home with me," Evie declared. "Family and friends can always find us."

Moving to a small home would be an adjustment, but not for long. Blueprints were already being made for a twenty eight by thirty eight foot addition to the little, red brick home. January first was a cold day for the final move, but January the sixth brought a winter thaw and the basement was dug. The blue prints included a large family room with a fireplace on the east wall. The family room extended to the dinette area, and open "U shaped" kitchen. It was just as Evie had often wished for when her family was home.

"We will at least have it for our grandchildren," Ray said. A dining room, bedroom with walk in closet and Master bath completed the expansion. An outdoor stairway led to the basement.

It was on Good Friday that Evie and Ray moved into the new part of their home. The dishwasher, refrigerator and stove were connected. It was just in time to have all the family for Easter dinner in the new dining room. Soon guests arrived from Sweden. Two sisters that the Millers visited, were now returning a visit. Evie was so proud to usher them to their private rooms and bath.

Ray planted his big garden. "No one has replenished that soil for forty years," Mr. Dean Alton informed Ray. Mr. Alton was the man that built the brick home. He knew more about the property than anyone else. He continued to relate the historical facts."It was during World War Two, when you could not buy lumber, that he tore down a good building and used the lumber to build the home. Evie and Ray looked at the pictures of the infant trees they faithfully watered. Mr. Alton was a retired block layer, and now Dean and and his wife, Florence, were next door neighbors.

Using the root cellar that Alton had so painstakenly built during the war for a foundation, Ray built a small gray barn. By this time Sunkist, the pony, was a permanent resident. He generously contributed fertilizer for the garden plot. The old patched fence was replaced with a white board fence and a new gate. The garden increased its production every year. Ray planted apple trees, set out strawberry plants and raspberry vines. Every fall Evie was making juice and jelly from the grapevines. Her freezer was packed with frozen corn, string beans, and berries. The root cellar sheltered potatoes, carrots, and squash for the cold winter ahead. The wood chopper's shed was filled with dry wood.

Ray found a project for every spring. Sidewalks, picnic, and entrance areas were cemented. Trees were trimmed. New neighbor and church friendships were cultivated.

The basement of the addition was now finished. Ma's old range was the center of attraction. It inspired Evie to collect antiques, as much like Ma's as possible. Among them was a wall phone, churn, tables, a baker's cabinet, sewing machine, dishes, pots and pans. Guests enjoyed the dinners that were cooked on the old wood stove. The black worn handle on the oven door could never be painted. "I can just see Mother peeking in to the oven filled with bread and smell the wonderful aroma," Evie said with a far off stare."No, I will never paint the handle to Ma's oven door."

As the sun was setting, the farmer and his wife were often in the wooden swing watching an old hen calling her chicks to the coop. It reminded them of farming days in their early marriage.

With the inevitable winter in the forecast, the farmer's conversation drifted to the stormy months of travel ahead. "It could storm so badly we could not get home," so the Millers decided to prepare for such days. Carpet was installed and a room papered in the basement of their shop. It was furnished with a hide-a-bed, table, hot plate and extra clothing. It was their home away from home, in the event that winter would prevent travel. Having walked the eight blocks to work for several years, it was a switch for Ray to travel seventeen miles by car.

"I love to hear the church bells playing those lovely old hymns," Evie repeated night after night as they marched into their new home. It seemed so country to see the snow on the evergreens, the old corn crib, and chicken coop.

"Come spring I am going to get some laying hens," farmer Miller stated, "and I am going to hire someone to haul out all that junk behind the farm buildings." Evie was just as busy choosing her draperies, curtains and wallpaper. She felt somewhat better until the addition was completed. The formaldehyde in the new carpet set off a severe attack of allergies. Evie never dreamed that carpet contained so many harmful fumes. As summer approached and doors and windows could be opened, the problem improved. Dr. Ameli recommended a strict, ten day cleansing diet. That relieved her immensely.

Ten more miserable years passed by. Evie returned to her office daily for a period of time, but could never lick her problems. She finally decided to move her business home.

One evening she listened to "Sixty Minutes" and shuddered as she compared her symptoms with others who suffered with side effects of mercury in their system.

Her mouth was filled with mercury. She contacted a dentist the following day and made an appointment to discuss her problems. A kind friend recommended a dentist that refused to put mercury in teeth.

Blood was drawn to send out of state for an analysis. With severe allergies, Doctor Hal Huggins from Colorado Springs prescribed a special formula for the caps for her teeth.

"Please remind the Doctor and his assistant not to wear any aftershave or perfumes of any kind," Evie told the receptionist when she called to make her first appointment. Evie had been confined to her home again, and could not be in any public place. Ray did all the shopping. "If I walked through the fresh vegetables in the store, I am choking before I get past the first section." She was now on such a restricted diet that most of her food had to come from health stores. Wheat, dairy products, (except butter) food coloring, additives, peanut butter, and on and on the list grew of "forbidden fruit."

After hours in the dental chair the horrible ordeal of having every tooth capped, and the root canals removed was completed. "I can't believe you can sleep in a bed," Ray remarked. Evie had been sleeping in a recliner and coughing continuously for weeks for over a fifteen year period. Within two weeks her lungs cleared up and she could lie down to sleep. "It is so good to have a roommate again," Ray said as Evie crawled in her own bed.

Still she was not enjoying perfect health. Her allergies would plague her at times. Going back on the ten day cleansing diet would relieve the allergies for a time. "I wonder if I am ever going to feel well?" Evie secretly wondered. Lack of minerals sent her to the hospital on Thanksgiving day of 1993. In 1994 Evie went to Preventive Medicine Clinic for treatments to clear her system of the years of accumulation of mercury. After numerous blood tests, she learned that mercury binds minerals. Her tests results revealed that she had minerals coated, but not usable. After the mercury was removed, minerals were replaced intravenously every

Friday for several months. Evie finally saw a light at the end of the tunnel. How difficult to believe Americans can tolerate putting the most poisonous metal in fifty per cent of silver fillings, and even tint false teeth with it. She has written letters to the Attorney General and the President. Thousands of dollars have gone down the drain for mercury fillings and then still more to have her teeth recapped, plus doctor bills. It takes such experiences to bring out the tiger in a woman. Thanks to the research of many, including the three doctors, Huggins, Jacobson, and Dole, Evie's health has improved. She is anticipating telling the whole wide world the entire story of no longer having to sleep in Ray's recliner or walk the floor in the lonely dark hours.

The Christmas letter to all Evie's family from the Ma's Old Range:

Merry Christmas

It was a cold winter day when I was set up in the country home of Elizabeth and Gus. I will never forget the excitement I created. The children cheered as Gus put up the stove pipe.

Elizabeth took a section of *The Fergus Falls Journal* and a few corn cobs, struck a match and I was in business. I could never have predicted what an important place I would play in that little home in the valley.

I served them faithfully for many years until the day I was replaced by an electric stove.

They set me up in the entrance to warm the boots and coats. It was quite a let down. I missed the pleasure of frying down the pork and baking bread. The real blow came when Elizabeth sold the farm, and the new owner carried me piece by piece to the junk pile. I thought it was the beginning of the end.

In time the oldest son returned and rescued me. He placed me in an old box car where I remained for eight years. I had heated the water for that boy's diapers. At least I was out of the rain, but still unassembled, confused, and very discouraged. My strong legs held and heated countless boilers of water over the years. My reservoir provided water for baths and washing the dishes. You could never imagine the number of meals I cooked.

One day one of my cooks came to visit me. She decided to take me home. I wondered if I was going back to my final resting spot. We stopped by a farm and a man stared in the truck and then said he would fix me for a price. I sat in an old shed awaiting my turn for an entire winter. Then the day for surgery finally arrived. When I came to and saw my reflection in another stove I could not believe they had blackened my nickel trim. When Evie came to get me she was just as shocked. She took me back to the cities and again. My trim was removed. In about three weeks I was reunited with all my shiny parts. To feel my old self again!

Now, I proudly fill a corner of Evie's antique kitchen. I hear the voices of little children and will once more bake the bread, boil the cranberries, and bake the turkey for Christmas dinner.

My advise to you is don't give up the ship! Keep your fire of faith blazing and don't eat too much pie, after all those mashed potatoes and trimmin's! Do come to visit me real soon.

Ma's Old Stove

37

Jane's Victory

Jane, Evie's youngest sister, had grown older, as did all of Elizabeth's children. The day Jane left home was the saddest day in the life of Gus and Elizabeth. They faced the reality, that they could no longer take care of little Jane. When Elizabeth reached fifty-seven and Gus was sixty-two, their health no longer permitted the extra burden.

As a toddler, Jane had recovered from the long siege of pneumonia just before Ray and Evie's marriage. But after having extreme temperatures for several hours, she would never again communicate words or the names of the people who loved her.

Elizabeth and Gus lived just one mile from Lahrman farm, where Ray and Evie lived. They took Jane to the Cambridge State Hospital when she was twelve years old. She sat between Elizabeth and Gus and sensed the finality of the long trip. After Jane was settled in her room, Ray assured them, "She will adjust to her new home." The aging parents walked slowly away.

Gus was always the person to say, "We better get movin'." But on that day he could not hurry away. "I would rather follow her to her grave," Gus said, after their final good-bye. The tired parents sat in the back seat, almost in silence, on the return trip. They had devoted all their energy to their youngest down syndrome child, almost forgetting that the other youngsters needed parenting as well.

Evie had sewn Jane seven new dresses to pack in her suitcase. She recalled the first dress, that she made Jane, when she was six months old.When Jane outgrew the little white dress trimmed in pink, the sentimental old sister tucked it away in her cedar chest. No other little girl could wear that dress, not even Evie's own daughters.

"Come over for dinner tomorrow," Evie said as they dropped the parents off at their farm home. They did not accept the invitation, so Evie delivered the dinner to their home. "We cannot eat a bite," they both echoed. Evie left the dinner regardless, only to bring another the following day to discover a dinner untouched in the refrigerator.

"I am going to make their very favorite meal today," Evie informed Ray. Gus met her at the door. He smelled the fried chicken, peeked at the mashed potatoes and gravy, and at last smiled. Evie joined them. They were hungry, though the conversation always drifted back to how they missed Jane.

"We are going to buy her a big swing," Gus remarked. "She enjoys swinging and rocking, more than anything." Later they requested to have Jane moved closer to home, to the Brainerd State Hospital. They could then visit weekly, unless old man winter interfered. In the summer they made a picnic dinner and took her to the outskirts of the property by car and ate their dinner each week. Jane enjoyed the swing, the food and her company. She also loved her weekly car ride.

It was a hot day in July, when the phone rang. It was Elizabeth calling all her children with the news of their father's heart attack. All of the children that could possibly do so, returned. Gus was dismissed from the hospital by the time the families arrived, but was flat on his back. Once again the dining room table was extended, as far as it could be stretched. "I wish I could see through that wall," he said. "I would like to see all my family surrounding the table once more."

One by one his family had to return to their homes and jobs, before Gus was able to join them around the table. Evie was at his bedside, and he was in tears as he made a special request. "Evie will you promise me that you will take on the responsibility of Jane?" Evie made that promise, not realizing the commitment would be over thirty years. Gus recovered to visit Jane several times in the next three years, before his final good-bye.

A call from Joy, in Montana, left the family numb. "Orpha is not expected to live! If you want to see her come as soon as possible. It was sobering to convey the message to Gus. Could his heart handle another blow? His response was, "Someone has to go! Evie, would you and Ruthie leave as soon as possible?"

The trains and planes were filled to capacity. The World's Fair made Seattle a popular place. The two sisters boarded the first departing bus for Montana. During every four hour stop, a call went through to the hospital, "Is Orpha Carlson still alive?"

The answer was always the same. "She is alive, but her entire left side is paralyzed. Her miraculous recovery was a thrilling chapter in the lives of the large family.

It was the March of 1992. Evie was up early one morning. Suffering with allergies, a constant cough, and fluid-filled lungs made sleeping difficult. She could only have her lactose free drink for breakfast. It was nutritional and full of energy. Ray was enjoying his coffee and favorite cereal.

"I must get to the store and find some summer clothes for Jane soon. There is enough money to purchase a bedroom set for her, too." Evie went on to elaborate, "Her roommate has a beautiful dresser and bed. There is no reason why Jane does not deserve beautiful things."

Jane had no audible way of requesting that she should keep up with the Joneses. Just the same Evie almost argued with herself that she may enjoy it more than we can ever imagine.

"If she has enough money, buy one. Why wait?" Ray responded as he raised his cup with the last swallow of coffee. "I don't feel up to it today, but if I go on that ten day cleansing diet again, I will be able to go into a furniture store without coughing my head off." The very thought made Evie cough before she could drink her herb tea.

"Do you realize Jane was forty-nine on March tenth? How I wish she could enjoy a card. I haven't been to see her for so long I am ashamed of myself," she confessed. Her birthday had come and gone, and every week Evie was sure she would feel well enough to make a trip to the Cambridge Treatment Center by the following week. The telephone interrupted the leisure breakfast hour.

"Hello! Yes, this is she. No! Not pneumonia again?! That poor girl has had that forty times, more or less." Evie recalled the horrible week a few years back when eight of the the family members sat vigil, by her bedside. "I can't bear to see her suffer again," Evie was stopped short by the gentle kind voice of the doctor on the other end of the line, trying to get a word in edgewise.

"Evie, she is not that seriously sick. I think we caught it early enough. Jane only has pneumonia in part of one lung. She is on antibiotics, and I am sure she will be back in her own bed soon. You may come to see her anytime. We just want to keep you posted, not alarm you." The doctor did not pause to allow Evie to voice her fears.

Evie wasted no time in calling the other local sisters. "Donna, do you think we should go today or tomorrow?" questioned Evie.

"June can't get away, Ruby has to work. Let's you and I go early tomorrow," Donna tried to sound so matter-of-fact.

Going to visit Jane was a time Donna and Evie enjoyed being together. The sisters were busy while raising their families.They had very little time alone the past years. They always managed to catch up on little details on trips such as this. "Are we in Cambridge already?" Evie could hardly believe the arrow pointing to Treatment Center.

The nurse motioned to a closed door. "Would the bacteria be contagious?" Donna inquired as she opened the door.

"No, Jane has been on antibiotics for four days," the nurse assured them.

Jane was in a room alone. The television was turned up, in hopes that Jane could hear with an ear infection. A broad smile spread across her feverish face as Donna embraced Jane. "I think she always thinks I am Ma," repeated Evie, almost every visit. Evie had just celebrated her sixty-eighth birthday, on January eighteenth, and was just Ma's height. Her hair was just as gray. There was no way of being sure if Jane understood that Ma had left this old world. Evie declared, she looked more like Ma then any of the eleven sisters. June was not along to make her point today. However, she maintained that *she* was the most like Ma, being even-tempered and all.

Donna had taken care of Jane so much in her childhood. Jane took much comfort in the tender touch of Donna's hand on her forehead. Donna would pause for a second and Jane would lean her head forward as if to say, "Please rub some more, Donna. It feels so wonderful to have your hand on my brow again." The afternoon wore on. Evie and Donna expressed their concern and love. Jane's smile exploded in a hearty laugh.

All too soon it was time for the big sisters, to bid her good-bye and leave her in the room alone. The nurse was confident she would improve daily. Reluctantly the sisters left and headed quietly towards the car. The trip home was with sobering thoughts. Donna was sure Jane was more sick than anyone could know. "Dad asked me to care for Jane as long as she needs me. But with the way I've been feeling lately, I can't help but wonder if she will outlive me." Evie's remarks were sincere.

Both Donna and Evie talked to the doctor often. "Jane is not recovering as we predicted. We are trying a different antibiotic today," she informed Donna. The families in California, Oregon, Kentucky, Michigan, and Oklahoma were notified of Jane's illness. We just wanted you to know she is sick, and we will keep you informed. The message reached anxious hearts. U.S. West conveyed every solemn change across the miles.

It was a cloudy cold day the last week in April. The phone rang early in the morning. Donna's voice sounded urgent. The doctor just called and said they have moved Jane to the city hospital. Donna added, "She has pneumonia in both lungs, and is not responding to any drug."

Any and all plans were quickly chucked. Could you meet me at June's house to save time? Within two hours, three sisters were following the sign to the emergency room and quickly spotted the room with the most activity. Little Jane was gasping for each breath. She would try to sit up. She squinted to see all the attached tubes and again tried to free herself from the restraining gadgets. At times she rolled her head near the guard rail, and changed positions hoping to pull the oxygen mask off, as if to say, "If I get this contraption off I could leave this old painful world."

Perhaps she was remembering in 1986 when she had a glimpse of heaven. The medics had carried out their orders to save her. The nurse on duty later confessed, "Jane seemed so disappointed when she was revived." She likely had a short visit with her mother or at least said hello to Baby Sarah for the first time.

Their first opportune moment, they talked with both of her doctors. Her chances of survival look very small.

"We do not want them to revive her, if she wants to

leave us," the sisters agreed. Her lungs were scarred, she had heart problems, and her kidneys were barely functioning.

"Still we will do all that is humanly possible for her," the promise came from the doctor, as nurses hurried to carry out his orders.

Two of the sisters stayed by her side. June, Donna, and Evie rotated the vigil. Ruby called and said, "Give Jane a message for me. Tell her, 'I want you to go sleep. You will have a gold chain swing, waiting for you in heaven.'"

Calls came from the family daily. One afternoon as Evie was getting dinner on the table, the phone rang. Evie rushed to receive the feared news. "Come now if you want to be with Jane! The nurse said she could go at any time," the tone of June's voice conveyed the urgency. "We thought she was gone for a few moments."

"I won't need to even take my tooth brush, I am sure I will not be spending another night at the hospital," Evie spoke. The sign to the hospital was visible, even through the veil of tears. She ran until she reached the elevator. The distance to the emergency room had surely lengthened.

Jane revived, off and on through the night. June decided to go home for the night, but Donna was determined to stay. Evie and Donna would take turns trying to rest. Perhaps each slept about one half hour during the night. Jane did appreciate family by her side. Though unable to express appreciation, they were sure she was aware of a family that loved her. The sun began to poke through the clouds and one of the longest night of their lives had ended. June, came back early that day. Evie returned home for a few hours and the phone rang.

"This is it! Evie, hurry back! Don't wait for anything." The car almost seemed to guide itself to Cambridge. It was raining, the second day of May. The wind was so strong, it almost blew light cars off the road. Under normal circumstances Evie would have stopped in the shelter of a building. But there was no turning back. She thought of Jane's life; how, like this day, it also had been filled with storms. Through the wind, tears, and rain, Evie saw the arrow pointing to the hospital.

Evie ran until she reached the elevator. "She is waiting to say good-bye to you," Donna said as if Jane knew Evie was returning.

Jane's social worker, Kim Palmer, Margaret Carlson and others from the State hospital were in the waiting room. They brought fruit and comforting thoughts of how Jane was loved. They reminded the sisters of her trick of crawling in bed and covering her head after dinner hour when she did not want to go to the game room. One of the aides pulled out a toy bear from the closet. When Judy first moved to Cambridge, pictures were purchased for her wall. The pictures were removed. "Pearl or Ruby would like these pictures. Those sisters took care of Jane her last days at home," Donna remarked.

Late in the afternoon Ray and his daughter, Beverlie, came into the hospital room. It had been a long time since Bev had seen Jane. Over an hour slipped by. It was now 7:15 p.m. when it happened: the moment they had actually prayed for—an end to Jane's suffering. It was with mixed emotions that they faced this moment. She always tried to pull the oxygen mask off. The nurse untied her hands as she gently said, "Let her die with dignity." The family joined hands with the kind nurse and repeated the Lord's Prayer. Slowly the color faded from Jane's face. How comforting for Evie to have Ray, her oldest daughter, and two sisters, by her side at times such as this. They lingered at the bedside until the nurse motioned for Evie to call the undertaker from Bertha.

Early that Sunday morning, Chuck and Irene arrived at the airport. All the family met to have dinner before they left for Bertha. The three hour trip gave them time to catch up on current events. Chuck wanted to ride with all his sisters and half hoped to get a word in edgewise, in moments of a lull in the conversation. How wonderful to be together again. Chuck had such a tender spot for baby Jane. It was in times like this that they recalled their childhood. They laughed and cried on their way, but arrived in Bertha a wee bit late. "This is not like Dad, he would never have been late," Irene said. He would have purchased some bananas to eat along the way, and not waited to be served a dinner at a busy restaurant.

All the arrangements were made. Jane would be placed in a child's size casket. She would have a steel vault. Her father would have been pleased with that decision. Jane looked like an angel. Flowers were placed on a band around her head. She held one flower in her hand, with her ring adorning one finger. She was no longer gasping for breath. Her mouth was relaxed. Jane was peaceful. Evie tried to imagine the grand homecoming Elizabeth and Gus were hosting for her, as Jane was being introduced to Baby Sarah.

All but three members of the brothers and sisters, cousins and family were in attendance. The simple ceremony was so meaningful. The Pastor preached a sermon to the living. A niece sang a solo, and old familiar hymns were sung by the congregation. Beverlie read a letter she had written to Jane the night she returned from witnessing Jane's home going.

The cars moved slowly over old familiar trails to reach the cemetery. Jane was placed near her parents and baby Sarah. A short prayer and comforting scripture, "ashes to ashes and dust to dust," was repeated as petals of flowers were placed on her coffin. It was over! The long, long night had past for one dear sister.

A few weeks later there was a beautiful memorial service for Jane at Cambridge. The video of Jane in her purple dress was shown, as the organist was playing hymns that Jane heard as a child. Busy nurses, teachers, social workers, and her doctor took time to pay their last respects. Tributes were paid as two sisters relived the life of Jane Branstner. It was a celebration of her entrance to a land free of pain and sorrow.

The following is a copy of the letter Beverlie penned

the evening of Jane's death.

I am just five years younger than Jane and have many memories of her. After hearing the sad news of her illness. I wondered why was she sent to us, and why does she have to suffer so much? I felt the need to see her while she was still alive. Jane was a real person, just like you and me. After I returned home that evening I wrote Jane this letter, because now I know she will understand it.

Dear Jane:

Forty Nine years old! To some that is "almost over the hill," yet I look at you and see hardly a gray strand in your auburn hair. You haven't needed a face lift. Natural eyebrows that I would die for(never suffering the pain of plucking them). Liz Taylor eat your heart out!!

I look at you and you're still twelve years old—enjoying life, the simple things—walking, swinging, riding in a car, and rocking in your favorite creaking rocking chair. Not a trouble in this world and giving joy to everyone around you.

All of this I know, because you have a family that loves you so much and you felt it, ten sisters and three brothers.

We ask ourselves why you had to struggle so until the end? You loved life and lived it to the fullest. It was worth it to you until the last breath of air—to slowly fade away. It gave us a chance to prepare ourselves for your departure. You taught us unselfishness(the most severe disease of all)You had the ability to to give yourself what you needed to be happy. That happiness was contagious and has taught others to experience it through you.

God sent examples to us, as he did in Jesus, just as he sent you. It reminds us of the important things in life. Judy, you knew the meaning of life. And now I say CONGRATULATIONS! We look forward to seeing you again one day. And after I say "Hi" to Jesus, I'd just like a chance to swing right next to you.

                                    All My Love,
                                    Beverlie

38

Bouquet For Mother

A letter arrived early in nineteen seventy five from nieces in California, announcing a Branstner reunion. They took full responsibility of collecting information, as to time and a date that would work out for all the relatives. The first response was "Let's wait until next year." Elizabeth was then seventy eight years old. "Mom is not well. We know she could enjoy it this year," members of the family insisted. "The reunion should not be delayed." And so the plans took root, and on June twenty Eighth nineteen seventy five. June and Evie hosted the reunion at the Wadena, Minnesota High School, and at Hewitt the next day.

Patchwork table cloths, small antiques, such as coffee pots, were center pieces. Elizabeth was Queen for a day. June presented her with a long black dress for the evening dinner. Family slides brought back memories, and grandchildren entertained the large crowd of over seventy in-laws and children. The only one outside the immediate family to attend the dinner was Uncle Lew. The following day was Open House for all the relatives.

The next spring Elizabeth suffered a stroke. She

could no longer stay alone in her comfortable apartment. Willy and Glenda, with three small children, and big hearts, lived in the home area. They invited Elizabeth to stay with them. With little ones, the load became too heavy. Ruthie and Willy lived in the area, and made arrangements to place Elizabeth in a Nursing Home. A phone call conveyed the sad message, "You must come up and help us move Mom, Evie."

"Now don't you children ever blame yourselves for this." Elizabeth said in all sincerity. "I need so much help, that no one can take care of me." "Would you like to go back to your apartment for a few days?" Evie asked. Ma beamed and said " I would just love to." With her walker she slowly made it to the car and back to her home on the second floor of the Humphrey Manor. The following days Evie packed up her earthly possessions, mainly at night, to protect her mother from the sad decisions.

She separated the gift items, to return to the respective donors. The furniture was left in place, and not a picture moved, until Elizabeth left her little nest. The jewelry was placed in one small suitcase along with her personal clothing. Evie loaded the trunk and back seat leaving enough room for Uncle Lew to sit in the back seat. Elizabeth hid her inner regrets, and endeavored to convince her daughter, "I will be fine, Evie." Evie would take one armload to the car, have a good cry, and then go back to face her mother. Last of all she wheeled Elizabeth to the elevator and down the hall to the car. She was surrounded by her old friends, with quivering lips and tearful eyes, they bade Elizabeth good-bye. Ruthie was in charge of a Board and Care in Bertha. Evie phoned her, "Can you go with us?" "I think I can get away an hour so," she replied. Ruthie would not take up much space in the front seat, weighing all of eighty-five pounds.

Evie visited her Mother as often as possible that summer. She took her to visit friends at the Manor, and to another nursing home to spend time with her sister, Tamma. Elizabeth fell and broke her hip on Thanksgiving day. She did not recover from this. All but two of her twelve living children attended her funeral on December 16, 1976. In memory of her, we mentally place a bouquet right by her headstone.

I salute you on this your day, Mother. In honoring you I honor all true Mothers everywhere. Now, that you are gone from us we will say many things to your credit for others to hear. We wish we could say them, for you to hear, and know and appreciate you for what you are and for all you have done.

In times that I cannot recall, and before I saw the light of day, you warmed my soul with deep and undying love, which you bore for my father. Not until I see with my eyes in the light of eternity will I fully evaluate what prenatal legacy has been worth to me.

You walked with courage to the very edge of the bordering shadows to bring me into life. I was not born to wealth, but thanks to your clean living and nutritional meals, I was granted health.

In honoring you I present you with this mixed bouquet.

Included in the arrangement is the Goldenrod. They speak of precaution and encouragement, which also remind me of you, Mother.

For variety, in the tulip family in the Roman Flower language they are significant of boldness and confidence. Christian Mothers require the boldness of lions portrayed in Proverbs 28:1. We have needed this brave influence to guide us through decisions and problems of our youth, and the courage to strive for the potential God has entrusted us with.

Our Bouquet was incomplete until we went to the Rockies in search of the Cherry Tree blossoms. They were beautiful beyond description. The cherry blossoms represent spiritual beauty. We chose five blossoms to represent motherly kindness, temperance, knowledge, and love.

We found sage to complete our arrangement, not merely for beauty, but because it suggests domestic beauty. Thank God we have mothers that taught by example this important virtue. You made our home inviting.

A most important addition to our bouquet was the violets of Modesty. It was the final touch that reminds us of you, our Mother.

We place this bouquet on your buffet, and say with Solomon of old, "Your children arise and call you blessed, your husband also. Let her own works praise her." Again I salute you! You have worked hard and well, and taken us as far as you could. You have guided us through the crowded harbor, you have pointed our faces to the open sea. If we do not safely make that crossing it will be no fault of yours.

Introduction To The Mixed Bouquet.

It is with joy that we place this mixed bouquet in the hand of our daughters tonight. Going back to the Middle Ages to the old Roman flower language, aided in our arrangement selection. We trust the professional florist will refrain from constructive criticism.

We began our search in deep waters for the Water Lily, to discover them waving their pure white faces in the breeze. These lilies were night-bloomers, continuing to bloom though seemingly unnoticed. We paused to thank God, that in this world of temptation, this lily is not extinct. It is with pride that we place it in the center of our bouquet.

We continue our search for a daisy to remind us of innocence. Though keenly aware that we are not born with the innocence of Adam and Eve. Our children were not blessed with a choice of the social, financial, or spiritual status in which they discovered life. May we as mothers guide them in their varied environments.

We trudged to the low pastures and hopped from bog to bog to collect the cowslip, the flower of youthful beauty, planted by God and watered by His early rains, in the precious age before the chimes of time, or sin could mar its beauty. In Proverbs 17:22 we are given the recipe for youthful beauty. A merry heart doeth good like a medicine. Bless the mothers that are creating this atmosphere in your home.

The gardenia, gives a special touch to our bouquet, as it suggests refinement. The home is the heart of developing this flower. It is here we cultivate the art of getting along with others, and weed out the unpleasant traits that rob us of inner beauty. Incidentally this process can be painful for both mother and daughter.

The crocus of gladness is a treasured addition to the arrangement. It adds both fragrance and beauty to any vase.

The touch of violets, in a rainbow of color, is symbolic of modesty. In a world that cultivates immodesty, it is comforting to know this flower is not extinct.

We placed a special order to Portugal for the cultivated Globe Amaranth. Thanks to the jet age it arrived in all its glory, representing immortality, because of the short time it retains its beauty. We must not stop with the physical needs of our precious bouquet, but must also care for the spiritual, by saturating with seeds of understanding, trust, truthfulness and Love. (Source of resources, God's letter to man.)

We thank God for the Bouquet he entrusted in our care. May we implant the thirst described in Psalms 43:1, "as the heart panteth after the water brook," thus we must water, to maintain our Bouquet.

In conclusion we present this Bouquet to our Daughters in a hand cut message on a beautiful Crystal Vase.

Bouquet For Daughter

When we first received the message, God was sending a Bouquet.

The day for it's arrival seemed so very far away.

We confess we often questioned "how much longer must we wait?"

And then we asked so boldly, "Are you sure it isn't late?"

But then special delivery brought a beautiful mixed bouquet.

"The long, long wait was worth it," was echoed every day. May we water carefully, its fragrance to retain.

Lest we mar the blossoms, and the leaves but then remain.

We love the daisy yellow, the innocence they portray.

How beautiful the cowslip, may its youthful beauty stay. Water Lily purity, may your color remain true;

The modesty of Violet, continue to blend your hue. Crocus with your gladness, may you maintain your glow.

When the skies of life have darkened may you keep on smiling so.

The Amaranth eternal, and Gardenia so refined,

You have made our life so happy and our clouds all silver lined.

May our schedule never be so full of trivial things,

That we fail to appreciate the joy our bouquet brings.

And when some handsome lover steals our mixed bouquet away, may the memories of its perfume forever with us stay.

Written for a Women's banquet May 1964

39
Evie Will
Never Forget

Ray and Evie's life pathway has been bordered with wildflowers and rugged stones. Sunrays have peeked through the clouds just when they needed its energy and warmth. Billowy clouds dropped refreshing rains at intervals when the trail became parched. Often in the form of humor. Let's take a walk.

"We must go visit Diane and Morrie," Ray said. Being tied to glass cutting and Shaklee over the years did not allow much time for travel.

Evie found a temporary replacement for her office, and they were off. During the day Diane was working, and the men were off to the golf course.

"I think I will drift over to that little shopping center," Evie breathed to herself. Her instincts lead her directly to a clothing shop with a "Summer Clearance" sign in bold, daring colors. As she walked in, she saw a woman leaning on the counter, concentrating on some papers. Evie followed the yellow brick trail to the clearance racks and tables. She found a few maybe's and was about to go to the fitting room, when suddenly it turned dark. Looking toward the only window and door in the shop, she heard the click of the door being locked. The lady was dashing away. "No! I am locked in this store!" Evie threw her choice outfits on a table and ran to the door. She knocked as loudly as her knuckles could tolerate. Just as the clerk stopped running to unlock her car door, she heard the frantic knock and returned to let "Lucy" out.

"I did not see you in the store, and I was just running out to do a few errands." Evie forgot all about her bargains. The lady had deadlines to meet, and Evie decided she could return at a more convenient season.

Another scene was back on their first little farm. Morrie and Bev, were sound asleep when Mommie and Daddy went to the barn. "I better check our children," Evie said as she finished milking a cow. Just weeks before she had sewn each child a pair of pajamas with feet attached.Mommie was so proud. "Now their feet won't get cold if they kick off their blankets." She shuddered when she saw the tykes running around in the living room, with jagged cuts at the mid calf of their new pj's. Evie had carelessly left her scissors in a drawer within reach. How upset could a seamstress get, though, when she considered to her relief that there was no physical harm.

As the playmates grew, they often played church. A favorite hymn, "When The Roll is Called A Piano," would likely be sung at every service.

Merv was four years old. It was before his sister, Jill, announced her coming. "Mervie, what is Mommie going to do when you leave me next year and go to school?"

"Mommie, I will never leave you, I promise," he answered. He kept that promise until he was twenty, and then he moved next door.

Cousin Phil and Brent were attending their Grandfather's funeral. They were surprised to see the deceased in a suit. On the way to the cemetery Brent said, "Phil, whatever we want to take with us, we will have to put in our pockets."

June and Hugh visited out of town friends. The house was immaculate. The children were cautioned not to touch the wall, as they ascended the stairs. The open stairway overlooked the living room—forbidden territory. Brent surveyed the room, proceeded to the kitchen, and asked the lady of the house, "What's that room for? Just to look at?"

"Well, I guess you could say that."

The three year old ran back upstairs to ask his mother, "Who does that woman think she is? My mother-in-law?"

Evie's sister June took care of her two and three year old grandchildren. They both climbed in a big rocker. Just before Grandma left the living room she cautioned them, "Now don't rock too hard, or you will tip over!" Shortly after she checked her cookies she heard the crash. "Why did you rock so fast?" Grandma questioned.

Heather picked up her dolly, and answered between sobs, "But Grandma, we were only going the speed limit!"

Ray's brother, Harry, was a very bashful boy. While trying to get to his place at the recitation bench, he stumbled over a girl's feet. The teacher asked, "What do you say Harry, when you step on someone's toes?" Harry stood up and looked the second grader in the eye and said, "Oops, did it hurt?"

One of the grandchildren, along with her family, were participants in an Easter Pageant at a large church. She heard the phrase, "in the name of God," over and over during rehearsals. The little three year old could manage taking care of herself quite well, with the exception of using the bathroom tissue. Mommie said, "Always call me and I will help you at this stage." One day Mommie was unable to answer the distress call, "Will somebody please wipe me?" She sent out an SOS several times, and waited patiently. Finally in desperation she called out, "In The Name Of God will someone *please* come and wipe me?"

Evie's daughter was living in Seattle, when Aunt June and Uncle Hugh stopped by for a visit. Emily was two years old. In leaving they said their good-byes in the apartment. Emily insisted on following the company to the parking lot. "No, we won't go to the car," Jill told her. A big disappointment spread across her face as she informed her Mommie, "I just want to watch them disappear."

Yes, Evie's life has been filled with enough laughter to make life fun; enough poverty to make her thrifty; enough sickness to appreciate health; enough sorrow to show empathy, and experiences that could fill another book.